# 'BEST BLACK TROOPS IN THE WORLD'

*British Perceptions and the Making of the Sepoy 1746-1805*

# 'BEST BLACK TROOPS IN THE WORLD'

*British Perceptions and the Making of the Sepoy 1746-1805*

CHANNA WICKREMESEKERA

MANOHAR
2002

First published 2002



ISBN 81-7304-426-0

*Published by*
Ajay Kumar Jain for
Manohar Publishers & Distributors
4753/23 Ansari Road, Daryaganj
New Delhi 110002

*Printed at*
Rajkamal Electric Press
Delhi 110033

In memory of
Mr. LIONEL WICKREMESEKERA

# Contents

*List of Illustrations* 8

*Acknowledgements* 9

*List of Abbreviations* 11

*Introduction* 13

CHAPTER 1
Europe and India: A Clash of Military Cultures 33

CHAPTER 2
British Perceptions and the Emergence of the Sepoy Army, 1746-1800 76

CHAPTER 3
The Sepoy Army in the Making: Recruitment, Command and Discipline, 1746-1800 96

CHAPTER 4
The Sepoy at War, 1746-1805 130

CHAPTER 5
The Sepoy and British Perceptions 158

*Conclusion* 181

*Appendix* 185

*Glossary* 187

*Bibliography* 189

*Index* 207

# Illustrations


MAPS

1. India in 1805 32
2. Anglo-French Conflict in the Carnatic, 1746-61 90

PLANS

1. The Battle of Buxar, 23 October 1764 137
2. The Battle of Tiruvannamalai, 26 September 1767 140
3. The Battle of Porto Novo, 1 July 1781 142
4. The Battle of Assaye, 23 September 1803 149
5. The Battle of Laswari, 1 November 1803 152

PLATES

1. Armed retainers or *burkundaz* 41
2. 'Battle of Plassey' from a contemporary hand coloured manuscript 80
3. Subedar, Bengal Army 113
4. Grenadier sepoy, Bengal Army 119
5. Madras sepoy with wife 127
6. The storming of Srirangapattanam, 4 May 1799 145
7. Sepoy and family with wife and children, riding a bullock, sepoy in undress carrying a sword 162

# Acknowledgements

SEVERAL PEOPLE and institutions have contributed immensely towards the successful completion of this thesis. The advice, patience and support of my Supervisor Professor Ian Copland and Associate Supervisor Dr. Ian Mabbett were indispensable in turning a mass of information and ideas into a logical and coherent thesis. Mr. Gary Swinton of the Geography Department at Monash University produced the maps and plans appearing in this work at short notice while the interlibrary loans staff of the Monash University Library readily obliged with difficult requests. Monash Asia Institute funded two research trips abroad while two scholarships provided by Monash University enabled me to survive four years as a graduate student.

Researching and writing this thesis provided constant reminders of the value and luxury of family and friends. I am eternally grateful to Sanjiva and Krysta Weerasooriya for providing support and encouragement that can never be measured. They took a personal interest in the completion of the thesis while cheerfully enduring excessive demands on their time, patience and computer. My research in London would never have been a reality without the wonderful hospitality of Mr. Lionel Wickremesekera and Charith and Deepa Wijeratne. The friendship and support of Mohana Dissanayake, Rajiva and Manoj Wickremesinghe and Supriya Wickremetilleke was also invaluable in making my research trips both useful and enjoyable while my parents and brothers have always remained a constant source of encouragement.

CHANNA WICKREMESEKERA

# Abbreviations

| | |
|---|---|
| Cons. | Consultations |
| BM | British Museum |
| FR | Factory Records |
| Home Misc. | Home Miscellaneous Series |
| MR | Military Records |
| Mil. | Military |
| NAM | National Army Museum |
| OIOC | Oriental and India Office Collections of the British Library |
| O.V. | Orme Various |
| Pol. | Political |
| Sec. | Secret |
| Sel. Com. | Select Committee |

# Introduction

THE BRITISH 'CONQUEST' of India was not simply a matter of the English East India Company extending a high degree of control over the politics and resources of the subcontinent. It was also a process of learning; with British dominion came the construction of knowledge about the country and the people over whom that dominion was extended. On the one hand, this was inevitable. Expansion brought the British into closer and more frequent contact with the people and the institutions of India. At the same time, as Warren Hastings pointed out, it was also good policy to know more about the country and the people being 'conquered':

> Every accumulation of knowledge and especially such as is obtained by social communication with people over whom we exercise a dominion founded on the right of conquest, is useful to the state. . . . [I]t attracts and conciliates distant affections; it lessens the weight of the chain by which the natives are held in subjection; and it imprints on the hears of our countrymen the sense of obligation and benevolence.[1]

Hastings' encouragement led to sustained scholarly inquiry into the salient features of the Indian civilization. Spearheaded by such scholars as William Jones and Charles Wilkins, and sponsored by organizations such as the Asiatic Society of Bengal, this early British quest for knowledge about India came to focus mainly on the translation of classical Sanskrit and Persian texts into English.[2]

[1] Cited in Bernard S. Cohn, *Colonialism and its Forms of Knowledge: the British in India*, Princeton, New Jersey: Princeton University Press, 1996, p. 45.

[2] The College of Fort William became the centre of British scholarly inquiry. Established in August 1800, the college offered courses in Muslim and Hindu law, jurisprudence, political economy, world geography besides teaching languages like Greek, Arabic, Persian and Sanskrit. David Kopf, *British Orientalism and the Bengal Renaissance: the Dynamics of Indian Modernization 1773-1835*, Berkeley: University of California Press, 1969, pp. 45-9.

These studies generated a lively admiration for Indian culture and literature. But, at the same time, there was a strong tendency to deny the Indian civilization equality with the West. The treatment of Indian political institutions was a case in point. For centuries, European imagination had held that Asian governments were headed by despotic tyrants, and despite their efforts to understand the complexities of Indian traditions, early British Orientalists failed to see beyond this age-old model.[3] The government of Indian rulers was seen as a classic 'Oriental Despotism', 'the nurse of the most abject slaves' according to the English historian Alexander Dow.[4] It concentrated all power in the arbitrary authority of the ruler, denying the rights of property to the common people. As such, it stood in sharp contrast to the more progressive constitutional monarchies and republics that characterized Western governments. Even William Jones who greatly admired Hindu culture agreed with the ancient Greek view that where political systems were concerned, Asia was the handmaiden of Europe.[5]

This portrayal of Indian backwardness continued to be an important aspect of the British construction of India in the nineteenth century. Indeed, it gathered momentum with the consolidation of British dominion. The reality of British supremacy in India and the growing

[3] Until increased commercial intercourse between Asia and Europe in the sixteenth and seventeenth centuries, Greek accounts of Asian tyrants—heavily influenced by Greek confrontations with the Persians—had formed the basis of European views of Asia. Increased contact only strengthened this opinion. Travellers returning from India and China provided detailed accounts of their experiences, rarely failing to describe Eastern monarchs as absolute rulers. The accounts of French travellers like Francois Bernier (1620-88) and Jean-Baptiste Tavernier (1605-89) who described the Mughal emperor as the owner of all land in the empire gained wide currency in this regard. Baron de Montesquieu, a leading figure of the Enlightenment gave the idea more concrete form in his major work *Espirit des Lois* (1748). See Ainslie T. Embree, *Imagining India: Essays on Indian History,* Delhi: OUP, 1989, pp. 36-8; and Inden, 'Orientalist', p. 421.

[4] Cited in Thomas R. Metcalfe, *Ideologies of the Raj*, The New Cambridge History of India, III.4, Cambridge: CUP, 1984, p. 7.

[5] Wrote Jones: 'Asia had no conception of freedom. If every reader of history would open his eyes to some very important conclusions which flow from the whole extent of it, he could not but remark the constant effect of despotism in benumbing and destroying all those faculties which distinguish men from the herd that grazes; and to that cause he would impute the decided inferiority of most Asiatick nations, ancient and modern to those in Europe who are blest with happier governments.' Cited in S.N. Mukherjee, *Sir William Jones: a Study in Eighteenth Century British Attitudes to India*, London: Sangam, 1987, p. 109.

technological and scientific progress in Europe combined to undermine even the limited admiration the British had for Indian culture. India came to be marked as stagnant, as a land of the past rather than the present,[6] rousing the reforming zeal of the early nineteenth century English utilitarians and evangelists. Hinduism was singled out as a religion that bred and nurtured servility while Indian languages were increasingly treated as unworthy of attention.[7] The policy of non-interference with indigenous traditions that dominated British attitudes for much of the eighteenth century was abandoned during the early decades of the nineteenth century in favour of change and 'improvement' through the inculcation of British values. The liberty of the individual and the 'rights' of 'private' property were to be respected and English education was to be introduced to disseminate these

[6] India was often seen as living in an age which Europe had experienced many centuries ago. According to the nineteenth century jurist Henry Maine, India had once been like ancient German society with communal ownership and patriarchal families. But while Europe progressed beyond this social structure, India lagged behind, the independent, self-sufficient, village communities that dotted the Indian countryside being the living proof of a society that had remained dormant for centuries. Clive Dewey, 'Images of the Village Community: a Study in Anglo-Indian Ideology', *Modern Asian Studies*, vol. 6, no. 3, 1972, pp. 306-7. Also see Adam Kuper, *The Invention of Primitive Society: the Transformation of an Illusion*, London: Routledge and Kegan Paul, 1988, pp. 33-5. Karl Marx also agreed, describing India as a land without history. 'What we call history,' he pointed out, 'is but the history of successive intruders who founded their empires on the passive basis of that unresisting and unchanging society.' Cited in Eric Stokes, *The Peasant and the Raj: Studies in Agrarian Society and Peasant Rebellions in Colonial India*, Cambridge: CUP, 1978, p. 20. As J.R. Seeley put it in one of his Oxford lectures in 1882, the dominion of England over India was 'the Empire of the modern world over the medieval'. Cited in G. Bennet (ed.), *The Concept of Empire: Burke to Attlee 1774-1947*, London: Black, 1962, pp. 279-80.

[7] The Rev. William Ward of the Serampore mission was one evangelist who denounced Hinduism with vigour. In his work on Hindu literature and history he launched into what he called a 'Brhamanical tyranny', describing Hindu beliefs as 'the most complete system of absolute oppression that perhaps ever existed'. William Ward, *A View of the History, Literature and Religion of the Hindus*, 4 vols., London, 1817-20, 1, p. 389, cited in Susan Bayly, '"Caste" and "Race" in the Colonial Ethnography of India', in Peter Robb (ed.), *The Concept of Race in South Asia*, Delhi: OUP, 1995, p. 176. In the words of historian and political theorist James Mill, 'despotism and priestcraft taken together, the Hindu, in mind and body, are the most enslaved portion of the human race'. James Mill, *History of British India*, with notes and continuation by H.H. Wilson, 9 vols., London: James Madden, 1840, vol. 2, pp. 166-7. On the development of contempt towards Indian religions see also P.J. Marshall, *The British Discovery of Hinduism in the Eighteenth Century*, Cambridge: CUP, 1970, pp. 41-3.

values among the subject population.[8] In short, the British were taking responsibility for the well-being of Indians, bestowing the gift of progress on them.

Scientific progress in Europe also served to add a racist dimension to British attitudes to India. The simple prejudice groups of people feel towards other groups with different customs and physical features, is probably as old as human civilization, and so it was with Europeans who came into contact with Asian and African peoples during the sixteenth and seventeenth centuries. But the racism which began to colour British attitudes towards Indians in the nineteenth century was not about simple prejudice but were based on the assumption that cultural or outward physical difference were manifestations of deeper, more fundamental causes. This belief had its roots in the European Enlightenment. Led by an interest in man's place in nature, eighteenth century European intellectuals began grading the diverse groups of people revealed to them by expansion of European trade and conquest according to their outward appearances. Not surprisingly, the fair-skinned European was considered decidedly superior to the Negro with his dark skin and 'ape-like' features.[9] Still, the basis of this assumed superiority was left largely undiscussed. But from late eighteenth century onwards, encouraged by the gradual expansion of European

[8] This is an attitude best summed up in Thomas Macaulay's famous Minute on Education where he envisages in India 'a class of persons Indian in colour and blood, but English in tastes, in opinions, in morals and in intellect'. Eric Stokes, *English Utilitarians and India*, Delhi: OUP, 1982; 1st pub. 1959, pp. 46-7. For Macaulay's views on the merits of English education see also Kopf, *British Orientalism*, pp. 236-52. Even Karl Marx, hardly an admirer of imperialism, could not but applaud British rule in India as a necessary evil rescuing the natives from the 'brutalising worship of nature'. See Shlomo Avineri, *Karl Marx on Colonialism and Modernization: his Despatches and other Writing on China, India, Mexico, the Middle East and North Africa*, New York: Doubleday, 1968, p. 94.

[9] As the English surgeon Charles White wrote in 1799, 'Ascending the line of gradation we come at last to the white European, who, being the most removed from brute creation, may, on that account, be considered the most beautiful of the human race. No one will doubt his superiority.' Cited in Paul Gordon Lauren, *Power and Prejudice: the Politics and Diplomacy of Racial Discrimination*, Boulder, Col.: Westview Press, 1996, p. 22. As explained by Leon Poliakov, all the leading figures in the French Enlightenment considered Negroes to be inferior to Europeans. Leon Poliakov, 'Racism from the Enlightenment to the age of Imperialism', in Robert Ross (ed.), *Racism and Colonialism: Essays in Ideology and Social Structure*, The Hague: M. Nijhoff Publishers for Leiden University Press, 1982, pp. 55-64. Referring to Winthrop Jordan's illuminating work, *White over Black*, Nancy Stepan suggests that European prejudice against the Africans went as far back as the sixteenth century when the Europeans

control over large areas of Asia and Africa, European scientists began toying with the concept that human civilization was closely related to 'essential' biological characteristics of the people concerned. Outward physical features came to be seen as indicators of these characteristics. The shape of the human skull in particular was deemed to determine the size of the brain and as a consequence, the degree of human intelligence.[10]

In the eighteenth century, the term 'race' had usually referred to people with a common descent including religious, cultural and linguistic ties and not necessarily biological connections[11] but in the nineteenth century quest for a scientific basis for human diversity, race came to signify a group of people with biologically determined, inheritable characteristics which in turn determined their culture and civilization.[12]

As the nineteenth century progressed, such 'scientific discoveries' enabled Europeans to rationalize the growing European ascendancy over Africa and Asia in racist terms. As the famous French typologist Count Arthur de Gobineau wrote, race 'dominates all other problems of history and holds the key to them all', adding that 'all civilisation derives from the white Race'.[13] But it was the emerging theory of evolution which put the stamp of racism firmly on European attitudes

---

were making their first contacts with Africa. The fact that the Europeans discovered the Negro and the great apes at the same time largely contributed to the identification of the Africans with these members of the animal world. Nancy Stepan, *The Idea of Race in Science: Great Britain 1800-1960*, Hamden, Connecticut: Archon Books, 1982, p. 8.

[10] The pseudo-science of phrenology had its origins in the late eighteenth century but it was only during the nineteenth century that it gained wide acceptance. Stepan, *The Idea*, pp. 21-8; Lauren, *Power and Prejudice*, pp. 36-7.

[11] Michael Banton, *The Idea of Race*, London: Tavistock Publications, 1977, p. 27. As Christine Bolt points out, the term 'race' was frequently used even to denote a group of animals. Christine Bolt, *Victorian Attitudes to Race*, London: Routledge and Kegan Paul, 1971, p. 2.

[12] In the words of Immanuel Kant, sometimes referred to as the 'founder of the modern concept of race', race was 'a question of innate natural characters which resides, which has its seat, in the composition of human blood'. Poliakov, p. 59. For this biological definition of race see also Peter Robb, 'South Asia and the Concept of Race', in Robb (ed.), *The Concept*, pp. 1-2; Louis L. Snyder, *The Idea of Racialism: its Meaning and History*, New York: Van Nostrand, 1962, pp. 7-18; and L. van de Berghe, *Race and Racism: a Comparative Perspective*, London: Wiley, 1967, pp. 15-25.

[13] Cited in Lauren, *Power and Prejudice*, p. 38. The Scottish anatomist, Robert Knox agreed, declaring that to him, 'race or hereditary descent is everything; it stamps the man'. Robert Knox, *Races of Men: a Fragment*, London: Renshaw, 1850, p. 6.

to non-white peoples. In the heady atmosphere of European expansion, Darwin's theory of natural selection expounded in his *Origin of Species* (1859) was distorted to create a view of natural destiny, laying the foundation for a 'very un-Darwinian anthropology'.[14] The contemporary world of European dominance over the non-European world was now seen as part of a natural order where superior races had gained mastery over the inferior as a part of an inevitable natural process. As an article in the *Saturday Review* of 1896 argued, in the 'global struggle for existence', strong races progressed while 'feeble races were being wiped off the earth'.[15]

Naturally, these developments in contemporary European thought had their impact on British attitudes to India and Indians. In the eighteenth century, the British attitudes to the people on the subcontinent had been largely free of racial prejudice. Although the term 'Blacks' was very often used by many Englishmen to refer to Indians in the seventeenth and eighteenth centuries it signified the appreciation of difference, rather than inferiority.[16] Englishmen mixed quite freely with Indians, many keeping Indian mistresses. Not that prejudice was non-existent. Contemporary British views of Indians, particularly Muslims, are replete with disparaging stereotypes. Robert Clive described the Nawab of the Carnatic, Mohamed Ali as the 'best

[14] Kuper, *The Invention*, p. 2.

[15] Cited in Lauren, *Power and Prejudice*, p. 51. As explained by James Belich, European conquest was now seen not 'derived simply from the fact that the British had more guns, or indeed from the conviction that they were superior soldiers, but from what was widely perceived as a Law of Nature'. James Belich, 'The Victorian Interpretation of Racial Conflict and the New Zealand Wars: An Approach to the Problem of one-sided Evidence', *The Journal of Imperial and Commonwealth History*, vol. 15, no. 2, 1987, p. 133. See also Michael Howard's engagement with the racialist interpretation of European expansion in Michael Howard, 'Empire Race and War in pre-1914 Britain', in Hugh Lloyd Jones, Valerie Pearl and Blair Worden (eds.), *History and Imagination: Essays in Honour of H.R. Trevor-Roper*, London, Duckworth, 1981, pp. 340-55. The attribution of 'primitive' racial characteristics sometimes extended to the social underclasses. As Henrika Kuklick points out, it was usual for European upper classes to describe their own social inferiors in language strikingly similar to that which was used to describe 'primitive' peoples. Henrika Kuklick, *The Savage Within: The Social History of British Anthropology 1885-1945*, Cambridge, New York: CUP, 1991, pp. 100-1. See also van de Berghe, *Race and Racism*, p. 17.

[16] K.N. Chauduri, 'From Barbarian and the Civilised to the Dialectic of Colour: an Archaeology of Self-Identities', in Peter Robb (ed.), *Society and Ideology: Essays in South Asian History*, Delhi: OUP, 1993, p. 44.

Mussalman' he ever knew[17] while the Governor of Madras, Lord Macartney listed 'pride, vanity, loquacity and undisguised treachery' among the defining features of a 'perfect Moorman'.[18] And even though many Europeans kept 'Black' mistresses it was a dubious indicator of their attitude to Indians. Intimate associations were largely encouraged by peculiar social circumstances; there were very few European women in India in the eighteenth century. As C.R. Boxer quips, necessity was not simply the mother of invention, but also the father of the Eurasian.[19]

But the fact is that the prejudices that informed British attitudes towards Indians in the nineteenth century were not marred by a belief in an essential Indian inferiority. Moreover, British attitudes to India in the eighteenth century also reflected the incipient state of current European thinking on race. Scholar-officials like William Jones believed that the Hindus and the Europeans belonged to the same 'Aryan' race.[20]

[17] Keith Feiling, *Warren Hastings*, London: Macmillan, 1954, p. 70.

[18] Cited in P.J. Marshall, 'Lord Macartney, India and China: the Two faces of the Enlightenment', *South Asia*, vol. 19 (special issue), 1996, p. 127. An even more scathing generalization was made by Robert Orme:

> A domineering insolence towards all who are in subjection to them, ungovernable wilfulness, inhumanity, cruelty, murders and assassinations, deliberated with the same calmness and subtlety as the rest of their politics, an insensibility to remorse for these crimes, which are scarcely considered otherwise than as necessary accidents in the course of life, sensual excesses which revolt against nature, unbounded thirst of power, and an expaciousness of wealth equal to the extravagance of his propensities and vices—this is the character of an Indian Moor, who is of consequence sufficient to have any character at all.

Robert Orme, *Historical Fragments of the Mogul Empire, of the Morattoes, and of the English Concerns in Indostan from the Year MDCLIX*, edited with an introduction by J.P. Guha, New Delhi: Associated Publishing House, 1974; 1st pub. 1782, p. 271.

[19] C.R. Boxer, *The Dutch Seaborne Empire*, London: Hutchinson, 1965, p. 229. Cited in G. Knaap, 'Europeans, Mestizos and Slaves: the Population of Colombo at the End of the Seventeenth Century', *Itinerario*, vol. 5, no. 2, 1981, p. 84. Sexual relations between the colonizer and the colonized had been part and parcel of European colonial expansion and it rarely, of ever, meant equality. As Van de Berghe points out, in South Africa under Dutch rule it was very common for young Dutch men to have sexual relations with Black women who were slaves. Van de Berghe, *Race and Racism*, p. 98. Likewise, the fact that Englishmen had Indian mistresses does not necessarily prove that there was a perception of equality between Europeans and the indigenous population. See the perceptive observations of Franklin and Mary Wickwire on this issue in Franklin and Mary Wickwire, *Cornwallis: the Imperial Years*, Chapel Hill: University of North Carolina Press, 1980, p. 90.

[20] For the British view of the Aryan origins of Europeans and Indians see Joan

There was also much ambiguity about the meaning of 'race'. To Jones, the 'Aryan race' meant a linguistic kinship.[21] Others used it more loosely, 'caste', 'race' and 'tribe' often being interchangeable terms. Thus we hear James Forbes speaking of the Nairs of southern India as a 'well made handsome race'[22] and Robert Orme describing the Brahmins as 'the tribe of the priesthood'.[23]

Towards the close of the eighteenth century, grim signs of changing attitudes began to appear. In 1789, Governor-General Lord Cornwallis wrote to Sir Robert Yonge at the War Office that Europeans in India generally looked down on Anglo-Indians 'on account of their colour and extraction'.[24] However, it was only in the following century that these seeds of racism found an ideal climate to sprout and grow. Social and political developments in British India ensured that. In the first half of the nineteenth century, the growing numbers of European soldiers and officials accompanied by European women gradually enhanced the sense of exclusivity among Europeans, encouraging a more closed European community.[25] The traumatic events of 1857 hastened this. The Indian now came to be viewed with increased contempt and loathing as the murderers of European women and children. As the shaken Whites closed ranks, the hated natives were recast as 'niggers'.[26]

The racist theories of European scientists found resonance in this environment of contempt and fear, providing a 'scientific' evidence of Indian inferiority. For those who believed in the Aryan origins of Europeans and Hindus, this provided a convenient explanation for the domination of the latter by the former. The Aryans who settled in

---

Leopold, 'British Application of the Aryan Theory of Race to India, 1850-1870', *English Historical Review*, vol. 89, no. 352, 1974, pp. 578-603.

[21] Bayly, '"Caste" and "Race"', p. 173; Marshall, *British Discovery*, p. 37.

[22] Cited in Bayly, '"Caste" and "Race"', p. 175.

[23] Robert Orme, *History of the Military Transactions of the British Nation in Indostan, From the Year MDCCXLV to Which is Prefixed a Dissertation on the Establishments Made by the Mahomedan Conquerors in Indostan*, 2 vols., vol. 2 in 2 parts, New Delhi: Today and Tomorrow's Publishers, 1975; 1st pub. 1778, 1, p. 3.

[24] Cited in Wickwire, *Cornwallis*, p. 90.

[25] See Percival Spear, *The Nabobs: a Study of the Social Life of the English in Eighteenth Century India*, London: OUP, 1963, pp. 126-45. Also Amaury de Riencourt, *The Soul of India*, London: Honeyglen, 1961, p. 219.

[26] Ragat Kanta, 'Race, Religion and Realm: the Political Theory of "The Reigning Raj Indian Crusade, 1857"', in Mushirul Hasan and Narayani Gupta (eds.), *India's Colonial Encounter: Essays in Memory of Eric Stokes*, Delhi: Manohar, 1993, p. 135.

India, it was now contended, had lost the purity of their blood by mixing with the aboriginal races of the subcontinent,[27] 'a very consoling conclusion for a dominant race' as an Indian writer put it.[28] So, an Indian hierarchy was gradually constructed. Peoples from the north, with their fair skin and 'noble features' were ranked closer to the Europeans and as a consequence, above the dark skinned peoples from the south and east, among whom the Bengali came to represent the stereotypical Hindu—feeble of both body and mind than the European and therefore destined to be conquered.[29] But racial stereotyping was not confined to the Bengalis. Other indigenous groups also suffered from the essentialization of characteristics. Thus, the Rajput was 'proud', the Marathi 'ambitious', the Pariah 'patient'.[30] This was not all. Closely related to the creation of inferiority was the perception of Indians as child-like. However, unlike European children, Indians did not grow up. Therefore, Indians were best ruled by a strong, paternalistic government; they needed the strong hand of the European. As one late nineteenth century British general pointed out, what India required was a 'good strong viceroy with a birch to smack naughty boys'.[31] It was an attitude best exemplified by the paternalistic 'Panjab Style' of government personified by John and Henry Lawrence.[32]

[27] Metcalfe, *Ideologies*, pp. 82-3.

[28] Cited in Leopold, 'British Application', p. 602 fn.

[29] As Macaulay noted, 'over the ages the Bengali had been trampled upon by men of bolder and more hardy breeds. Courage, independence, veracity are qualities to which his constitution and his situation are equally unfavourable.' Cited in F.G. Hutchins, *The Illusion of Permanence: British Imperialism in India*, Princeton, New Jersey: Princeton University Press, 1967, p. 72. To the Victorian Englishman, steeped in the ideas of masculinity with its attendant moral and physical virtues, the slightly built Bengali was a ready example of femininity and sensuousness. Mrinalini Sinha, 'Gender and Imperialism: Colonialist Policy and the Ideology of Moral Imperialism', in Michael S. Kimmel (ed.), *Changing Men: New Directions in Research on Men and Masculinity*, Newbury Park, Calif: Sage Publications, 1987, pp. 225-9.

[30] The apparent distinction of upper and lower castes by colour in the Hindu *varna* system was now eagerly cited by British racialists as evidence of the recognition of colour-based inequality even within the Hindu tradition. Bolt, *Victorian*, pp. 157-205.

[31] Cited in David Omissi, *The Sepoy and the Raj: the Indian Army 1860-1940*, Bassingstoke: Macmillan in association with King's College, 1994, p. 194.

[32] Lewis D. Wurgaft, *The Imperial Imagination: Magic and Myth in Kipling's India*, Middletown, Connecticut: Wesleyan University Press, 1983, pp. 18-26. Bernard Cohn attributes this paternalism to the 'revalorising' of the model of despotism as 'one of the paradigms that formed the ideological infrastructure of British rule in India'. According to this paradigm, Indians were seen as best responding to a firm hand rather than rational laws and regulations. Cohn, *Colonialism*, p. 65.

Thus, the construction of Indian cultural and racial inferiority was a key element in the knowledge created by the British about India. This has led some scholars to describe the British epistemological engagement with India as a purely hegemonic exercise, casting the Indians in dependent role to rationalize British dominion over the subcontinent as necessary and inevitable. This view owes much to Edward Said whose influential work *Orientalism* set the tone for much of the discussion in recent times on British colonial discourse. Said describes 'Orientalism'—the study of the Orient—as an imperialist discourse which enabled the European colonizer to 'manage—and even reproduce—the Orient politically, sociologically, militarily, ideologically, scientifically and imaginatively'.[33] To this end, Orientalism generated stereotypes which 'explained' colonialism in terms of a technically and morally superior West taking responsibility for a decadent East. Although *Orientalism* deals only with the Middle East, in his other major work, *Culture and Imperialism*, Said suggests that these insights hold good for India as well.[34]

Said's view has gained much support among other scholars. Ronald Inden has forcefully applied Said's views to India, explaining the hegemonic nature of the colonial discourse, with particular reference to its treatment of the caste system. The construction of Indian society as dominated and regulated by caste, he contends, enabled the British to portray Indians as being incapable of independent thinking. 'People of India are not even partially autonomous agents. They do not shape and reshape their world. Rather they are the patients of that which makes them Indian—the social, material reality of caste. The people of India are not the makers of their own destiny. A hidden, substantialized agent, Caste, is the maker of it.'[35]

[33] Edward Said, *Orientalism: Western Conception of the Orient*, New York: Patheon Books, 1978, p. 3.

[34] Elsewhere Said argues for the Indian case mainly with reference to Kipling's *Kim* (1901): 'The division between white and non-white in India as elsewhere was absolute and is alluded to throughout *Kim* as well as the rest of Kipling's work; a sahib is a sahib, and no amount of friendship or camaraderie can change the rudiments of racial difference. Kipling would no more have questioned that difference and the right of the white European to rule, than he would have argued with the Himalayas.' Edward Said, *Culture and Imperialism*, London: Chatto and Windus, 1993, pp. 194-5. For a lengthy discussion of the imperialist ideology contained in Kipling's works see Lewis D. Wurgaft, *The Imperial Imagination*.

[35] Ronald Inden, 'Orientalist Construction of India', *Modern Asian Studies*, vol. 20, no. 3, 1986, p. 428.

However, not everybody agrees with Said and Inden. In his major work on south India, Eugene Irschick questions the view that the British construction of the Orient was an epistemological project undertaken by the British alone with neither contribution nor participation from Indians. Speaking of south India, he argues that the British simply did not have the kind of dominance necessary to impose their perceptions on a passive people.[36] On the contrary, the British hold was so tenuous that many voices other than that of the British had the opportunity to be heard and that the construction of meaning about south India during the colonial period was the result of this collaborative effort. One major example cited by Irschick is the emergence of the idea of a 'decadent' or 'amoral' society in contemporary south India as opposed to a 'Golden Past'. The idea was not a mere 'creation' of British officials but the product of a complex situation the British and the Indians found themselves in. To evade taxes, the landowners resorted to various tactics, like providing false information and abandoning their fields. Such acts, which were perfectly rational strategies of survival for the landowners, appeared as signs of a decaying moral order to the British who sought to stabilize their tax base by harking back to a 'Golden Age' when life was more sedentary and morally responsible.[37] Thus the construction of a 'Golden Past' for south India was the result of both the British and the Indians pursuing their interests.

Christopher Bayly has echoed Irschick's views, pointing out that although there was an element of hegemony in the British construction of knowledge about India, that hegemony was not absolute. He cautions about analysing the leading ideas of Anglo-India through its master texts:

> These ideas were abstractions from a body of competing and fractious ideas, principles and rules of thumb which were generated by the routine collisions and alliances of colonial politics. British assessments of crime, religion and native lethargy were more often reflections of the weakness and ignorance of the colonisers than a gauge of hegemony. Again, forces were at work in colonial India more general than those unleashed by the East India Company itself. British attempts to describe their Indian subjects in more rigid categories of race, religion and region, for example, were inflected by an international information order which mirrored the creation of a global economy and the

[36] Eugene F. Irschick, *Dialogue and History: Constructing South India 1795-1895*, Berkeley: University of California Press, 1994.

[37] Ibid., pp. 14-66.

rise of the nation state. Orientalism, in Edward Said's sense, was only one among a variety of localised engagements between power and knowledge.[38]

These critiques may have checked the initial vigour of the concept of Orientalism, but the debate is far from concluded. However, the debate on Orientalism has thus far been grounded by and large in the fiscal, political and social aspects of British colonialism. But it must be noted that there was a prominent military dimension to the British interaction with India and that the EIC's army in particular, had great potential to contribute to the British understanding of India and Indians. The army was the institution that spearheaded conquest and conquest involved long and violent exposure to the military traditions on the subcontinent. And interestingly, the great majority of the soldiers who fought the Company's wars of conquest were Indians drawn from that same indigenous military culture which the Company confronted. As such, the formation and development of the Company's army has the potential to reflect the British perception of Indian military culture in particular and Indian society in general.

What were the perceptions that informed British attitudes to their Indian soldiers? The few scholarly attempts to investigate this has so far focussed largely on the Indian army in the nineteenth century. These works, which show the influence of the 'Orientalist' view of colonial discourse, reveal that the major influence on British military thinking was the emerging concept of race. As scholars like Douglas Peers, David Omissi and Lionel Caplan have shown, it was only too easy for the British authorities to see the sepoys as an inherently inferior breed of soldier—worthy, malleable, tough, yet ultimately childlike, condemned by their natural inferiority to be led by men of a superior race.[39] As Brigadier John Jacob explained in the mid-nineteenth century, it was their 'habitual nobility of being' which enabled British officers to command Indian troops.[40] Yet in true paternalistic style, the British

[38] C.A. Bayly, *Empire and Information: Intelligence Gathering and Social Communication in India 1780-1880*, Cambridge: CUP, 1996, p. 143.

[39] See Omissi, *Sepoy*, and Douglas Peers, 'The Habitual Nobility of Being: British Officers and the Social Construction of the Bengal Army in the Early Nineteenth Century', *Modern Asian Studies*, vol. 25, no. 3, 1991, pp. 545-69, and *Between Mars and Mammon: Colonial Armies and the Garrison State in India 1819-1835*, London and New York: Tauris Academic Studies, 1995; Lionel Caplan, 'The Bravest of the Brave: Representations of the Gurkha in Modern British Military Writings', *Modern Asian Studies*, vol. 25, no. 3, 1991, pp. 571-97, and *Warrior Gentlemen: 'Gurkhas' in the Western Imagination*, Providence: Berghahn Books, 1995.

[40] Cited in Peers, 'Habitual Nobility', p. 545, fn.

military officer set himself up as more than a commander; he strove to be also a father-figure to his men, taking care of their needs.[41]

Racist stereotyping of the Indian sepoys formed an important part of the overall imperial construction of the Indian soldier's inferiority. For instance, in the early nineteenth century, Arabs were typically ranked next to Europeans in bravery while Gurkhas and Malays were considered ideal for light duties.[42] But this racial thinking had its highest expression in the theory of martial races which divided 'races' in India into martial and non-martial races according to their perceived military virtues. The major impetus for this came from the Russian threat to the north-west in the late nineteenth century which raised the concern that only some 'races' of Indian soldiers would be able to handle a European enemy.[43] The resultant search for the martial races of India decided heavily in favour of north Indian peoples. Jats, Gurkhas and Sikhs became highly prized as soldiers while southern peoples like the Tamils and Gujars were overlooked.[44] But the British admiration for the fighting qualities of the northern peoples did not undermine their sense of racial superiority. The Jats and Gurkhas may have been brave, but they were also considered slow-witted and—that term again—childlike. Lionel Caplan has explained this construction of the

[41] See Jeffrey Greenhunt, 'Sahib and Sepoy: an Inquiry into the Relationship Between the British Officers and Native Soldiers of the British Indian Army', *Military Affairs*, vol. 48, no. 1, 1984, pp. 15-18.

[42] Peers, 'Habitual Nobility', p. 566.

[43] As Lord Roberts said in 1882, it was 'no use trying to persuade ourselves that the whole of the Native Army is capable of meeting an enemy from Central Asia or Europe'. It was not a question of efficiency, he argued, but of courage and physique. Cited in Omissi, *Sepoys*, p. 1. See also Stephen P. Cohen, *The Indian Army: its Contribution to the Development of a Nation*, Berkeley, University of California Press, 1971, pp. 47-8. Sir George MacMunn, another prominent advocate of the martial races theory, claimed that one of the main differences between the East and the West was that in the East 'only certain clans and classes can bear arms' while the others did not possess the 'physical courage necessary for the warrior'. Cited in Omissi, *Sepoy*, p. 24. See also Sir George MacMunn, *The Martial Races of India*, London: Sampson Low, Marston & Co., 1933, p. 2.

[44] The 'handbooks' which introduced these races to the British officers described men from different 'races' as if they were specimens. Thus, the handbook on Madras castes described the Pallan as 'a stout, short, jet black man, sturdy, a meat eater, and not overclean in person or habits'. Cited in Omissi, *Sepoy*, p. 31. Racial stereotyping was now at its peak. The Pathans were considered 'independent' and 'calculating', the Dogras 'proud' and 'shy' and the Gurkhas 'playful' and 'bloodthirsty' in combat. Cohen, *Indian Army*, p. 51.

identities of the martial races with regard to the British attitudes to their Gurkhas. The Gurkhas were often seen as a perfect martial race—obedient, loyal and brave but also extremely dim-witted. Even their bravery, which the British admired much, did not quite measure up to European standards for the courage of the Gurkha was seen as physical courage, which was much inferior to the moral courage which their British officers were blessed with:

> Like all martial races the Gurkhas were invariably brave, tough in an unthinking, instinctive, 'gung-ho' sort of way as befitted their somewhat simple, unimaginative character. As such they did not entirely replicate their officers whose courage was deliberate and directed to high moral purposes—in short Aristotelian. Such courageous propensities, moreover, could only hope to be acquired in the cultured social and ideological ambiance of the institutions in which the officer was nurtured and in which his persona was formed. These attributed were therefore out of reach of even of Gurkhas as of other martial races.[45]

Thus, racist attitudes were important to the development of the Indian army in the nineteenth century. But in the nineteenth century, the Indian army was already a well established force and the racist attitudes originated primarily in Europe and not as a result of interaction with the Indian military culture. It was in the eighteenth century that the English East India Company raised an army of Indian soldiers trained and equipped in the European manner during intense and violent interaction with the indigenous military culture. What were the were the perceptions that informed British thinking on their Indian soldiers during this interesting period?

Work on the sepoy army in the eighteenth century is still largely dominated by standard narrative histories like Wilson's voluminous history of the Madras Army[46] and Patrick Cadell's work on the Bombay Army[47] which deal almost exclusively with its organization and the military services. Such works, while providing us with a wealth of information, are largely silent about the British attitudes that informed the organization and employment of the sepoy army. Indeed, in recent times, Gerald Bryant has examined the EIC's army in the eighteenth century from a more 'modern' perspective, focussing on aspects of

[45] Caplan, *Warrior Gentlemen*, p. 155. For British views of the perceived low intelligent of the martial races see also Omissi, *Sepoy*, pp. 26-7.

[46] W.J. Wilson, *History of the Madras Army*, 5 vols., Madras: Government Press, 1882-8.

[47] Patrick Cadell, *History of the Bombay Army*, London: Longmans Green, 1938.

command, control and employment of the Company's army, but the sepoy army as an institution does not figure prominently in his inquiries.[48]

The exception is Seema Alavi's recent work on the Bengal Army.[49] Alavi for the first time has examined the impact the Company's sepoys had on the rural societies from which they were drawn. She also explores the influence the indigenous military culture had on the Company's approach to raising its native army, demonstrating that in raising the Bengal Army, the Company's preference for soldiers from particular social backgrounds was largely informed by the recruitment strategies of contemporary Indian rulers as well as by the military thinking in contemporary Europe. The high caste-dominated armies of local rulers like the Benares Raja, Cheyt Singh, functioned as a model for the Bengal Army, which drew its sepoy recruits from the same social base.[50] As a result, caste became the category that dominated British attitudes towards their sepoys, reflected in the allowance made for the observance of religious scruples within the army.[51] Such views sit comfortably with the general view of British India in the eighteenth century as a racially accommodating period when Englishmen admired Persian poetry, smoked the hookah and enjoyed the company of their Indian concubines.

Broadly speaking, we have no quarrel with this interpretation. But although Alavi deals admirably with the impact British perceptions of Indian culture had on recruitment and general management of the sepoy army, its command structure, training and more importantly, its deployment in the pursuit of the English East India Company's military

[48] See Gerald James Bryant, 'The English East India Company and its Army 1600-1778', unpublished Ph.D. thesis, University of London, King's College, 1975; 'Officers of the East India Company's Army in the Days of Clive and Hastings', *Journal of Imperial and Commonwealth History*, vol. 6, no. 2, 1978, pp. 203-27; 'East India Company and the Crisis in Madras 1783', *Journal of the Society for Army Historical Research*, vol. 62, no. 249, 1984, pp. 13-27; 'Pacification in the Early British Raj 1755-85', *Journal of Imperial and Commonwealth History*, vol. 14, no. 1, 1985, pp. 3-19.

[49] Seema Alavi, *The Sepoys and the Company: Tradition and Transition in Northern Indian Military Culture 1770-1830*, Delhi: OUP, 1995.

[50] Ibid., p. 39.

[51] Ibid., pp. 76-80. Douglas Peers also suggests that caste was the most important criterion that influenced the organization of the sepoy army in the eighteenth century. He refers to the Burma War of 1824-6 as the turning point in the transition of the Bengal Army 'from an army modelled on caste lines to one that rested principally on race'. Peers, 'Habitual Nobility', pp. 545-6.

objectives remain out of the scope of her work. Although this is understandable in the case of Alavi's work, the importance of the need to view the organization, training and the deployment—in addition to recruitment—of the sepoy army in the eighteenth century within the context of contemporary British perceptions of India and Indians cannot be emphasized too much. As noted earlier, the British construction of Indian backwardness originated in the eighteenth century which was also the period when the EIC's sepoy army was formed. And the formation of the sepoy army was not simply a matter of recruiting and arming thousands of men. It was also about organizing an Indian army to fight in the European manner, and, interestingly, implicit in this transition from Indian to European style of fighting is a basic value judgement which run parallel to the general British discourse on India at the time—that the Indian way was inferior to the European. The transition also suggests another, even more interesting assumption; that the Indian soldiers had the potential to assimilate to the European system.

This implied inferiority of the Indian military system on the one hand and the recognition of the ability to assimilate that is implicit in the formation of the sepoy army opens a totally new dimension in the exploration of British attitudes to the formation of the sepoy army in the eighteenth century. It suggests the possibility that there were broader perceptions of the Indian soldier based on value-judgemental contrasts between the Indian and European cultures influencing the formation of the sepoy army. But the recognition of this possibility is not sufficient. We need to explore its full extent and determine the nature of its impact on the formation of the sepoy army. This is what we intend to do in this thesis through an examination of the formation of the English East India Company's sepoy army during the latter half of the eighteenth century.

We shall base our inquiry on some basic questions neglected by most scholars: how did the British perceive Indian soldiers and how did this perception influence the formation of the sepoy army in the eighteenth century? We shall begin to answer these questions by examining the British perception of the contrast that existed between Indian and European military systems and proceed to examine the impact this had on the recruitment and organization of the sepoy army. In doing this, close attention will be paid to the implementation of European-style discipline and command over the sepoy army. Last but not least, we shall explore the influence of British perceptions on the employment of sepoys in military operations. The findings, as we shall see, will be quite interesting.

## SOURCES

As befitting a research on British attitudes, this thesis is largely based on British sources. These include the voluminous minutes of various committees set up by the three presidencies of the English East India Company which dealt with military matters. They provide an insight into the attitudes that prevailed in the official circles and are particularly important in exploring the Company's attitude towards the organization of the sepoy army. The Home Miscellaneous Series in the British Library's Oriental and India Office Collections also contains a wide range of documents, both official and private, which deal with various facets of the organization and employment of the sepoy army during the latter half of the eighteenth century. The European manuscripts departments of the Oriental and India Office Collections and the British Museum contain many private papers which are also extremely useful in this regard as they often offer a glimpse into personal opinions of British officers and officials which are not usually available in official documents. They are particularly rich in details about the operational aspects of the sepoy army. The Orme collections (Orme Various and Orme India) are indispensable in this regard; they contain hundreds of letters, journals and narratives of many Company officers who took part in the first British military campaigns on the subcontinent later used by Robert Orme to write his *History of the Military Transactions of the British Nation in Indostan* (New Delhi, 1975; 1st pub. 1778). Other private collections include the Coote and Carnac papers as well as numerous other journals and letters.

Contemporary publications also form an important source of information on British attitudes towards their sepoys and the Indian military culture in general. Orme's work has already been noted. It provides a highly detailed descriptions of the military operations conducted by the EIC from 1746 to 1761, but it is ultimately Orme's version of the events and is best used in conjunction with other primary sources, especially the Orme manuscripts on which the work was largely based. There are also many other contemporary publications most of which, like Innes Munro's *A Narrative of the Military Operations on the Coromandel Coast* (London, 1789) and Edward Moor's *A Narrative of the Operations of Captain Little's Detachment* (London, 1794) are accounts of military campaigns written by participants. Like the private papers, they provide a personal view of events, albeit meant for a larger audience than the journals and letters found among the private collections.

There is little that is unique about these sources. Almost all these documents have been previously scrutinized by meticulous researchers and many of the British observations and remarks about Indian soldiers cited in this thesis have been previously noted. The novelty of the present research lies in the treatment of these sources. These sources have never been used in a systematic inquiry into the development of British perceptions about Indian soldiers and the impact of these perceptions on the formation of the EIC's sepoy army. This is particularly the case with the study of the deployment of sepoys. As noted above, most works on the EIC's army during the eighteenth century deal with operational aspects and almost all are based on the same sources consulted in this thesis. But none of the standard works on the EIC's military operations in the eighteenth century recognize the potential of the operational details available in the sources for revealing British perceptions about sepoys.

The primary sources are supplemented by secondary sources. Again, these are mainly English language sources. They include the standard works on the different presidency armies which are rich in details about military organization and campaigns. Secondary works have also been consulted copiously with reference to the discussion of the contrast between Indian and European military systems which function as a necessary prelude to exploring British perceptions about Indian soldiers and the Indian military culture. The works on the Indian military culture include classics like William Irvine's *The Army of the Indian Mughals* (2nd edn., New Delhi, 1962) and Surendranath Sen's *The Military System of the Marathas* (Calcutta, 1959), as well as the works of modern scholars like Norman Ziegler, Dirk Kolff and Stewart Gordon. The discussion of the European military system in particular is almost exclusively based on secondary sources. But this, I believe does little to impair the validity of the conclusions drawn from this discussion. As for European military history, the Early-modern period has been analysed rigorously enough to produce a fine crop secondary works by historians like Christopher Duffy, John Childs, Geoffrey Parker and Jeremy Black that adequately answers our purpose.

The heavy dependence on British and other European sources does not create the problem of possible bias, considering that the thesis is primarily about British perceptions. This however, does pose a problem with regard to the discussion of the Indian military culture where a lack of Indian voices may prove a drawback. But I believe this weakness has been largely offset by the use of secondary works that rely extensively on Indian sources. The use of British sources to explore British attitudes is also not without its pitfalls. There is always the problem of the determining the extent to which personal opinions and observations represent collective views. There are several ways of getting over this problem. One is to consider the sheer weight of evidence; another is to check perceptions against practice. I have endeavoured to do both in this thesis.

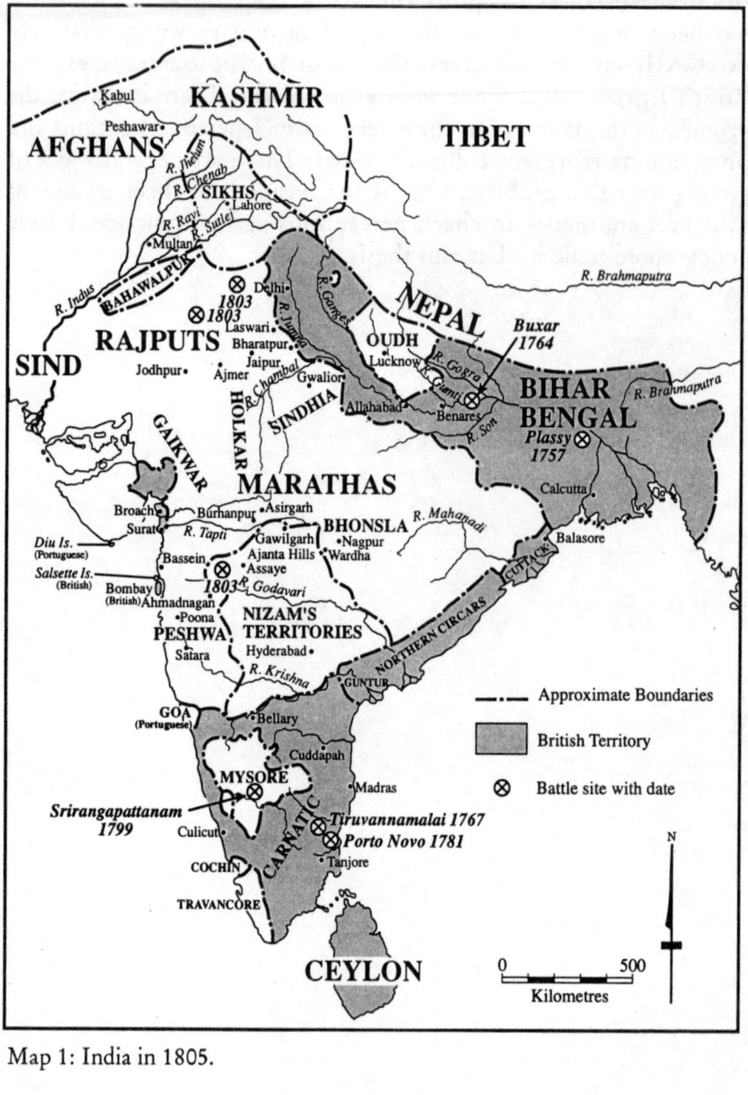


Map 1: India in 1805.

*One*

# Europe and India: A Clash of Military Cultures

A CRUCIAL FACTOR in the English attitude towards employing native soldiers was their perception of the differences that existed between the European and Indian military cultures. Indeed, these differences were very considerable. Warfare on the subcontinent stood in sharp contrast to that in Europe in all major aspects, from the organization of armies down to the martial values of the soldiers. The purpose of this chapter is to examine these differences in order to set the stage for exploring British perceptions of the Indian military system.

## WAR IN INDIA

### *Rulers and Soldiers*

We shall begin our examination of the Indian military system with an obscure military campaign in southern India in the seventeenth century. In 1676 the Governor of Golconda, Sher Khan, was at war with the ruler of Gingee in southern India. To further his military campaign, he requested the French East India Company to help him capture the Fort of Tindivanum, the stronghold of a local chief loyal to the ruler of Gingee. The French despatched one of their senior employees, Francois Martin with 100 Frenchmen and 600 Indian infantry. On the way Muhammad Raza, one of Sher Khan's captains joined him, with 50 cavalry and 200 infantry. A little later, their small force was further strengthened by 300 troops brought by Kolaique Achamail Nayak, a local chief or won over from Nasir Muhammad.[1]

[1] Francois Martin, *India in the Seventeenth Century (Social, Economic and Political): Memoirs of Francois Martin 1670-1694*, trs. Lotika Varadarajan, 2 parts, Delhi: Manohar, 1983, part 2, pp. 543-53.

Not long after, Martin suggested to Muhammad Raza that he should attack a prosperous village close to Tindivanum but the cavalry captain refused, saying, 'it was not customary for his men to keep so much to the forefront'. A few days later another cavalry captain joined the party with 44 horsemen. Before long Achamail Nayak became disgruntled over the non-payment of his troops and decided to decamp; only some earnest persuasion by Martin prevented him from doing so. Meanwhile, another local chieftain had joined the little army with 800 men. On 10 November the combined army moved towards the village of Tindivanum and appeared before the raja's fort which, Martin believed, was in a poor state of defence. But Martin's calls to action fell on deaf ears: 'I again suggested to the officers that they should form the men into detachments. Showing them the crumbling bastion, I pointed out how easy it would be to carry the fort from there if we could only act with a little vigour. Not one of them wished to cooperate.'[2]

But more was to come. Not long after this episode, the rear of the Franco-Golconda force was attacked by a sally from the fort. Martin, who was leading the party turned back to help, but found his allies dragging their feet. 'The men turned round as if to follow me but marched slowly, while the cavalry also advanced but at a tardy pace', he noted. After a short engagement the enemy was driven inside the fort, yet Martin felt that a golden opportunity had been lost. 'Had our men given us the backing which they could have very well done our momentum would have carried us right inside the fort, but unfortunately the men held back. Muhammad Raza even went to the extent of staying outside the village with his band of fifty horsemen', he bitterly complained.[3]

The army which Martin struggled to hold together and lead in battle may be considered a minute version of a 'typical' Indian army of the time as far as the system of command was concerned. The armies of Indian rulers consisted of numbers of individuals skilled in arms, but not subjected to anything approaching a uniform system of discipline and control. The root cause lay in a segmented structure of political control which favoured military units which, in terms of command and control, approximated to war bands rather than to a disciplined army.

[2] Ibid., p. 552.
[3] Ibid., p. 553.

The mud forts that lay scattered around the countryside were ample testimony to this inescapable reality. These strongholds symbolized the power of the local lineages and of their kin—feudatory chiefs—called *zamindars* in northern India and *deshmukhs* or *palaikkars* in southern India—who articulated power through armed bodies of retainers drawn from their caste and kinship networks and from the general population. Such military power enabled these lineages to maintain control over the surplus produced by the local peasantry. In the words of Irfan Habib, armed force was 'the first historical prerequisite for the establishment as well as the retention of *zamindari* rights'.[4]

Regional overlords drew on the allegiance of local chiefs to maintain authority over a larger number of people and their revenue. For example, in the south Indian kingdom of Puducottai, the Tondaiman Raja's power depended on the allegiance of the local chieftains, known as *sardars*[5] while the Muslim power in sixteenth century Telengana and coastal Andhra rested largely on an accommodation between the Telugu warrior aristocracy in the countryside and a ruling elite of Persian and Deccani Muslims.[6] Likewise, Maratha landowning families or *deshmukhs* allied to the southern Muslim kingdom of Bijapur helped maintain Bijapuri power in the region of Maharashtra.[7]

Burton Stein has described the above type of political control as a 'pyramidally segmented type of state, so-called because the smallest

[4] Irfan Habib, *The Agrarian System of Mughal India*, New York: Asia Publishing House, 1963, p. 163. Some of these chiefs could muster very substantial forces. For example, the Burdwan Raja in Bengal maintained a force of nearly 30,000 men. P.J. Marshall, *Bengal, the British Bridgehead: Eastern India 1740-1828*, The New Cambridge History of India II. 2, Cambridge: CUP, 1988, p. 55. According to the seventeenth century traveller, Niccolo Manucci, these lineages included 'many powerful men who could place in the field, more or less, forty thousand soldiers'. Niccolo Manucci, *Storia do Mogor or Moghul India 1653-1708*, trs. William Irvine, 4 vols., Delhi: Editions Indian, 1965, vol. 2, p. 417. The militarization of the Indian countryside is also discussed in Dirk A. Kolff, *Naukar, Rajput and Sepoy: Ethnohistory of the Military Labour Market in Hindustan 1450-1850*, Cambridge: CUP, 1990, pp. 1-31.

[5] Nicholas B. Dirks, *The Hollow Crown: Ethnohistory of an Indian Kingdom*, Ann Arbor: University of Michigan Press, 1993, pp. 168-92.

[6] John F. Richards and Velcheru Narayan Rao, 'Banditry in Mughal India', *Indian Economic and Social History Review*, vol. 17, no. 1, 1980, p. 95.

[7] Stewart Gordon, *The Marathas 1600-1818*, The New Cambridge History of India II. 4, New York: CUP, 1993. See Chapter 1, especially pp. 23-36.

unit of political organization—a section of a peasant village—was linked to ever more comprehensive units of political organization of an ascending order'.[8] Those at the top and bottom of this pyramid derived their power and legitimacy from the acknowledgement of each other's positions. An overlord needed the allegiance of lesser powers to establish himself as a superior power while the lesser powers required the sanction of higher authority for their power to be legitimate. As Dirk Kolff explains, such alliances 'had little of the nature of sacred treaties and seem to have been regarded very much like service contracts, temporary agreements of an auxiliary character'.[9]

Thus, in the eighteenth century, 'conquest' usually meant the successful suborning of lesser ruler and chiefs by a superior power.[10] Under such circumstances, the demonstration of overwhelming power and generosity could result in large-scale submission and the formation of extensive alliances.[11] Kingdoms rose and fell and empires expanded and contracted in South Asia with the making and unmaking of such alliances. On the subcontinent, kingdoms were separated by frontier zones rather than by clearly marked boundaries such as existed by then between most sovereign states in Europe. The 'frontier' of a

[8] Burton Stein, *Peasant State and Society in Medieval South India*, Delhi: OUP, 1980, pp. 264-5. See also Bernard Cohn's discussion of the political system in eighteenth century Benares. Cohn describes the power structure in Benares as having a number of 'levels': the imperial, headed by the Mughal emperor, secondary, consisting of Mughal officials and administrators, the regional comprising petty rajas and other regional overlords and finally, the local lineages. Bernard Cohn, *An Anthropologist Among the Historians and Other Essays*, Delhi: OUP, 1987, pp. 483-99. The segmentation of political power in pre-modern India is also discussed in Karen Leonard 'The Hyderabad Political System and its Participants', *Journal of Asian Studies*, vol. 30, no. 3, 1974, pp. 569-82; Richard G. Fox, *Kin, Clan, Raja and Rule: State Hinterland Relations in Pre-industrial India*, Berkeley: University of California Press, 1971; Andre Wink, *Land and Sovereignty in India: Agrarian Society and Politics Under the Eighteenth Century Maratha Swarajya*, Cambridge: CUP, 1986; J.C. Heesterman, *The Inner Conflict of Tradition: Essays in Indian Ritual, Kingship and Society*, Chicago: University of Chicago Press, 1985, pp. 10-26.

[9] Kolff, *Naukar*, p. 91.

[10] See for example, Stewart Gordon's description of the Maratha 'conquest' of the Mughal province of Malwa. Stewart Gordon, *Marathas, Marauders and State Formation in Eighteenth Century India*, Delhi: OUP, 1994, pp. 58-9.

[11] Kolff, *Naukar*, p. 91.

kingdom was the fringes of the area over which a ruler had a large measure of control and from which he could draw an assured revenue. According to Benedict Anderson, boundaries in pre-modern South Asia were 'porous and indistinct' facades where 'sovereignties faded imperceptibly into one another'.[12] The Indian situation was basically no different.

The Mughal empire was also essentially a large network of alliances which incorporated different levels of regional and local power. This reflected the imperial strategy of domination through accommodation. The Mughal nobility comprised Rajputs, Indian Muslims, Afghans, Iranis and Turanis, all wielding varying degrees of authority in different regions of the subcontinent.[13] Likewise, Maratha leaders were gradually integrated into the network after the empire pushed to the south in the latter part of the seventeenth century. The troublesome Maratha leader Shivaji himself was offered a post as a Mughal commander as the price of his submission. As a part of the deal Shivaji was also ordered to conquer Bijapuri territory around Goa.[14] As J.C. Heesterman explains, the 'fall of the Mughal empire' was no more than the retreat of Mughal influence towards a core area and the growth of the influence of other contenders for empire so that 'the empire, though never

[12] B. Anderson, *Imagined Communities: Reflections on the Origin and Spread of Nationalism*, London: Verso, 1991, p. 226. Cited in Elizabeth Nissan and R.L. Stirrat, 'The Generation of Communal Identities', in Jonathan Spencer (ed.), *Sri Lanka: History and the Roots of Conflict*, London: Routeledge, 1990, p. 25. The Burmese response to a British query about the boundary of the kingdom in 1823 illustrates this perfectly. When asked by British officials to show the boundary between Bengal and Burma, the Burmese officials replied that their king knew the extent of his dominions and that 'no one can set limits to it but himself'. Cited in Ainslie T. Embree, *Imagining India*, p. 72. As Stewart Gordon explains, a 'frontier' in pre-modern India was 'a broad band between two heartland areas, in which the Deshmukh or petty rajah might pay taxes and offers loyalty to either side or none or both, depending on the perceived relative strength of the kingdoms'. Gordon, *The Marathas*, p. 38.

[13] For a good description of the various ethnic and regional interests represented within the Mughal nobility see Satish Chandra, *Parties and Politics at the Mughal Court*, Delhi: People's Publishing House, 1972. On the early expansion of Mughal dominance in India see Douglas E. Streusand, *The Formation of the Mughal Empire*, Delhi: OUP, 1989, pp. 57-81.

[14] Shivaji's son Shambaji was also offered a command in the Mughal army. Gordon, *Marathas*, pp. 74-5.

actually overthrown, naturally and irrevocably shrivelled again into a local sphere of influence, or "little kingdom" at the mercy of the new would be empire builders such as the Marathas, the Afghans and eventually the British'.[15]

Segmented states resulted in segmented armies. Armies in early modern India consisted largely of men brought together by the principal figures who formed political alliances. As such, the army of a powerful Indian ruler actually consisted of a number of separate armies commanded by the leaders who raised and maintained them. Their size varied according to the power and influence of their commanders.

The armies of the two great empires of early modern India—the Mughals and the Marathas—are very good examples of this phenomenon. The Mughal cavalry was made up of the forces contributed by the numerous elite who were placed in a hierarchy known as the *mansabdari* system whereby the nobility was assigned the task of supplying troopers to army according to their means.[16] Thus, the Mughal 'army' actually included a number of separate armies raised and controlled by independent commanders. There was no uniform structure of command to control and direct these independent units; the *mansabdars* formed little more than a conglomeration of independent commanders owing allegiance directly to the emperor.[17] Important nobles with large contingents employed numbers of subordinate officers, mostly family members. Sometimes, some of these officers also

[15] Heesterman, *The Inner Conflict*, pp. 16-17.

[16] A *mansabdar's* position within the military hierarchy was denoted by two basic ranks—*sat* and *sawar*. The former merely indicated the mansabdar's position in the hierarchy while the latter corresponded to the number of troopers he was required to maintain. M. Athar Ali, *The Mughal Nobility under Aurangzeb*, Bombay: Asia Publishing House, 1996, pp. 38-40. See also William Irvine, *The Army of the Indian Moghuls: its Organisation and Administration*, New Delhi: Eurasian Publishing House, 1962, pp. 3-11. Until early seventeenth century, *sat* ranks of over 5,000 were reserved for the Mughal princes. But in the early decades of the seventeenth century, this policy was reversed to allow commoners to be admitted to the upper echelons of the hierarchy. W.B. Moreland, *India at the Death of Akbar*, Delhi: Atma Ram and Sons, 1962, p. 61. The *sawar* rank was usually either equal to the *sat* rank or less. Abdul Aziz, *The Mansabdari System and the Mughal Army*, Delhi: Idarah-i-Abiyat-i-Delhi, 1972, pp. 45-6.

[17] Athar Ali, *Mughal Nobility*, p. 39. See also John F. Richards, *The Mughal Empire*, The New Cambridge History of India I. 5, Cambridge: CUP, 1993, pp. 63-5, and Irvine, *Army*, p. 183.

held *mansabs*, mainly through the patronage of the noble, creating what John Richards has aptly termed a 'cluster' of lesser *mansabdars* gathered around a greater noble. This often resulted in large separate armies armed with their own artillery.[18]

In addition to this heavy cavalry, the *mansabdars* also enjoyed the services of numerous local lineages that came within their jurisdiction. These mostly contributed the infantry strength since the localized revenue base of the *zamindars* often did not permit them the luxury of cavalry.[19] But the numbers of infantry they could muster could be staggering. The *zamindari* infantry within the Mughal empire in the sixteenth century is calculated by Abu'l Fazl in excess of 4,00,000.[20]

Towards the latter part of the sixteenth century however, the rise of the *jamadar* or jobber-commander as a broker of military service provided another valuable source of infantry. Kolff suggests that the *jamadar* emerged in the wake of the Lodi conquest of eastern Hindustan in late fifteenth century. He argues that the Afghan soldiery, which helped the Lodis to conquer eastern Hindustan in the 1490s, had a negative impact on the chances of military employment for the numerous local *zamindari* troops, with the result that many peasant soldiers looked to external sources of employment. The *jamadars* emerged as the contractors of this pool of military labour emancipated from *zamindari* patronage, operating mainly from the pilgrim town of Buxar on the Ganges, became a key recruiting station for these soldiers.[21]

[18] John F. Richards, 'Norms and Comportment among Imperial Mughal Officers', in Barbara Metcalfe (ed.), *Moral Conduct and Authority*, Berkeley: University of California Press, 1984, pp. 260-1.

[19] Habib, *Agrarian*, pp. 166-9. Manucci, *Storia*, 2, p. 417. The French missionary Abbe J.A. Dubois who was in India between 1792 and 1823 paints a similar picture with regard to the forces of the *palaikkars* of south India: 'poligars rarely have any cavalry, the smallness of their revenues and the character of the country they inhabit rendering it almost impossible to maintain them'. Abbe J.A. Dubois, *Hindu Manners, Customs and Ceremonies*, trs. Henry K. Beauchamp, London: OUP, 1959, 1st pub. 1906, p. 677.

[20] Habib, *Agrarian*, p. 163.

[21] Kolff, *Naukar*, pp. 159-92. Rafi Ahmad Khan points out with regard to the recruitment of infantry during Shah Jehan's reign that they were almost all Rajputs recruited from Buxar. Rafi Ahmad Khan, 'New Light on Mughal Cavalry', in Irfan Habib et al. (eds.), *Medieval India: a Miscellany*, Bombay: Asia Publishing House, 1972, vol. 2, p. 78.

How did *jamadari* recruitment work? Colonel John Caillaud, an eighteenth century English officer, has left the following description:

> Every Jemydar [*sic*] raises his own men and makes the best terms with them as he can for their subsistence, which is not fixed nor regulated but varies according to circumstances and some particulars relative to the order and conditions of those who offer their service: thus in the infantry a man who hath his own arms, and these happen to consist of a good firelock, he receives more monthly pay than one with a matchlock and so on for those who have but pikes or swords. The Jemydars may have some arms of his own, and in that case he receives for the use of them so much a month from the sepoys to whom they are delivered.[22]

By the early eighteenth century, the *jamadari* system of recruitment had become widespread, turning the *jamadars* into a considerable source of military labour. For instance, the army with which Siraj-ud-Daulah expelled the English from Bengal included 20,000 musketeers all raised by *jamadars*.[23]

Like the *zamindari* war bands, the *jamadari* contingents varied greatly in their numbers, reflecting the power and influence of the individual *jamadars*. Some units had as many as 1,000 while others had as few as a hundred.[24] Both the *zamindars* and *jamadars* enjoyed a patron-client relationship with their troops, the former as a member of the local elite and the latter as a provider of employment. As such, it would not be misleading to say that, like the *zamindari* war bands, the *jamadari*

[22] OIOC, Orme India III, p. 3748, Orme, probably speaking of this mode of recruitment, says that the native commanders 'receive a fixed price for every man, and hires out everyman at a different and less price'. Robert Orme, *Historical Fragments*, p. 268. *Jamadars* also recruited cavalry. Cavalrymen were paid more than the foot soldiers and cavalrymen who provided their own mounts, or *silahdars* as they were known, received higher pay than the *bargirs* or those who were mounted by their *jamadars*. However, pay was not the only source of income for these mercenaries; plundering and the levying of protection money under the threat of plundering were also very common. Jos Gommans, *The Rise of the Indo-Afghan Empire c 1710-1780*, Leiden: E.J. Brill, 1995, pp. 135-41.

[23] S.C. Hill (ed.), *Bengal in 1756-57: a Selection of Public and Private Papers Dealing with the Affairs of the British in Bengal During the Reign of Siraj-ud-Daulah*, 3 vols., New York: AMS Press, 1968 (1st pub. 1905), vol. 1, p. 265. In volume 1, *jamadars* are often mentioned with regard to the Mughal army that captured Calcutta in 1756.

[24] Kolff, *Naukar*, p. 174.

Plate 1: Armed retainers or *burkundaz*; inscribed: 'Asiatick infantry soldiers called Back-um-dang.' By a Calcutta artist *c.* 1798-1804. OIOC Add. Or. 1160.

units were also private armies, although unlike the *zamindari* forces which were associated with locality, the services of the *jamadari* units were negotiated in the open market by their 'proprietors'—the *jamadars*.

Thus, the Mughal army was actually made of a number of separate armies controlled by independent commanders. If there was no uniform chain of command within the Mughal army, the armies of the Marathas were not much better served in this regard. During the days of Shivaji the army consisted of the followers of numerous Maratha families who were attracted to the Chatrapati Maharaja by his leadership qualities. With the expansion of Maratha power under the Peshwas, the Maratha armies came to consist of prominent leaders personally loyal to the Poona government who incorporated numerous smaller bands within their forces.[25] The Maratha *sardars* or captains were rewarded for their military contributions with large estates.[26] But during the latter decades of the eighteenth century, the Marathas also turned increasingly towards mercenaries supplied by *jamadars*.[27]

Apart from their loyalty to the principal leaders, there was no chain of command to hold all these bands together and naturally it did not favour uniform plans of action for the coordinated use of all the fighting units in the field. Under such circumstances, it is not surprising if leading and controlling Indian armies itself often became an exercise in diplomacy rather than military command—as Francois Martin found when he tried to invest Tindivanam in 1676. In the case of Martin's expedition, the relatively simple task of capturing a lightly defended fort was bungled by the difficulty in getting the chiefs to agree to any form of united action. Martin's energies were largely wasted in futile attempts to persuade Muhammad Raza to support him and in chasing after the *palaikkar* Kolaique Nayạk rather than in actual fighting. One

[25] Gordon, *Marathas*, pp. 106-13. See also Wink, *Land and Sovereignty*, pp. 37-8. Also John Pemble, 'Techniques and Resources in the Second Maratha War', *Historical Journal*, vol. 19, no. 2, 1976, p. 398.

[26] According to the mid-eighteenth century English traveller, John Henry Grose, the Maratha cavalry was not always paid in cash 'but in rice, tobacco, salt, pieces of cloth and the other necessities of life'. John Henry Grose, *A Voyage to the East Indies with Observations on Various Parts there*, London: S. Hooper and A. Morely, 1757, p. 124.

[27] See Surendranath Sen, *The Military System of the Marathas*, Calcutta: K.P. Bagchi, 1979; 1st pub. 1959, pp. 66-7.

can easily imagine the difficulties associated with managing similarly organized armies numbering in their thousands on a battlefield.

*Tactics, Weapons and Training*

The problem of command and control, I believe, go a long way in explaining the rather simple tactical approaches adopted by armies in India which suited the internal cohesion of units formed by patron-client relationships rather than externally imposed discipline. They were aggregations of individuals brought together by resourceful leaders. And that is how they fought—as aggregates of individuals and not as cohesive bodies of soldiers.

Mughal battles are a case in point. The battle developed in two main stages. First came a massive bombardment by heavy artillery, placed at the front of the line, with the wheels of carriages tied together with chains or rawhide. Infantry armed with matchlocks took station behind the guns and heavy cavalry occupied the wings. After the guns had delivered their fire, the chains linking the carriages were unhooked to let the cavalry through. Then, to the sound of huge kettledrums, the cavalrymen descended on the enemy with their bows and bared swords.

The cavalry charge was delivered according to guidelines laid down by the Mughals' ancestor Amir Timur centuries earlier. Timur's army, composed mainly of cavalry, was divided into four parts: the vanguard (*harravval*), the right wing (*barangar*); the left wing (*jarangar*); and the centre (*gol* where the emperor himself took station). In battle each section was hurled at the enemy in successive charges. If all these failed, the centre, consisting of select warriors and the royal guard had to be thrown in led on by the emperor himself.[28]

[28] Paul Horn, *Das Heer und Kriegswesens der Grossmughals*, Leiden, 1894, pp. 143-51. M.K. Zaman has reproduced the section relating to the development of the cavalry charge as it appears in Timur's own 'Political and Military Institutes of Tamerlane'. M.K. Zaman, *Mughal Artillery*, Delhi: Idarah-i-Abiyat-i-Delhi, 1983, pp. 45-6. A description of the deployment of Timur's army also appears in Syed Jamulluddin, *The State under Timur: a Study in Empire Building*, Delhi: Har-Anand Publications, 1995, p. 173. A very good example of a classic Mughal battle is the Battle of Samugarh fought between two claimants to the Mughal throne, Dara Shukoh and Aurangzeb in May 1653. Interesting descriptions of this battle have been left by two European eyewitnesses, the Frenchman Francois Bernier and the Italian Niccolo Manucci. See Francois Bernier, *Travels in the Mughal Empire, A.D. 1656-1658*, trs.

The Marathas challenged Mughal supremacy by adopting cavalry themselves. But they avoided the ferocity of the Mughal heavy cavalry and concentrated on their main weakness—the slow moving artillery and baggage train. The supply lines of the vast Mughal armies became the prime targets of Maratha light cavalry, mounted on small country-bred horses. Such strikes, despite their fleeting nature, added to the frustration of the enemy. For instance, in their campaign against the Nizam of Hyderabad in 1727-8, better known as the Phalked campaign, the Marathas armed only with sabre, lance and bow were greatly out-gunned. Yet they led the Nizam's army, encumbered as it was with baggage and heavy artillery, on a merry dance, finally crippling it by cutting off its lines of supply.[29] Often, as Orme noted, it was simpler and less costly in lives to buy the Marathas off, rather than to fight them. What is more, this expedient saved the country at large from the constant bane of Maratha raiding parties.[30]

Although both the Mughals and the Marathas used artillery they were put to very limited use in the field. The main role of Mughal artillery was to 'soften up' the opposition through an initial bombardment after which they remained largely silent. As a result, Mughal guns were usually very large, heavy and extremely cumbersome, requiring a stupendous effort to move.[31] The Maratha guns were no

---

Archibald Constable, New Delhi: S. Chand, 1968; rpt. of 1891 edn., pp. 49-54 and Manucci, *Storia*, 1, pp. 263-70. For a comprehensive account of Mughal military campaigns see also Gordon, *The Marathas*, pp. 37-40.

[29] Sir Jadunath Sarkar, *A Military History of India*, Bombay: Orient Longman, 1970, pp. 152-3. See also William Irvine and Sir Jadunath Sarkar, *Later Mughals*, Calcutta: Sarkar, 1922, pp. 299-306.

[30] Robert Orme, *A History*, 1, p. 45. See the description of the Maratha incursion into Bengal in 1742 in Sir Jadunath Sarkar, *The Fall of the Mughal Empire*, 4 vols., New York: AMS Press, 1949-50, vol. 1, pp. 44-5.

[31] According to Bernier, many of the heavy guns in Aurangzeb's army required as many as 20 yoke of oxen to drag them. In addition, an elephant was usually required to push the carriage over difficult ground. Bernier, *Travels*, p. 352. The need for large numbers of draught cattle and the elephant's role is also mentioned by Orme with regard to the artillery deployed by the Nawab of Bengal, Siraj-ud-Daulah at the Battle of Plassey in 1756: 'These machines were drawn by 40 or 50 yoke of white oxen of the largest size, bred in the country of Purnea; and behind each cannon walked an elephant, trained to assist at difficult tugs, by shoving with his forehead against the hinder part of the carriage.' Cited in Irvine, *Army*, pp. 121-2.

better, their clumsy carriages often carrying the army's baggage in addition to the gun. Predictably, they were used mainly in siege work.[32]

Once battle was joined it turned in to a series of fights around the leading chiefs on either side. Indeed, the fall of leaders quite often decided the fate of battles since leader-less troops, deprived of their principal reason for being there, promptly dispersed to their villages. 'The victory is commonly decided by the fall of the principal chief. These begin the onset, and are followed by the hardiest of their partisans. . . . The greatest slaughter falls around the commander in chief, as the victory is confirmed by in the instant of his death.'[33] But it was not only the death of the leaders that effected the outcome of battles; the defection of leaders could also influence the fortunes of an army. The close relationship between political power and military command meant that military confrontation itself often took the form of negotiation, bribery acting as the chief weapon. A hefty sum could usually induce a rival commander to switch his allegiance during the heat of the battle or the commander of a garrison to deliver the fort. Frequently, the display of impressive wealth and force alone was sufficient to persuade opponents to come to terms; a massive artillery train, a large stable of richly caparisoned elephants and a sprawling bazaar could impress in the mind of an enemy the wisdom of negotiation.[34]

[32] Edward Moor, *A Narrative of the Operations of Captain Little's Detachment and of the Mahratta Army Commanded by Purseram Bhow; During the Late Confederacy in India Against the Nawab Tippoo Sultan Bahadur*, London, 1794, pp. 78-9. According to Moor, who was with the Maratha Peshwa's army during the Second Mysore War (1790-2), the baggage obscured the gun to the extent that nobody could possibly conceive it was a piece of artillery 'were it not for the number of bullocks dragging it'. Like the Mughal cannon, the Maratha guns also frequently required the assistance of an elephant to push it over rugged terrain.

[33] Orme, *Historical Fragments*, p. 269; Irvine, *Army*, p. 235; Indian commanders usually rode to battle on elephants in order to allow themselves a better view of the battlefield as wells as to reassure their troops. At Samugarh in 1758, Dara alighted from his elephant and mounted a horse in order to lead his men but his troops, concluding by the empty howdah that their leader had fallen, took to their heels. See Bernier, *Travels*, pp. 54-5 and Manucci, *Storia*, vol. 1, pp. 269-70.

[34] See Jos Gommans, 'Indian Warfare and Afghan Innovation During the Eighteenth Century', *Studies in History*, n.s., vol. 11, no. 2, 1995, pp. 265-6. Both Bernier and Manucci attribute Dara Shukoh's fatal decision to alight from his elephant at Samugarh

Traditional Indian battle-tactics—the charge leading to close-order combat as practiced by the Mughals and harrying tactics adopted by the Marathas—provided ample scope for the talents of individual combat—a freedom epitomized by the Maratha trooper 'who lounged his horse about near the 74th [King's Regiment], and every now and then dashed forward and killed a European' at the Battle of Assaye in September 1803.[35] This scope for individual expression was reflected, too, in the armaments of soldiers. The sword was a favourite weapon of Indian soldiers[36] but many individuals carried a variety of weapons that reflected personal choice rather than tactical considerations. According to Major Dirom the Marathas who joined the English army on its campaign against Mysore in 1792 were 'armed with sword and shield, with lances bows and arrows, and every variety of ancient and modern arms and armour'[37]; and another English officer observed with regard to the Nizam's army in 1791 that 'no national or private collection of ancient armour contains a weapon or article of equipment which might not be traced in this motley crowd'.[38]

Thus, soldiers also took an individualistic approach to training for war, and the individual soldier prepared primarily for inter-personnel combat. He trained hard at the dexterous use of his weapons of choice—swordplay ranking highest in the training regime.[39] There was no formal

---

to the treachery of one of his commanders, Kalliullah Khan, who persuaded his master to lead the troops from horseback. Bernier, *Travels*, pp. 52-4; Manucci, *Storia*, vol. 1, pp. 269-70.

[35] Mountstuart Elphinstone to William Strachey, 9 October 1803, quoted in T.E. Colebrooke, *The Life of the Honourable Mountstuart Elphinstone*, 2 vols., London: John Murray, 1884, vol. 1, p. 76.

[36] The Mughals and the Rajputs opted for the curved blade while the Marathas preferred the straight bladed weapon. See Gordon, *Marathas, Marauders*, pp. 182-208.

[37] Major Alexander Dirom, *A Narrative of the Campaign in India Which Terminated in the War With Tippoo Sultan in 1792*, Delhi: Asian Educational Publication Services, 1985; 1st pub. 1793, p. 24.

[38] Cited in Irvine, *Army*, p. 73; Dubois, *Hindu Manners*, p. 676.

[39] As pointed out by Seema Alavi, Mughal soldiers were expected to be skilled in the use of the sword both on foot and on horseback. Alavi, *Sepoys*, p. 12, fn. Henry Grose speaks highly of Maratha swordsmanship: 'Their swords are, generally speaking, of an admirable temper, and they are well trained up to the exercise of them so that on all occasions of battle, they quit their muskets and betake themselves to them

instruction but individuals honed their skills in jousts with their friends and rivals. Sometimes these contests resulted in fatal injuries. However, by a process of elimination, the survivors became very expert indeed—as the English found when they tried to storm the fortress at Madurai in 1751. The 'forlorn hope' thought they had an easy passage when only three native swordsmen stood at the breach barring their entry. But in the event it took a collective effort on their part to bring down just one of them.[40]

Weapons-training aside, the Indian soldier also paid great attention to his physique—conditioning his body through physical exercises such as wrestling and gymnastics.[41] The athletic prowess achieved by some of these individual warriors is evident from the charge made by a select corps of Arabs on the British positions at Sitabaldi in November 1817. 'Their manner of advancing was exceedingly imposing.' Explained Lieutenant Colonel Fitzclarence. 'Being perfectly undisciplined they advanced in a crowd; the bravest being in advance and taking high bounds and turning two or three times round in the air, they rushed forward to the sound of small drums, accompanied by the perpetual vociferation of the war cry "Din! Din! Muhammad!"'[42]

## *The Ethos of Individual Skill and Courage*

Given the militarized nature of Indian society and the place of individual fighting skills in warfare, it is not surprising if military values had an ideological significance in South Asia. From ancient times the ruling elite sought to demonstrate their fitness to rule through the perfection

[swords] with great success. Cited in Surendranath Sen, *Military System*, p. 70. The Marathas, however, also used the spear or the lance quite often and with great dexterity which made individual Maratha horsemen 'very dangerous persons to say anything to'. John Shipp, *Memoirs of the Extraordinary Military Career of John Shipp, late a Lieutenant in His Majesty's 87th Regiment*, Chichester, London: T.F. Unwin, 1890; 1st pub. 1829, p. 85.

[40] OIOC Orme India II, p. 273.

[41] The seventeenth century English traveller Peter Mundy was fascinated by the sight of soldiers training at a military camp on his way to Patna from Agra. He wrote: 'They would tugg [*sic*] and wrestle with one another, tumble on the ground, beatinge [*sic*] and thumpinge [*sic*] themselves in a strange manner and posture.' Cited in Kolff, *Naukar*, p. 28.

[42] Cited in Irvine, *The Army*, p. 187.

of military skills. And it was the commitment to fighting which distinguished the members of the martial classes or the Kshatriya from the rest. In the *Mahabharata* the hero, Arjuna, laments the possibility of having to kill his close relatives and teachers. His charioteer, who is really Lord Krishna, is quick to respond, reminding Arjuna of his moral obligations as a Kshatriya:

Casting thy eyes on the prescribed duties of thy order, it behoveth thee not to waver, for there is nothing else that is better for a Kshatriya than a battle fought fairly. Arrived of itself and like unto an open gate of heaven, happy are those Kshatriyas, O Partha, that obtain such a fight! But if thou dost not fight such a just battle, thou shalt then incur sin by abandoning the duties of thy order and thy fame. . . .[43]

Thus, to the Kshatriya, fighting was a matter of honour. At the hands of warrior elites like the Rajputs, this ancient military ethos found new expression. The Rajputs did not constitute a caste or kinship-based group; rather, they were a political elite that had acquired the values and norms of the ancient Kshatriyas in order to legitimize their political ascendance.[44] Accordingly, the 'ideal' Rajput was fearless and skilled in the use of weapons, the classic Rajput battle a contest between picked warriors or champions, fought on foot, almost ritualistic in its observance of formalities as shown by the following example quoted by Norman Ziegler from a sixteenth century Rajput court epic:

Then Kumbho got down [from his horse]. . . .went into the camp and bowed to Hemo. Hemo said. 'Very fine, Kumbho!' Then Hemo said, 'Kumbho! You inflict a wound.' Kumbho said, 'Hemoji! You inflict a wound.' Hemo said, 'Kumbho! You are a boy. I have had nim leaves bandaged on many [a wound].' Then Kumbho was saying, 'Hemoji! You inflict a wound.' Hemo said, 'Kumbho! Your body has yet felt no sword; you are a boy. You inflict a wound. I am an elder; why should I inflict the [first] wound?' Kumbho said, 'Hemoji! In years you are elder, but in rank I am senior. You have taken my grain in the hem of your clothes; you are my military servant [and] therefore, I am senior; you inflict [the first] wound.' Then Hemo said, 'What should I do? You allow

[43] Cited in Joel Larus, *Culture and Political-Military Behaviour: the Hindus in Pre-modern India*, Calcutta: South Asia Books, 1979, p. 99.

[44] See Kolff, *Naukar*, and B.D. Chattopadhyay, 'The Emergence of the Rajputs as Historical Process in Early Medieval Rajasthan', in Karine Schomer (ed.), *The Idea of Rajasthan: Explorations in Regional Identity*, 2 vols., Delhi: Manohar, 1994, vol. 2, pp. 161-91.

me no choice.' Then Hemo wounded Kumbho. The blow [of his sword] severed Kumbho's helmet, split [his] skull [as though smashing] a clay bowl, sliced between his eyebrows and lodged [itself] at the top of his ear, Kumbho inflicted a wound; [he] cut Hemo in two part. Hemo fell down. Then Kumbho drew his dagger and stabbed [it] into Hemo's chest.[45]

Of course it is very doubtful whether all or even most Rajputs followed the elaborate, exaggerated politeness in combat as shown by the two combatants in this example. But they probably set an example of proper conduct which Rajputs and other warrior-elites were expected to embrace as part of their ethos. But bravery was not the only virtue of an ideal Rajput warrior. In a clear recognition of the importance of the patron-client relationship to the political and military organization on the subcontinent, the Rajput code of honour also stressed the loyalty to a master as the sacred obligation of a warrior.[46]

Similar values prevailed in southern India as well. A sixteenth century Portuguese observer, Duarte Barbosa describes how the Nayars or the military castes the south-eastern coastal region of Kerala emphasized the importance of weapon training and other martial arts in the education of young boys.[47] Personal courage was high on list of elite virtues in the Nayaka states of south India too, as underlined by the following incident. In September 1673 Madurai forces were poised to overwhelm Tanjavur. The ruler of Tanjavur, Vijayaraghava, seeing his son cut down before his eyes and realizing that he himself was doomed, called out to the Madurai leader to pull back his matchlockmen. 'You must order your men not to shoot their guns (*tupakkulu*) but to fight only with swords and spears,' he admonished, adding, 'Do you want to know why? Because if one dies from some lousy bullet shot from a distance, he fails to enter heaven (*paralokhani*)—that is nothing like a

[45] Cited by Norman Ziegler, 'Evolution of the Rathor State of Marvar: Horses, Structural Change and Warfare', in Karine Schomer (ed.), *The Idea of Rajasthan: Explorations in Regional Identity*, vol. 2, pp. 205-6.

[46] Shyam Singh Ratnawat, *Rajput Nobility: With Special Reference to the Kachchawaha Nobility of Jaipur During 1700-1858*, Jaipur: Panchsheel Prakashan, 1989, pp. 193-6. See also Norman P. Ziegler, 'Some Aspects of Rajput Loyalty During the Mughal Period', in John F. Richards (ed.), *Kingship and Authority in South Asia*, Wisconsin: University of Wisconsin, 1972, p. 225.

[47] Cited in K.M. Panikkar, *A History of Kerala 1498-1801*, Annamalainagar: Annamalai University Press, 1960, p. 11.

warrior's death (*ayudhamaranamu*). Don't you know all this yourself?' The wish was granted and Vijayaraghava rushed at his opponents, sword in hand and attained the right kind of death in the right kind of fighting—interpersonal combat.[48]

To recap then, the military culture on the subcontinent stressed personal allegiance and individual bravery. This was the result of a system of political and military organization which favoured war-bands formed around individual leaders. Armies thus created consisted of soldiers with little collective discipline but great skill in the use of weapons. Likewise tactics were elementary and combat mostly hand-to-hand, which in turn valorized a concept of ideal warriorhood, based on individual courage.

How did this contrast with the European military system? When the English East India Company started raising an army of Indian soldiers in the mid-eighteenth century, warfare in Europe had reached an interesting stage, thanks to a series of momentous developments now familiar to historians as the 'military Revolution'. Dated between the sixteenth and the eighteenth centuries, the military revolution witnessed the emergence in Europe of armies much larger and better controlled than at any previous time in European history.[49] These large armies were also being increasingly dominated by drilled infantry using firearms and gradually turned into professional bodies of soldiers controlled directly by the state. In the following section of this chapter, we shall examine in detail the main features of these developments and their importance for the expansion of European military power in South Asia.

[48] Velcheru Narayana Rao, David Schulman and Sanjay Subramaniyam, *Symbols of Substance: Court and State in Nayaka Period Tamilnadu*, Delhi: OUP, 1992, p. 236.

[49] The concept of a 'Military Revolution' in Europe between 1560 and 1660 was first advanced by Michael Roberts in an inaugural lecture delivered at the Queen's University, Belfast in 1956. It is published in Michael Roberts, *Essays in Swedish History*, London: Weidenfield and Nicholson, 1968, pp. 195-225. Although the broad outline of Roberts' thesis has been generally accepted by military historians, some, like Geoffery Parker in his *The Military Revolution: Military Innovation and the Rise of the West 1500-1800*, Cambridge, New York: CUP, 1988, and more recently Jeremy Black, *European Warfare 1660-1815*, London: UCL Press, 1994, have sought to extend the time frame to embrace the early part of the eighteenth century as well.

## WAR IN EUROPE

### *The Revolution in Tactics*

The advent of musket-bearing infantry fighting in line was the result especially, of the development of the hand-held firearm's potential as an infantry weapon. The importance of infantry however, had been demonstrated in European battlefields long before gunpowder weapons had made their appearance. In the fourteenth and fifteenth centuries the pike-wielding infantry of the Swiss cantons had successfully tested the vulnerability of the mail-clad knights—the dominant feature of contemporary European warfare—of their Hapsburg and Burgundian overlords.[50] But, unlike the pike, firearms increased the footsoldier's potential by enabling him to strike from a distance. Although crude, hand-held firearms had been in use since the fifteenth century it was not until early sixteenth century that a reliable version was developed. This was the harquebus; a weapon fired by a simple mechanism called the matchlock whereby a slow-burning match was pressed into the touch hole at the pull of the trigger. The musket, introduced in mid-sixteenth century, was an improved version of the harquebus, longer and heavier but having a greater range than the harquebus. They both had the advantage of being easier to master than the bow. As a result, by the mid-sixteenth century, the harquebus and the musket came to replace the bow as the premier missile weapon in European armies.[51]

Early firearms however, suffered from a number of drawbacks. The musket and harquebus took much time to reload, and while this occurred, they were at the mercy of enemy cavalry. Thus, from the sixteenth century, musketeers were often used in conjunction with pikemen formed into solid blocks like the Swiss phalanxes of the previous century. The musketeers, taking position along the edge of this formation, could now seek security within it during the laborious process of reloading.[52] This combination of 'shot and pike' clearly

[50] John McCormack, *One Million Mercenaries: Swiss Soldiers in the Armies of the World*, London: Leo Cooper, 1993, pp. 14-15. See also Charles Oman, *The History of the Art of War in the Middle Ages*, 2 vols., New York: Burt Franklin, 1924, 1, pp. 253-61; and Bert S. Hall, *Weapons and Warfare in Renaissance Europe: Gunpowder, Technology and Tactics*, Baltimore, Maryland: John Hopkins University Press, 1997, pp. 36-8.

[51] Parker, *The Military Revolution*, pp. 17-18.

[52] Fritz Redlich, *The German Military Enterpriser and His Workforce: a European*

established the primacy of infantry in European battlefields, relegating the cavalry to the role of supporting infantry.

However, the search for enhanced firepower continued. A major breakthrough was made in early seventeenth century when the Dutch under Maurice of Nassau, Prince of Orange, introduced a revolutionary change to infantry tactics. Maurice organized his musketeers in a linear form no more than five to six ranks deep and made the first rank retire or 'countermarch' to the rear to reload after firing, allowing the second rank to follow suit. In this manner a continuous flow of fire was maintained. Maurice also made his soldiers practice a standard series of movements to load and fire the matchlock, so that they could perform the routine collectively at a word of command for each movement. The resulting mechanistic behaviour of the musketeers ensured a steady rate of fire as well as close fire-control—one of the features conspicuously absent in contemporary Indian warfare.[53]

Two further innovations in firearms in late seventeenth century greatly contributed to the completion of the musketeers' dominance of the infantry. One was the introduction of the flintlock firing mechanism. The flintlock consisted of a flint-holding arm which struck sparks off a metal plate into the priming pan to set the charge alight. This greatly facilitated loading. The other was the bayonet whose widespread adoption in the early eighteenth century rendered the pike virtually useless, as the musketeer was now self-sufficient in both offensive and defensive means. This increase in the firepower and the independence of the musketeer was underlined by the reduction of the ranks in the line to two to three by the middle of the eighteenth century.[54]

Such developments also brought with them major changes in

---

*Economic and Social History*, 2 vols., Wiesbaden: Steiner, 1964, vol. 1, p. 124. This tactic was perfected by the Spanish during the sixteenth century. Their squares of firearms and pikes, called tercios had 3,000 men were divided into twelve companies, ten of pikemen and the rest musketeers and harquebusiers. Hall, *Weapons and Warfare*, p. 178.

[53] Hans Delbruck, *History of the Art of War Within the Framework of Political History*, trs. Walter J. Renfroe, Jr., 4 vols., Westport, Connecticut: Greenwood, 1975-85, trs. of 3rd German edn., 1920, vol. 4, p. 158. John Childs, *Armies and Warfare in Europe*, Manchester: Manchester University Press, 1982, p. 122.

[54] Childs, *Armies*, p. 124. Delbruck, *The History*, vol. 4, p. 270.

organization. Maurice broke up his army into smaller units to facilitate drill and control. A unit of 550, called a battalion, became the basic tactical unit. By further subdividing the battalion into companies within the command structure of the battalion Maurice made it possible for battalion commanders to exercise closer control over the training and fighting of their troops through subordinate officers.[55] The battalion remained the basic tactical unit for most European armies throughout the eighteenth century and regiment and battalion was often interchangeable terms. A battalion was sub divided into companies, their numbers varying from country to country. By early eighteenth century, two of the companies were designated as grenadier companies and comprised the tallest and strongest men who were called upon to spearhead attacks, especially against fortified positions. For marching, eighteenth century battalions were deployed in a columnar formation. This meant that the companies in a battalion marched one behind the other with sufficient intervals between them to allow them to change into line by wheeling 90 degrees to left or right. When threatened by cavalry, infantry adopted the formation of a hollow square, usually by pulling back some of the companies deployed in line. The perfection of such evolutions required constant practice, bringing drilling in to its own. Even the process of loading and firing the flintlock musket involved a fairly complex sequence that comprised 26 separate movements.[56]

The firepower of the infantry was greatly augmented by artillery. Artillery, like hand-held firearms, first made its appearance in the shape of crude, cumbrous cannon in the first half of the fourteenth century. For instance, the English at the Battle of Crecy in 1346 'fired off some cannons which they had brought to the battle to frighten the Genoese'.[57] But it was not until well into the next century that more powerful and accurate cannon were developed; and even then cannon

[55] William H. McNeill, *The Pursuit of Power: Technology, Armed Forces and Society Since A.D. 1000*, Chicago: University of Chicago Press, 1982, pp. 128-9.

[56] This was without the bayonet. Fixing the bayonet required seven additional movements. David Chandler, *The Art of War in the Age of Marlborough*, London: B.T. Batsford Ltd., 1976, pp. 102-3. On the manoeuvers relating to the formation of line and square see Christopher Duffy, *The Military Experience in the Age of Reason*, London: Routeledge and Kegan Paul, 1987, pp. 198-204.

[57] Philippe Contamine, *War in the Middle Ages*, trs. Michael Jones, Oxford: Basil Blackwell, 1984, pp. 198-9. Also Hall, *Weapons and Warfare*, pp. 45-6.

continued for some time to function mainly as siege weapons. Not until the early decades of the seventeenth century, when the Swedish King, Gustavus Adolphus attached four light guns to each of his infantry regiments, was there a decisive break with tradition;[58] and it took almost another half a century for the practice to become widespread. But once the break has been made, the results were devastating.[59] By the early eighteenth century most states in Europe were using two basic types of cannon in their field armies: a heavy artillery train for siege work and a larger number of lighter pieces to provide close support for the infantry.[60]

But firepower did not completely eliminate cavalry. As suggested by the square formation, cavalry still retained a place of importance despite infantry becoming the dominant arm. The armoured knight was replaced, first, by horsemen wearing breastplates (cuirass). Armed with pistols and carbines they performed a form of countermarch of their own by trotting up to infantry in troops to discharge their weapons before retiring. But by the late seventeenth century this approach had given way to the straightforward charge with sabres in close formation. Such tactics were particularly deadly against infantry broken by musketry or artillery.[61]

Thus, by the early part of the eighteenth century, European battlefields had come to be dominated by disciplined infantry fighting in linear formations two to three ranks deep. Battles fought between such formations of infantry however, were chilling affairs because fire was delivered in volleys at close, almost point-blank range (due to the

[58] Parker, *The Military Revolution*, p. 23.

[59] A French officer in Napoleon's army has left a graphic description of the devastation caused by enemy artillery on their army during an action near Leipzig in October 1813: 'As soon as we arrived our thin line was ploughed by enemy's balls. Officers and men fell like ears of corn before the reapers sickle. The cannon balls ploughed through our ranks from first to last, each fire sweeping away at least thirty men when they took a column full on.' Jean- Baptiste Barres, *Memoirs of a Napoleonic Officer*, trs. Bernard Miall, New York: The Diall Press, 1925, p. 184.

[60] B.P. Hughes, *Open Fire: Artillery Tactics from Marlborough to Wellington*, Chichester, Sussex: A. Bird Publications, 1983, p. 12. Also Chandler, *The Art*, pp. 179-80.

[61] On cavalry tactics see Christopher Duffy, *The Military Experience*, pp. 221-7; and Chandler, *The Art*, pp. 50-61.

musket remaining notoriously inaccurate at any greater distance).[62] But at close range, musketry could be very deadly to troops packed tightly together. The firefight made even the bayonet largely redundant since few opposing armies now grappled with each other in hand to hand combat. Charge with the bayonet usually came only after a side was broken by musketry and already in retreat. Of the wounded French soldiers admitted to the Invalides in 1762 only 9 per cent were wounded by bayonets while more than 80 per cent suffered from bullet wounds.[63] While the bayonet still had a role to play in attacks on strongly defended entrenchments, in the field, the musket ball, not cold steel would henceforward prove decisive.

Thus, by early eighteenth century, military tactics in Europe had undergone a radical transformation. Fighting had become an issue between closely controlled bodies of footsoldier's firing at each other at close range. The adoption of firearms and the introduction of drill had been largely responsible for this tactical transformation, but drill and muskets alone did not produce efficient armies. In order to utilize armies of disciplined soldiers to the best advantage, the governments and rulers who employed them had to have control over them. This, however, was not an easy thing to achieve.

[62] Childs, *Armies*, p. 123. An interesting episode from the Seven Years' War (1756-63) illustrates this perfectly. During the storming of a German town a French officer put on a bonnet abandoned by a Hessian grenadier and fifty French grenadiers mistaking him for an enemy fired at him from a distance no more than thirty paces. Only two of the balls hit the target: one knocking the bayonet off the officer's musket and the other passing harmlessly through his coat. Lee Kennet, *The French Armies in the Seven Years' War: a Study of Military Organisation and Administration*, Durham: Duke University Press, 1967, p. 116. Nor did accuracy improve when the target was considerably bigger. During the War of American Independence, an English officer described what happened when the enemy approached:

> When they were about 100 yards from each other both parties fired, but I did not observe any fall. They still advanced to a distance of 40 yards or less, and fired again. I then saw a good number fall on both sides. Our people then rushed upon them with their bayonets and the others took to their heels; I heard one of them call out murder! lustily.

Cited in Christopher Duffy, *The Military Experience*, p. 200.

[63] Kennet, *French Armies*, p. 116.

*Military Organization and the European State*

Apart from the fact that they were used in a different kind of warfare, the companies and battalions of infantry that came to dominate European battles in the sixteenth and seventeenth centuries had some similarities to Indian armies of the eighteenth century. They were very similar to the *jamadari* units in India in that they were more or less the 'property' of those who raised them. The soldiers were mercenaries pure and simple and were recruited by contractors who received commissions from embattled rulers to recruit a certain number of 'regiments' and a lump sum to cover the costs of arming and equipping them. These military entrepreneurs or 'colonels' as they were usually called would then employ 'captains' to recruit smaller groups or companies.[64] Some major entrepreneurs like the Count Albrecht von Wallenstein of Bohemia recruited, armed and commanded entire armies on the continent.[65] Furthermore, these armies drew recruits from all over Europe. According to an English chronicler an army gathered for the king of England in the mid-sixteenth century contained 'so many depraved, brutish soldiers from all nations under the sun—Welsh, English, Cornish, Irish, Manx, Scots, Spaniards, Gascons, Portingals, Italians, Arbannoises, Greeks, Turks, Tartars, Almains, Germans, Burgundians, Flemings, who had come there . . . to have a good time under the king of England'.[66] The chronicler may have been indulging in some willful exaggeration, but the polyglot nature of the army he is describing is unmistakable.

[64] Redlich, *The German*, p. 218. See also Andre Corvisier, *Armies and Societies in Europe 1494 -1789*, Bloomington: Indiana University Press, 1979, pp. 44-5. In a clear reflection of the contemporary military tactics the forces raised by these entrepreneurs were very often combined-arms units comprising archers, hand-gunners and cavalry. See Dennis E. Showalter, 'Caste, Skill and Training: the Evolution of Cohesion in European Armies from the Middle Ages to the Sixteenth Century', *Journal of Military History*, vol. 57, no. 3, 1993, p. 422.

[65] During the Thirty Years' War (1618-48), Wallenstein controlled a vast territory extending from the Baltic to Bohemia while his armaments industries manufactured arms and equipment for the Imperial armies on a massive scale. Michael Howard, *War in European History*, London: OUP, 1970, p. 29. Also Michael Duffy, 'Military Revolution and the State 1500-1800', in Michael Duffy (ed.), *The Military Revolution and the State 1500-1800*, Exeter: University of Exeter, 1980, p. 2.

[66] Cited in Gilbert John Millar, *Tudor Mercenaries and Auxiliaries 1485-1547*, Charlottesville: University Press of Virginia, 1980, p. 145.

At first sight, it might seem surprising that states entrusted military recruitment to outsiders. But it made a lot of sense. Then as now 'outsourcing' was convenient and (arguably) cost-effective. Then as now, it saved the bureaucracy, the difference being that sixteenth century governments did not possess the administrative infrastructure in the first place. As it was, some governments did try to implement a centralized recruiting system—Spain being one. But significantly, Spain abandoned direct recruitment after the 1580s and thereafter devolved the responsibility to local authorities and private entrepreneurs.[67] Thus, by the time the Thirty Years' War (1618-48) broke out, the private military enterpriser had established himself as the main supplier of troops to almost all armies of Europe.

Mercenary armies were an attractive option for several reasons. Firstly, they gave their employers a degree of control which was absent from the armies of feudal levies. The cash nexus that dominated the relationship between the military entrepreneurs and their warlord employers enabled the latter to impose conditions on their military troops—for example through the condottas or contracts signed between the Italian cities and their mercenaries (or *condottieri*) which laid out precisely the details of the troops the *condottieri* were to provide.[68] Secondly, employing mercenary soldiers—particularly foreigners—was politically advantageous. Foreigners were attractive politically because rulers were reluctant to trust their subjects with arms, particularly firearms. And they were also more reliable when it came to suppressing local rebellions.[69]

But, in the long run, the disadvantages of relying on mercenary armies became too burdensome for European rulers. What were the disadvantages? Firstly the colonels and captains who recruited the mercenaries retained greater control over them than the governments

[67] See I.A.A. Thompson, *War and Government in Habsburg Spain, 1560-1620*, London: Athlone Press, 1976, pp. 103-43.

[68] Michael E. Mallet, *Mercenaries and their Masters: Warfare in Renaissance Italy*, London: Bodley Head, 1974, pp. 80-5; Mcneill, *Pursuit*, pp. 74-5; Contamine, *War*, p. 160.

[69] For instance, after being rebuffed by rebels in Castile and Valentia in 1520, Charles V returned with 4,000 Germans and 74 guns two years later and Lord Russell took hundreds of Ladesknechtes and Italian harquebusiers to suppress Cornish rebels in 1549. V.G. Kiernan, 'Foreign Mercenaries and Absolute Monarchy', in Trevor Aston (ed.), *The Crisis in Europe 1560-1660*, London: Routeledge, 1965, pp. 128-9.

in whose name they fought. The soldiers looked to the military entrepreneurs rather than the warring kings and princes as their employer. Secondly, and related to this lack of government control, was the scope the arrangement presented for corruption. Mercenary captains were often guilty of peculation, the natural tendency being to charge their employers for the pay of dead and deserted soldiers.[70] Thirdly, apart from corruption, there were also other strains on the economy. The contractual nature of their service meant that mercenaries had to be disbanded after wars only to be raised afresh when a new military situation loomed. Added to this drain on the government's purse was the threat of disbanded mercenaries devastating the countryside.

The answer to these problems was found in the creation of the permanent, standing army. Actually, permanently employed soldiers were nothing new. Most European rulers had long maintained small bodies of personal bodyguards and household troops, which were always on the payroll. But the practice of employing substantial numbers of soldiers on a permanent basis became common from around the middle of the fifteenth century. In 1445-6, Charles VII of France established the *ordonnance* companies, which comprised 1,800 men-at-arms, 3,600 archers and 1,800 swordsmen. These numbers continued to be maintained during his successor, Louis XI's time, so that, by the end of the fifteenth century, France had a permanent force of almost 25,000 men.[71] Early the following century the Spanish followed suit when they opted to keep their large army in Flanders in a state of permanent mobilization from 1567 till 1706.[72] And by 1620 the Netherlands States General was employing a standing force of 30,000 foot and 3,600 cavalry.[73] However, still, it was the segmented, mercenary armies rather than permanent forces that was the norm. The real watershed in this regard was the Thirty Years War. After the treaty of Westphalia in 1648 most European rulers decided to continue maintaining the forces with which they had ravaged much of Central Europe during the previous three decades.[74] Over the next century, these permanent armies matured into viable instruments of state power

[70] M.S. Anderson, *War and Society in Europe of the Old Regime, 1618-1789*, London: Fontana, 1988, pp. 47-8.

[71] Contamine, *War*, pp. 169-71.

[72] Parker, *The Military Revolution*, p. 80.

[73] Delbruck, *The History*, vol. 4, p. 163.

[74] Childs, *Armies*, pp. 28-30.

dependent solely on the state for their existence. Moreover, the state had also taken over the key functions of military administration—recruitment, supply and training, making soldiers directly dependent on the state bureaucracy that was gradually expanded to enable governments to extend their control to these area of administration.

Late seventeenth century France provides a good example of the extension of state control. As a first step the intendants or royal officials were appointed to supervise specific areas of military organization. Although the standard procedure of recruitment remained much the same as in the heyday of mercenary armies (colonels undertook contracts to raise regiments with the money they received as a lump sum from their employers) the way in which the recruiters spent the money was now closely scrutinized by the intendants who reported on their findings to the Secretary of State for War.[75] Secondly, during the 1680s the practice of identifying regiments and companies by the names of their captains and colonels (as a mark of their 'ownership' of these units) was discontinued in the French army, thereby undermining the proprietorial claims of officers to military units.[76]

As a third step, the French tried to regulate the system of supplying armies. Mercenary armies had largely subsisted off the land, more often than not through straightforward plunder.[77] The Intendance sought to limit such indiscriminate plundering by providing more dependable sources of supplies, for example, by the establishment of permanent magazines at strategic places which were stocked ahead of campaigns with essential items such as flour, fodder and spare ammunition. In France, the fortresses along its eastern borders were used as the main supply depots for the army.[78] But magazines could provide an army with supplies only while operating within or close to the borders. When in enemy territory soldiers still had to 'live off the land'. However this

[75] Michael Howard, *War*, pp. 64-5. See also Andre Corvisier, *Armies and Societies*, pp. 74-6.

[76] Anderson, *War*, p. 105.

[77] The horrendous destruction of life and property during the Thirty Years' War was largely the result of armies treating the countries through which they passed as the only source of supplies. According to a saying that gained currency during the Thirty Years' War, every soldier needed three peasants: 'One to provide his wife, one to give up his lodgings and one to take his place in hell.' Cited in Geoffrey Parker, *The Thirty Years' War*, London: Routeledge and Kegan Paul, 1984, p. 200.

[78] Childs, *Armies*, p. 113.

process was now regularized to enable the 'systematic exploitation' of the countryside instead of wholesale plunder. The inhabitants were required to provide the army with supplies at prices fixed by the Intendants, thereby ensuring a steadier supply of food and forage than would have been the case if the inhabitants were threatened by hordes of plundering soldiers.[79]

Finally, the French State began to make an active contribution to its soldiers' welfare, particularly in the area of health. From the late seventeenth century onwards, the French government spent large sums of money on regimental medical staff, field hospitals and garrison infirmaries. In 1708 alone, fifty military hospitals were created and the numbers increased steadily during the course of the century. Coordination was provided by the establishment of a hospital inspectorate which also monitored the quality of the health care given to soldiers.[80] Incidentally, such measures greatly increased the hold the state had over its soldiers.[81]

Where France led, others followed. Although England remained a notable exception to the absolutist style of government, that did not stop the country from developing a strong state-controlled army. For a long time, the English had staunchly resisted the idea of a standing army, choosing to rely on militia and 'trained bands'. But following the Restoration in 1660 the nucleus of a standing army, consisting of a number of selected Royalist units, came into being. And James II took the move further by gradually increasing the numbers and replacing many Protestant officers with Catholics. Although the latter tendency was reversed in the Glorious Revolution completed under William of Orange[82] the English involvement after 1688 in conflicts with continental powers, above all, France with her massive professional army, and the threat of Jacobite rebellion at home, convinced Parliament

[79] Martin van Creveld, *Supplying War: Logistics from Wallenstein to Patton*, Cambridge: CUP, 1977, pp. 27-8.

[80] Colin Jones, 'The Military Revolution and the Professionalisation of the French Army the Ancien Regime', in Michael Duffy (ed.), *The Military Revolution*, p. 41.

[81] As one French official pointed out, 'there is nothing which produces better effect in armies than that the sick and wounded are looked after'. Cited in ibid., p. 41.

[82] See John Childs, *The Army, James II and the Glorious Revolution*, Manchester: Manchester University Press, 1980.

of the necessity for maintaining a strong standing army.[83] Thus, while the British army, which rose into prominence during the War of Spanish Succession (1702-13), was the instrument of a government run by the parliament, not by a monarch, the mechanisms of central control were well in place.[84] The Secretary at War was responsible for military administration, recruitment, supplies and billeting, while the Secretary of State took in hand the task of planning campaigns. The Board of Ordnance was responsible for furnishing the army with ordnance and other military munitions. At the same time, the army became more specialized, with separate branches for the engineers and the artillery.[85] Significantly, the English now began to follow the French practice of identifying regiments by numbers rather than by the names of their commanding officers.[86]

Thus, military organization in pre-modern Europe was gradually being transformed into a government enterprise so that the soldiers now saw the government for which they fought as a real employer and not as a distant authority as it had been during the era of mercenary armies. In the words of John A. Lynn, the common soldier 'evolved from an easily discarded hireling into a state servant provided with better medical care and the promise of a decent retirement'.[87]

Conversely, as the state's hold on the soldiers grew the 'feudal' authority the officers had enjoyed over their men weakened, laying

[83] Parliament succeeded in getting the army reduced to a mere 7,000 after the campaign on the continent in 1697, but the outbreak of the War of the Spanish Succession brought parliament back to its senses. Substantial increases to army numbers followed, reaching almost 20,000 at the end of Marlborough's campaigns. Leonard W. Cowie, *Hanoverian England 1714-1837*, London: Bell, 1967, pp. 198-9.

[84] A major clause in the Declaration of Rights presented to William III when summoned the Convention of Estates was that 'The raising and keeping of a standing Army within the kingdom in time of peace, unless it be with the consent of parliament is against the law'. The Mutiny Act, passed in 1689 and renewed each year thereafter, gave the parliament further control over the way the army was run. See David Ascoli, *A Companion to the British Army 1660-1983*, London: Harrap, 1983, pp. 22-6.

[85] Dorothy Marshal, *Eighteenth Century England*, London: Longman, 1965, pp. 47-8; Anderson, *War*, p. 103.

[86] Anderson, *War*, p. 105.

[87] John A. Lynn, 'The Evolution of Army Style in the Modern West 800-2000', *International History Review*, vol. 18, no. 3, 1996, p. 519.

the foundation for a professional officer corps. This professionalism was also enhanced by the introduction of uniformity in drill and equipment. In the mercenary armies different regiments followed different training regimes and were armed with a variety of muskets. But the new standing armies, from the early part of the eighteenth century, were being increasingly armed with standardized weapons provided by their governments, while gradually adopting uniform drill procedures.[88] Indeed, uniform came to be the order of the day, applying not just to drill and weapons. Mercenary armies were no strangers to uniforms but there was hardly any regularity about them, different units wearing different clothes reflecting the fancy of their officers. But the standing armies of the eighteenth century were issued with regular uniforms in bright colours, which provided the soldiers with a distinct sense of corporate identity. Thus, the British infantryman coming to be associated with his red coat and the Frenchman with the grey.

By the middle of the eighteenth century, European armies were well on their way to becoming efficient, professional forces. Indeed it was the control over such well-drilled and organized armies which placed the stamp of 'absolutism' on the *Ancien Regime* of Europe, because standing armies gave European monarchs the ideal instrument for overawing domestic challengers to their authority. At the same time, the tactical and political foundations of these armies also helped to mould the martial values of the officers and men who served them.

### *Officers and Men*

A major achievement of the new standing armies in the sphere of political control was the incorporation of the nobility into the officer corps. The emergence of infantry as the main element of armies and the military entrepreneur as the key figure in military organization had undermined the world of the nobility where military primacy went hand in hand with political and social dominance. In the aftermath of the Thirty Years' War, European monarchs strove to utilize this dejected nobility in a constructive role within the new order of military organization by filling the ranks of their officer corps with them. In this way, the disgruntled aristocracy was conveniently found a role where they could reclaim a semblance of their former status as the

[88] Ibid., pp. 105-7.

'natural leaders' of the people while accepting the authority of the state.[89]

The emerging aristocratic-military nexus had important cultural implications. In the eighteenth century the officer corps developed into something of a distinct, international class with its own culture and ethos—an ethos which bore a remarkable resemblance to medieval chivalry in its emphasis on sacrifice and exposure to danger as matters of honour.[90] For example, at the Battle of Fontenoy the French officers invited their English counterparts to partake of the 'honour' of firing first ('Gentlemen of the English Guard please fire'), only to have it politely refused with an invitation for the French to open fire first![91] To the men of this class, taking cover or removing marks of distinction under sniper fire smacked of cowardice;[92] the receipt of wounds, of heroism. As John Keegan explains, it was

> the receipt of the wounds, not the infliction of death, that demonstrated an officer's courage; that demonstration was reinforced by his refusal to leave his post even when wounded, or by his insistence on returning as soon as his wounds were dressed; and it was by a punctiliousness to obeying orders which made wounds or death inevitable that an officer's honour was consummated.[93]

If the officers came from the top of the social hierarchy, the common soldiers came from the bottom. The majority of the soldiers were volunteers but they invariably came from the rootless and economically hard-pressed elements of society that found in the army a refuge from the wretched lives they led. 'Life in the Army, with its relative regularity of pay, a suit of clothes every eighteen months or two years, a square meal every day and a roof over one's head, was not only highly attractive to many of the poor but frequently a great deal better than their current lot.'[94] Despite this, conscription was also resorted to widely, particularly

[89] Black, *European*, p. 92; Childs, *Armies*, pp. 76-8. In the armies of the major European powers, the aristocracy made up more than two-thirds of the officer corps. See Steven T. Ross, *From Flintlock to Rifle: Infantry Tactics, 1740-1866*, London: Frank Cass, 1996, pp. 17-18.

[90] As Frederick the Great explained, he chose his officers from the aristocracy because 'the nobility had a sense of honour'. Cited in Childs, *Armies*, p. 87.

[91] Ibid., p. 4. The quote from Major-General F.M. Richardson, *Fighting Spirit: a Study of Psychological Factors in War*, London: Leo Cooper, 1978, p. 52.

[92] Christopher Duffy, *The Military Experience*, p. 76.

[93] John Keegan, *The Face of Battle*, London: Jonathan Cape, 1976, p. 179.

[94] Childs, *Armies*, p. 61.

in Prussia and Russia where the landed nobility filled their regiments with their enserfed peasants.[95] In most countries, the enlistment of the lower classes—whether peasants or the urban poor—was seen as an effective way of maintaining control over the troublesome sections of society and reinforcing the natural social order within the military environment.[96]

Discipline in the new standing armies was tough, as turning recruits into veritable soldiers in the eighteenth century-style required much time and effort. They had to be transformed from men into machines that were capable of repeating a series of movements in response to words of command in battle conditions. Training men to perform these mechanical tasks was hard enough, but when the men were drawn from the least educated strata of society drastic methods had to be resorted to mould them, the whip and rod being liberally employed. On the parade ground, blows were laid on for such trivial oversights as 'spots of water on the gaiters, badly polished coat buttons, mishandling of the musket or making a half-turn too early, too late or just without enough snap'.[97] Military service in pre-modern Europe may have been preferable to starvation; it was far from an easy life.

Discipline, though—however harsh—was not merely the means of attuning the soldier to the immediate physical demands of battle. The regular army was a world separate from society where everybody had a clearly defined place and purpose, subject to a distinct code of norms and values. Discipline was the means by which conformity to these

[95] Ibid., p. 78; Max Beloff, *The Age of Absolutism*, London: Hutchinson University Library, 1967, pp. 108-9.

[96] Christopher Duffy, *Military Experience*, pp. 89-90. A large proportion of these men were still foreigners; the Dutch and British armies that fought the War of Spanish Succession (1702-13) had more Germans than their own nationals. Geoffrey Treasure, *The Making of Modern Europe 1648-1789*, New York: Methuen, 1985, p. 214. Towards the end of the eighteenth century, the German state of Hesse-Kessel became a key supplier of troops to European states. Kiernan, 'Foreign Mercenaries', p. 136. For example, 17,000 of the 32,000 men collected by the British near New York City in 1776 were Hessians. Ross, *Flintlock*, p. 21. But state control meant that these soldiers were not mercenaries in the sixteenth and early seventeenth century sense, but troops who were subject to the close control of the bureaucracy of the state which employed them.

[97] Christopher Duffy, *The Army of Frederick the Great*, Melbourne: Wren, 1974, p. 62.

rules was ensured. The cardinal virtue which discipline sought to instil in the soldiers was mechanical unquestioning obedience, even in such seemingly minor; ritualistic details as polishing a button.[98]

Nevertheless, the highest expressions of this virtue were glamorized as 'bravery'. What it meant, actually, was to stand fast in the face of approaching death, and to kill when ordered without question or hesitation. In fact even taking anything more than a short side step to avoid a cannon ball was considered undignified,[99] a British officer at Waterloo berating his men who had slightly dipped their heads to avoid an incoming cannon ball with the taunt: 'For shame, for shame! That must be the second battalion I am sure.'[100] Conversely, troops who stood firm performed 'bravely' even if it meant gaining only a psychological edge over their adversaries. 'the kind of soldier who acts only under pressure will be frightened to see the enemy come so near and will often seek safety in flight without attempting to defend himself', observed the eighteenth century French tactician Comte de Guibert. 'The closer you approach the enemy the more fearsome you become, and a coward, who will fire at a brave man at one hundred paces, will not dare to so much as aim at him at close range.'[101]

It is fair to say then, that by the eighteenth century, the face of European warfare was been drastically altered by the dominance of infantry armed with muskets. From a ritualistic hand to hand test of strength and skill between individual noblemen, it had turned into the exchange of deadly musketry between solid blocks of commoners over 'distances at which suburbanites swap neighbourhood garden

[98] In his illuminating work on the relationship between dance and drill, William McNeill contends that drill allowed soldiers 'recruited from the fringes of an increasingly commercialized society—individuals for whom the cunning and constraints of the marketplace was repugnant and unworkable—to create a new, artificial primary community where comradeship prevailed in good times and bad and where old fashioned principles of command and subordination gave meaning and direction to life'. William H. Mcneill, *Keeping Together in Time: Dance and Drill in Human History*, Cambridge, Massachusetts: Harvard University Press, 1995, p. 131.

[99] Richardson, *Fighting Spirit*, p. 51. Corvisier describes how, since the seventeenth century, death as a result of maintaining order in the ranks came to be seen as a noble sacrifice. Corvisier, *War and Society*, pp. 183-8.

[100] Cited in Keegan, *The Face*, p. 156.

[101] Cited in Christopher Duffy, *Military Experience*, p. 206.

hints' to borrow John Keegan's apt phrase.[102] Shock had been replaced by firepower and the valour of the individual subsumed in the steadiness of the company and battalion. As on the Indian subcontinent, this approach to war was not simply a matter of weapons and tactics. The centralized political and administrative structure contributed immensely to the efficiency of well-disciplined armies with their rigid chains of command. Behind the serried ranks of infantry armed with muskets was a bureaucracy, which catered to its maintenance, enabling the army to function as a purely military institution.

Thus, by mid eighteenth century, when the English East India Company stood poised to take its first steps towards the 'conquest' of the subcontinent, very considerable differences existed between the Indian and European military systems. However, the fundamental nature of these differences only became clear during the latter half of the eighteenth century when the armies of the English and French East India Companies began active military operations on the subcontinent.

### *European Superiority and the 'Indian Military Revolution'*

The European armies of mid-eighteenth century were not only fundamentally different to Indian armies; drilled infantry armed with muskets and field artillery also had a clear superiority over the massive, disorderly armies of Indian rulers. They were organized to make optimum use of the available firepower and therefore, were able to deny the Indian soldiers the opportunity to employ their skill in hand to hand combat. Quick firing, mobile field artillery and volley-firing infantry could stop heavy cavalry from a distance and out manoeuver large Indian armies weighed down with their cumbersome cannon.

The outbreak of the Carnatic Wars in the 1740s and 1750s provided ample scope for the demonstration of this superiority of artillery and drilled infantry. Field artillery in particular made a strong impact on Indians who had not seen quick firing, mobile field guns at work until then. Indeed so awed were the people on the subcontinent by field artillery that sometimes the mere presence of guns was deemed sufficient to impress an opponent. Asked by Abdul Jalleel, the brother of Nawab Mohamed Ali, for the loan of a mortar, the Fort St. David

[102] Keegan, *The Face of Battle*, p. 148.

council replied that the Company could not spare anybody skilled in its use. But this did not worry Jalleel in the least. He only wanted to possess one as 'being possessed of such a thing would greatly intimidate his enemies and was the only use he intended it for'.[103]

The combination of field artillery with drilled infantry may have inspired awe in Indian rulers but it was not long before they began to desire a similar efficiency for their own armies. To be sure, military innovation in India had begun before the demonstration of the superiority of European forces. As Jos Gommans points out, the Afghans had introduced new ways of fighting to India—such as mounted musketeers and camel artillery—many years before the Carnatic Wars broke out,[104] but the fact that the demonstration of European military superiority led to a scramble for the adoption of European methods of fighting cannot be denied. The mechanics of this transmission were the availability—in abundance—of European 'expertise' in the form of deserters from the European trading companies. European deserters had been welcome at the courts of Indian rulers since the early sixteenth century as artillery experts. As early as 1503, two Milanese gunfounders defected from the Portuguese to take up service with ruler of Calicut as artillerymen and they were soon followed by four Venetians.[105] By the mid-seventeenth century, the Mughal artillery was being handled by a rather curious collection of Portuguese, English, Dutch, German and French deserters.[106] By the early eighteenth century, such personnel had turned the area just outside

[103] FSD. Cons., 11 November 1749, OIOC FR G/18/6, p. 412. In 1751, a highly exasperated king of Mysore who begged the English to come to his help against the French, saying that he was 'by no means acquainted how to deal with an army of that complexion who fought with muskets and cannon'. OIOC Orme India II, p. 527.

[104] Gommans, 'Indian Warfare', pp. 270-80. See also Jos Gommans, 'War-horse and Gunpowder in India c. 1000 - 1850', in Jeremy Black (ed.), *War in the Early Modern World*, London: UCL Press, 1999, pp. 109-12.

[105] C.R. Boxer, 'Asian Potentates and European Artillery in the 16th-17th Centuries: a Footnote to Gibson-Hill', *Journal of the Malayan Branch of the Royal Asiatic Society*, vol. 38, 1996, p. 159.

[106] Bernier, *Travels*, p. 217. Another mid-seventeenth century French Traveller, Jean-Baptiste Tavernier, found most of the gunners at Daulatabad in southern India to be either English or Dutch. Jean-Baptiste Tavernier, *Travels in India: Six Voyages de Jean-Baptiste Tavernier 1605-1609*, trs. V. Ball and William Crooke, 2 vols., Delhi: Oriental Books Reprint Corporation, 1977, vol. 1, pp. 144-5.

the Kabuli Gate in Delhi's Red Fort in to a Firanghipura or a European quarter.[107]

But during the latter half of the eighteenth century, renegade Europeans were eagerly sought after for another service—to train Indian armies to fight in the European style. And their influence soon changed the complexion of many Indian armies. Under the guidance of an adventurer called Walter Reinhardt (better known by his infamous nickname 'Sumroo'), and some Armenian mercenaries, the Nawab of Bengal, Mir Cassim, built up a force of several battalions of drilled infantry in the early 1760s.[108] Around the same time, the Nawab of Awadh was boasting of up to eighteen battalions of disciplined infantry.[109] The fall of Pondicherry, the French headquarters in the Carnatic, to the English in January 1761 sent scores of disbanded French soldiers in to the service of Hyder Ali of Mysore. With the help of these French personnel, Hyder and his successor Tipu Sultan formed a large contingent of disciplined infantry dressed in red and green uniforms and armed with French and English muskets.[110] By the time of the Second Mysore War (1780-4) their numbers had risen to nearly 20,000.[111] This army was also highly centralized. Both

[107] Irvine, *Army*, p. 172.

[108] N.N. Raye, *The Annals of the Early English Settlements in Bihar*, Calcutta: Kamal Book Depot, 1927, p. 223.

[109] P.J. Marshall, 'Western Arms in Maritime Asia in the Early Phase of Expansion', *Modern Asian Studies*, vol. 14, no. 1, 1980, p. 27.

[110] Innes Munro, *A Narrative of the Military Operations on the Coromandel Coast Against the Combined Forces of the French, Dutch and Hyder Ali Cawn, From the Year 1780 to the Peace in 1784*, London, 1789, p. 130. Hyder became interested in European-style warfare during the siege of Tiruchirapalli by French and Mysorean forces in 1752-4. He started repeating in his camp the military exercises he had seen performed by the French and British troops. At the same time, he succeeded in luring some of the French officers into his service. See Nikhilesh Guha, *Pre-British State System in South India: Mysore 1761-1799*, Calcutta: Ratna Prakashan, 1985, pp. 61-2; and Lord Egerton of Tatton, *A Description of Indian and Oriental Armour*, London, 1896, p. 31. For the training of Mysorean troops in the European fashion in later times see M.M.D.L.T., *Hyder Ali and the Revolution in India (the History of Hyder Shah Alias Hyder Ali Khan Bahadur*, Delhi: Daya Publishing House, 1988; 1st pub. 1848, pp. 143-5.

[111] A narrative of the Second Mysore War attributed to one Major Sydenham gives the disciplined infantry in the Mysore army that fought at Porto Novo in July 1781 as 18,402 men organized in twenty-three battalions. OIOC Home Misc., 248, p. 89.

Hyder Ali and Tipu Sultan did away with the traditional method of granting land revenue assignments or *jagirs* in lieu of military service, preferring to maintain a paid, standing army much in the style of contemporary European monarchs.[112]

The Mysoreans however, did not place heavy dependence on their regular infantry, continuing to rely mainly on their light cavalry to harass and intimidate their enemy, particularly the British with their slow moving infantry columns. When they offered pitched battles, as they sometimes did against British forces, the Mysoreans showed a marked reluctance to engage their enemy in an infantry firefight. A British officer noted that as soon as any part of the British army approached within musket shot of the Mysorean line, 'a great body of horse, rocketeers and poligars throw themselves into the opening; and all the rest of the infantry and cannon get off as fast as they can'.[113] Both Hyder and Tipu preferred to defeat British forces piecemeal by surrounding and overwhelming small British detachments with superior force. A good example is the defeat of a detachment of nearly 600 Europeans and about 3,000 sepoys under Colonel William Baillie in September 1780. Baillie, on the way from the northern Circars to join the main British army at Conjeewaram, was harassed by Hyder and Tipu for nearly a week before finally being overwhelmed at Pollilore, within 8 miles of Conjeewaram.[114] Such a strategy enabled the Mysoreans to leave the British with mainly hollow victory until in the Third Mysore War the Company enlisted the help of the Marathas with their light cavalry to deny Tipu his advantage.[115]

Unlike the Mysoreans, the Marathas eagerly embraced regular infantry. The Maratha flirtation with European-style forces started very

[112] See Kate Brittlebank, *Tipu Sultan's Search for Legitimacy: Islam and Kingship in a Hindu Domain*, Delhi: OUP, 1997, pp. 90-1 and 106-9; Tipu in particular made certain that none of his key military officers established secure localized power bases by regularly shifting them from place to place. Pradeep Barua, 'Military Developments in India 1750-1850', *Journal of Military History*, vol. 58, no. 4, 1994, p. 602.

[113] 'Memoranda of Colonel Robert Kelly'. OIOC Mss. Eur. D. 1146/6, p. 56.

[114] For a description of this encounter given by a survivor of Baillie's detachment see *Memoirs of the War in Asia from 1780 to 1784 Including a Narrative of the Imprisonment and Sufferings of Our Officers and Soldiers by an Officer of Colonel Baillie's Detachment*, London, 1789, pp. 146-62.

[115] Barua, 'Military Developments in India 1750-1850', *Journal of Military History*, vol. 58, no. 4, 1994, pp. 602-4.

early, when they suffered at the hands of the French and their sepoys in 1751. But their first attempt to secure European expertise was unsuccessful, and they had to settle for two Arabian adventurers. These men in turn were commissioned to raise a force of sepoys in the European style.[116] But the real flowering of the Maratha military revolution occurred after 1784 when the Maratha chief Mahadji Scindia enlisted the services of Benoit de Boigne, a Frenchman formerly in the service of the English EIC, to raise a European-style infantry for him. De Boigne proved a resounding success. By 1789 he had raised an infantry force of three brigades, each consisting of ten battalions of 750 men each. Following Mahadji's death in 1795 de Boigne retired from Maratha service, but his command now passed over to another Frenchman, Pierre Cullier, or 'Perron'. Soon, Perron had increased the strength of the Maratha regulars, by two more brigades.[117]

The army raised by de Boigne and passed over to Perron stood fair comparison with contemporary European armies in many respects. Each battalion had five pieces of field artillery attached to it—2 six pounders, 2 three pounders and 1 carronade. All were supplied with 45 rounds of grape, 12, and 400 rounds each for the three and six pounders. Each gun also had 1 tumbril. Armaments were at first smuggled in from the Company's territories but soon de Boigne enlisted a competent gun founder named Sangster who established a gun foundry at Agra.[118] The artillery cast at this foundry was of excellent quality and well-served. The guns captured at the Battle of Delhi (11 September 1803) were even considered superior to British ones[119]

[116] They were known as the *gardis*. Sen, *Military System*, p. 112. Twelve battalions of these soldiers, drilled in emulation of the French sepoys and armed with flintlock muskets, took part in the Battle of Panipat fought between the Marathas and the invading Afghan forces of Ahmad Shah Abdali in January 1761. Irvine, *Army*, p. 106. The majority perished at the battle, but a small *gardi* force continued to function as the nucleus of the Peshwa's army well into the 1790s. Edward Moor, *A Narrative*, p. 83.

[117] S.P. Sen, *The French in India 1763-1816*, Calcutta: Firma K.L. Mukhopadhyay, 1958, p. 544.

[118] OIOC Home, Misc., 388, pp. 83-5.

[119] An anonymous British participant of the battle wrote: 'The scientific men say it is the best ordnance they have ever seen; they are all made of brass and have elevating screws & ca, and of a much better constitution than the English cannon.' OIOC Mss. Eur. B. 401. See also William Thorn, *Memoir of the War in India Conducted by General Lord Lake, Commander-in-Chief and Major-General Sir Arthur Wellesley,*

while a British officer, Captain John Blakiston, describes how the Maratha guns taken at the Battle of Assaye (23 September 1803) were 'found laid a few degrees below the point blank, just what they ought to be for the discharge of grape or canister at a short distance'.[120] The Maratha infantry also had many similarities to the Company's army. Each brigade had five battalions of regular and three battalions of irregular infantry. The regulars were drilled in the British fashion, according to the 'old English system' of 1780. They were clothed in the same manner as the Company's sepoys while the troops even marched to military tunes 'played perfectly in the European style'.[121]

This was indeed a belated adoption of the fruits of the European 'Military Revolution' by Indian states. But rather than being a successful transition it only served to highlight the fundamental nature of the contrast between the European and Indian military systems. The innovating Indian rulers only adopted the outward manifestations of European military superiority like field artillery and disciplined infantry. The centralized command structure, which underpinned the efficiency of these tactical aspects, was almost completely neglected, resulting in outwardly potent yet intrinsically weak military forces.

---

*Duke of Wellington; From its Commencement in 1803 to its Termination in 1806, on the Banks of the Hyphasis*, London: Military Library, 1818, pp. 117, 233.

[120] Blakiston also says that so rapid was the Maratha fire at Assaye that 'officers left with the baggage and who were out of sound of small arms could not compare the sound of the guns to anything less than musketry'. Captain John Blakiston, *Twelve Years' Military Adventures in Three Quarters of the Globe or, Memoirs of an Officer Who Served in the Armies of His Majesty and of the East India Company, Between the Years 1802 and 1814, in Which are Contained the Campaigns of the Duke of Wellington in India, and his Last in Spain and the South of France*, 2 vols., London: Henry Colburn, 1829, vol. 1, pp. 176-7. On the excellence of Maratha artillery see also R.G.S. Cooper, 'Wellington and the Marathas 1803-04', *International History Review*, vol. 11, no. 1, 1989, pp. 31-8.

[121] Charles (later Lord) Metcalfe, who was assistant to the British Resident with Scindia in 1802 made the following first hand observation on Scindia's army in March 1802: 'The uniforms of the sepoys are the same as the Company's. So are the accoutrements with the exception that they carry a sword as well as a bayonet and musket. The band which was in full tune, as they marched by my little camp, played nothing but English tunes, perfectly in the European style.' John William Kaye, *Life and Correspondence of Charles, Lord Metcalfe*, 2 vols., London: Bentley, 1854, 1, p. 67.

The Maratha regular army was a case in point. The Maratha State had very little control over the European officers on whom it depended for leadership of their army. These officers were a polyglot band of mercenaries who had been lured into native armies by the promise of vast fortunes. Indeed one of the conditions which made service with the Marathas attractive to them was the 'freedom of leaving the service and remitting their property without restraint'.[122] Yet the future of the wealth they accumulated depended largely on the English EIC. They relied on the latter—which now had the command of the seas—for a safe passage to Europe for both them and their wealth. Many had invested thousands of pounds in savings in EIC paper.[123] De Boigne himself transferred his wealth to France with the help of contacts in the British settlements and it was with this in mind that he included in his contract with Scindia a clause which relieved him of the responsibility of fighting the British.[124]

A considerable number of English officers also fought for the Marathas. Again however, fighting for the Marathas (or any other native power for that matter), was for these men nothing more than an easy way to make money. Not only did they feel a lack of loyalty to their employers, but the mercenary rewards of Maratha employment tended to attract less competent types. Some, like de Boigne, did have some military experience but there were also a substantial number who had dubious military credentials. For example Cullier Perron who succeeded de Boigne was a runaway sailor and Louis Bourquin who replaced him later was an ex-pastry cook![125] The crucial thing though is that the Marathas did little to remedy the situation. Unlike in the case of

[122] Mark and Murray Hammick Wilks, *Historical Sketches of the South of India*, 3 vols., London, 1818, vol. 3, p. 352.

[123] Dirk H. Kolff, 'The End of an Ancien Regime: Colonial War in India 1798-1818', in J.A. Moor and H. Wesseling (eds.), *Imperialism and War: Essays in Colonial War in Africa and Asia*, Leiden: Universitaire Press, 1989, p. 36.

[124] 'Sketches of De Boigne's Life', published in *The Telegraph*, 1797 and 1798; in Lewis Ferdinand Smith, *A Sketch of the Rise, Progress and Termination of the Regular Corps Formed and Commanded by Europeans in the Service of the Native Princes of India with Details of the Principal Events and Actions of the Late Maratha War*, Calcutta, 1805, p. 77.

[125] Herbert Compton says with sarcasm that 'Bourquin's craft in culinary matters was superior to his skill in military matters'. Herbert Compton, *A Particular Account of the European Military Adventurers in Hindustan*, London: OUP, 1976; 1st pub. 1895, p. 341.

Mysore, the Maratha State's relationship with the mercenaries actually enhanced its mercenary character. Thus, de Boigne was remunerated in true 'feudal' fashion—with a *jagir* incorporating fertile land on both sides of the Yamuna.[126] This effectively freed the mercenaries from the control of any authority higher than that of de Boigne. But de Boigne himself was no less a mercenary than the rest; and while he was a genuine soldier by training, his position as 'general' in Scindia's army probably owed more to the absence of other competent personnel at the time he offered his services to the Gwalior ruler than to any extraordinary military ability on his part. The *jagir* suited him as it gave him undeniable power. He had at his disposal one of the richest provinces in north India and this combined with his command provided him with ample scope to create an army that served his mercenary interests. Predictably, he made certain that his position was secure within the army, particularly in the face of the influx of many like-minded Europeans. He personally controlled the finances of the army; determined the pay of all soldiers and officers; maintained a tight grip over the flow of information by not delegating authority or establishing a proper chain of command; personally supervised the medical facilities, supplies and the making and designing of equipment; and he is said to have been his own adjutant general and quartermaster.[127] Thus, in many ways, de Boigne was more of a feudal chieftain than a military commander in the contemporary European mould.

Following de Boigne's departure, the 'ownership' of Scindia's army passed over to Perron who went a step further than de Boigne by playing his French officers against the English and rewarding those who displayed sufficient allegiance to him with higher positions within the army irrespective of their military talents.[128] Thus, most of the upper echelons of the officer corps came to be filled with Perron's stooges. 'Low they were in every sense of the word', says Lewis Ferdinand Smith, the biographer of the mercenaries, 'wretches were raised from cooks, bakers and barbers to be the majors and colonels, absurdly entrusted

[126] Sen, *Military System*, p. 119.

[127] Shelford Bidwell, *Swords for Hire: European Mercenaries in Eighteenth Century India*, London: John Murray, 1978, p. 82.

[128] Ibid., p. 168. According to Major Thomas Skinner, one of Perron's Anglo-Indian officers, 'Instead of being a good plain honest soldier, beloved by his soldiery and esteemed by all about him, he [Perron] began to turn his ear to flattery and neglect merit while his favourites got all the good opportunities'. Cited in Compton, *A Particular*, p. 333.

[129] Cited in Sen, *Military System*, p. 121.

with the command of brigades and shoved into paths to acquire lakhs'.[129] Ironically, Perron was finally ousted by one such favourite of his, Louis Bourquin, who orchestrated a mutiny at the outbreak of the Second Maratha War.

The efficiency of this curious army with its disciplined infantry commanded by European officers but under a distinctly Indian style of segmented political authority was severely tested by the outbreak of the Second Anglo-Maratha War in 1803-5. Now, the European mercenaries in Maratha service faced a real threat to what was dear to them—their relationship with the Company. Knowing this well, the English offered an amnesty to all the mercenaries in Maratha service and the response was a mass exodus.[130] Perron himself negotiated a safe passage to Lucknow with all his wealth. The English officers displayed a remarkable patriotism, three of the English mercenaries serving the Maratha chief Jaswant Rao Holkar preferred to suffer execution rather than fight their countrymen[131] while one of Perron's English officers, one Captain Lucan, volunteered to show Brigadier-General Lake the way to the gate of the Aligarh fortress, greatly facilitating the subsequent British storming of the place.[132]

As for the few officers who were left, they deserted soon after the commencement of the war. Bourquin, who commanded at Delhi, took off even before the British infantry had struck the decisive blow.[133] Another French officer named Drudgeon, who led a relieving force sent from the Deccan, surrendered to the British as soon as he heard of the defeat at Delhi.[134] And the Hanoverian officer, Pohlman, who was in command at Assaye, was so reluctant to fight that he is said to have been closely guarded by one of his fellow officers who showed a

[130] The first proclamation of this amnesty was made on 25 August 1803 and was followed by another on 1 September, setting 1 November as the deadline. The amnesty offered the mercenaries employment in the Company's army on their present pay for the duration of the war and 'a reasonable remuneration' upon its termination. John Pemble, 'Techniques and Resources', pp. 393-4. See also Smith, *A Sketch*, p. 49; and Dennis Holman, *Sikander Sahib: the Life of Colonel Thomas Skinner 1778-1841*, London: William Heinemann Ltd., 1961, pp. 86-7.

[131] Compton, *A Particular*, p. 419.

[132] Ibid., p. 369.

[133] Hugh Pearse, *Memoir of the Life and Military Services of Viscount Lake*, London: Robert Blackwood, 1908, p. 225.

[134] Compton, *A Particular*, p. 350.

rare enthusiasm for Scindia's cause.[135] But such individual acts of loyalty could not stem the tide of wholesale desertion and the Maratha army was left stranded, virtually leaderless on the fields of Assaye, Delhi and Laswari.

To reiterate, the defeat of the Maratha regular army showed that the fundamental differences that existed between the European and Indian military systems lay not simply in military tactics but also in the system of political control that underpinned them. Maratha army collapsed when the British exploited its segmented political control by negotiating with its officers—just as it often happened in contemporary Indian military culture. As we shall see in the next chapter, the English also perceived the contrast between their armies and those of Indian rulers, but in a quite different way from the Marathas.

[135] Barry Close, British Resident at Poona, to the Governor-General, 16 October 1803. Raghubir Singh (ed.), *Poona Residency Correspondence, volume 10: The Treaty of Bassein and the Anglo-Maratha War in the Deccan in 1803-04*, Bombay: Sri Gauranga Press, 1951, pp. 156-7.

*Two*

# British Perceptions and the Emergence of the Sepoy Army, 1746-1800

IN THIS CHAPTER I shall examine the emergence of the English East India Company's sepoy army in the context of the prevailing European, particularly British attitudes towards Indian soldiers. I shall start by looking at the way in which Europeans perceived the Indian military system and then move on to examine the origins and expansion of the Company's sepoy army.

## THE INDIAN SOLDIER THROUGH EUROPEAN EYES

It was explained in the previous chapter that one of the factors that separated Indian and European armies in the pre-modern era was the absence of collective discipline in the Indian forces. European visitors to the subcontinent had noticed this from an early time. Francois Bernier found the Mughal army 'marching with the irregularity of a herd of animals'[1] while to his contemporary, Niccolo Manucci, the Mughal troops that gathered at Samugarh in May 1658 appeared to have been deployed too close together, like 'trees in a pinewood'.[2] Nearly a century and a half later the Abbe' Dubois also observed how Indian armies lacked 'all the skilled dispositions by which it is possible to manoeuvre large bodies of troops without confusion'.[3] To many Europeans, Indian armies with their disorderly multitudes of soldiers and sprawling bazaars resembled large moving fairs more than armies. 'In the armies of India one merely sees colours, flags and standards, one is continuously overwhelmed by the noise of timbals, trumpets, oboes and fifes and so on', wrote Jean Law de Lauristen, the head of

[1] Bernier, *Travels*, p. 55.

[2] Manucci, *Storia*, vol. 1, p. 266.

[3] Dubois, *Hindu Manners*, p. 674.

the French factory at Kasimbazar in the mid-eighteenth century.[4] Yet, despite their lack of order, such armies could also impress European observers with their grandeur as Captain John Dalton discovered when he came across the combined armies of the Nawab of the Carnatic and the King of Mysore in 1752:

> Trichinapoly plains were now covered for a considerable way with innumerable swarms of horse, foot elephants and camels and both armies having—according to the eastern custom—a surprising number of silk colours and standards of different sorts afforded a very extraordinary prospect and notwithstanding their irregularity in point of Marshalling their armies, there was something grand in their appearance.[5]

If Europeans were fascinated by the way Indian armies moved, they were intrigued by the way they fought. Noted Manucci of the Battle of Samugarh: 'I noted in this action as in so many others where I was present, that the only soldiers who fought were those well to the front. Of those to the rear, although holding their bared swords in their hands, the Moguls did nothing but shout "bakush bakush" and the Indians "Mar, Mar"—kill, kill. If those in front advanced those behind followed the example; and if the former retired, the others fled. A custom in Hindustan quite contrary to that in Europe.'[6] To Orme, an Indian battle appeared very much like a melee with fighting taking place in clusters around the principal commanders.[7] The Maratha tactic of ravaging the country was particularly striking to some British observers as evident from the following description of the devastation caused by the army of Purseram Bhao during the Third Anglo-Mysore War (1790-2):

> This part of the country was the richest we had yet seen, abounding in villages and towns, so thick that the night we came to this ground we counted ten villages in flames at the same time. It was by no means uncommon to see six or eight burning at once in several parts of this fine country.
>
> In this style do the Marathas carry on a war; it is indeed the only way in which, as enemies, they are at all formidable; they can pour on an enemy's country an inundation of a hundred thousand horse; and when we consider the ruin and

[4] Quoted in Gommans, 'Indian Warfare', p. 263.
[5] OIOC Orme India III, p. 533.
[6] Manucci, *Storia*, vol. 1, p. 266.
[7] Orme, *Historical Fragments*, p. 269.

devastation spread by such a host of locusts, we are inclined to think that the curse of God could not have fallen on Egypt in a more destructive form.[8]

One aspect of Indian warfare that rarely failed to draw European attention was the state of the Indian artillery. We have already noted some European observations on the weight and size of Indian cannon. Their inefficiency was also commented on. According to Orme, the Mughals 'had no conception that it was possible to fire with execution the same piece of cannon five or six times; for in the awkward management of their own clumsy artillery, they think they do well if they fire once in a quarter of an hour'.[9] Although the artillery of the regular Maratha armies were praised by the British, the guns traditionally used by the Marathas did not receive such approval. William Tone, a British officer who served with the Peshwa's army thought the gun carriages were clumsily constructed although the cannon were 'tolerably cast'. Moreover, he also believed that the wrought iron cannon balls used by the Marathas had the potential to spoil the bore, affecting the precision of firing.[10] This was not all. Like their artillery, Indian fortifications also seemed crude to Europeans. According to James Mill the Indians' knowledge of fortification was 'elementary', and mostly consisted in 'surrounding the place with a mud wall and ditch, or availing themselves of the natural advantages which water or impervious thickets could afford'.[11] Indian approach to attacking fortresses was equally ridiculed. I am tempted here to quote the frequently cited description left by Edward Moor of the Maratha attempt to breach Dharwar fort in 1791:

A gun is loaded, and the whole of the people in the battery sit down, talk and smoke for half an hour, when it is fired and if it knocks up a great dust it is

[8] Moor, *A Narrative*, p. 141. The predatory warfare of the Marathas impressed many Europeans. It is interesting to hear Orme describing them as the 'Normans of India'. OIOC O.V., 28, p. 158.

[9] Orme, *History*, vol. 1, p. 74. The mid-eighteenth century English military historian Richard Cambridge was also very critical of Indian artillery, pointing out that nothing was more harmful to the Indians than 'the false notion that is generally entertained amongst [*sic*] them, and chiefly their commanders, in relation to artillery. They are terrified with that of the enemy, and put a foolish confidence on their own, and what is the most fatal mistake, they place their chief confidence on the largest pieces which they neither know how to manage nor move.' Richard Owen Cambridge, *An Account of the War in India Between the English and the French on the Coast of Coromandel from the Year 1750 to the Year 1761*, London: printed for T. Jeffreys, 1762, p. 11.

[10] Cited in Sen, *Military System*, p. 103.

[11] Mill, *History*, 1, p. 209.

thought sufficient; it is reloaded, and the parties resume their smoking and conversation. During two hours in the middle of the day, generally from one to three, a gun is seldom fired on either side, that time being, as it would appear, by mutual consent, set apart for meals.[12]

Other aspects of Indian military organization did not escape the notice of observant Europeans. We have already seen Colonel Caillaud describing *jamadari* recruitment. While outlining the mode of recruitment, Caillaud also noted the power of the *jamadars*, which he thought was 'unlimited and uncontrolled'. He also noticed the mercenary character of their service, saying that it was 'a matter of great indifference to them who they serve'.[13] Others agreed, Law declaring that 'loyalty and patriotism are virtues unknown in India'[14] while William Tone disdainfully described the Maratha regulars as 'mere soldiers of Fortune' who 'would plunder their native village without pang'.[15]

All these views were obviously Euro-centric. Europeans, familiar with their centralized armies of neat columns and lines of drilled infantry and the rapid-firing, mobile field artillery could not but marvel and snigger at the massive unwieldy armies and equipment of the Indians. In short, they were creating Indian difference in the military sphere. The eighteenth century watercolour painting of the Battle of Plassey (see p. 80) provides an eloquent pictorial representation of this perception of difference. On the left are the neat lines of British infantry with their field guns while the right is occupied by a shapeless mass of elephants, cavalry, infantry and artillery. The contrast is total.

Significantly, Europeans also felt that such disparities conferred on European armies a decided superiority over their Indian counterparts. 'I could never see these soldiers', mused Bernier, 'without reflecting upon the ease with which five and twenty thousand of our veterans from the army of Flanders would overcome these armies, however numerous'.[16] Bernier was certainly not alone. Jean-Baptiste Tavernier, who was in India in late seventeenth century, concluded that one

[12] Moor, *A Narrative*, p. 30.

[13] Orme India XIII, p. 3746. Charles Malet who was the British Resident at Poona in the early 1790s described the commanders of the Maratha cavalry as being extremely corrupt and having absolute control over their men. OIOC H.M. 242, pp. 35-6.

[14] Quoted in Gommans, 'Indian Warfare', p. 264.

[15] Quoted in Sen, *Military System*, p. 120.

[16] Bernier, *Travels*, p. 55.

Plate 2: 'Battle of Plassey' from a contemporary hand coloured manuscript. Note the contrast between the disorderly mass of Mughal soldiers and the neat lines of British and sepoy infantry as perceived by the anonymous British artist. Source: Jackdaws Publications no. 52, a Collection of contemporary documents compiled by David Johnson, published and distributed by Jonathan Cape Ltd. Bedfordshire, London. Date of publication unavailable.

hundred European soldiers 'would scarcely have much difficulty in defeating a thousand soldiers from the army of Golconda'.[17] As for English attitudes, in 1739, the Bombay government dismissed the Marathas as a military threat in terms strikingly similar to those employed by Bernier to describe the Mughals, pointing out that, although the Marathas could field armies many thousands strong, 'their soldiers have but the least order or discipline and indifferently provided with ammunition and military accoutrements . . . their greatest number would hardly stand against any regular body of Europeans.'[18]

As we have seen in the previous chapter, such confidence was not misplaced. When hostilities broke out with the French and their allies in the Carnatic in the 1740s, mere handfuls of disciplined European infantry and field artillery regularly dispersed large masses of Indian troops. According to Colonel Caillaud, artillery in particular came to be the 'great object of terror to an Indian enemy' because 'the distance at which it doth [*sic*] execution damps their first spirit and generally throws them into confusion and if they are bold enough to come nearer their effects are so devastating that they seldom fail, soon deciding the fate of the day'.[19]

Such devastating firepower made Indian armies reluctant to venture closer to British troops. An interesting consequence of this was that Indian soldiers and resolute behaviour came to be considered almost mutually exclusive. According to a British sergeant present at the siege of Arcot in 1751 it was with '*bravery uncommon to Blacks*' that Chanda Sahib's troops crossed the moat to storm the breach[20] and when in 1752, the Mysorian cavalry charged to within 50 yards of a British position in the Carnatic, it was considered remarkable. 'I never saw Black fellows do so before', was the comment of a stunned English officer.[21] Similar sentiments were expressed by the Bengal council in describing a decisive victory obtained by Major Adams over the troops of Patna in September 1764. According to the council, the battle was

[17] Tavernier, *Travels*, II, p. 391.

[18] Quoted in W.S. Desai, *Bombay and the Marathas up to 1744*, Delhi: Munshiram Manoharlal, 1970, pp. 100-1. An English sergeant serving at Fort St. David in 1749 described the Tanjorian army in equally derisive terms saying, 'the enemy gives great encouragement to Europeans. It is no hardship to raise 30 or 40 thousand, but they are cowardly and very ill disciplined.' James Miller, 'The Diary of James Miller', *Journal of the Society for Army Historical Research*, vol. 3, no. 14, 1924, pp. 222-3.

[19] OIOC Orme India XIII, p. 3739.

[20] OIOC Orme India II, p. 284.

[21] OIOC Orme India III, p. 666.

hard fought and the enemy retreated only 'after a resolute and most uncommon stand for troops of this country'.[22] However, it was Richard Cambridge who best summed up the strength of this perception, ironically through a fervent plea for its urgent revision: 'It is owing entirely to an ignorance of the manners of Asiatics, that many people imagine that they can never be made soldiers. . . . But those are greatly mistaken, who attribute their dread of firearms, and particularly artillery, to an invincible timidity.'[23]

Cambridge's tone suggests that he was in the minority when it came to dismissing negative impressions about Indian soldiers. Evidently, the British were developing a strong prejudice against Indian soldiers based on what was observable on the battlefield. However, it would be too hasty to condemn this prejudice as racist. British stereotyping of Indian troops as timid and cowardly was probably not much different from the opinions European nations had about the military character of each other. For example, the Russians were considered 'long enduring, tough and insensitive', the Polish 'proud, obstinate and pleasure loving' while the English were seen as violent and patriotic.[24] Moreover, Indians themselves were not passive victims of European prejudice and generalizations. Mark Wilks relates how, during a lull in the fighting in the Second Mysore War (1780-4) Mysoreans rode upto the British lines, challenging British soldiers to single combat.

[22] Bengal to Madras, 5 September 1764. Madras Mil. and Sec. Cons. 11 October 1764. OIOC, P/251/49, p. 263. Narratives and correspondence of European officers are replete with similar observations. For example, at the Battle of Chengama in 1767, Colonel Henry Cosby described how the British troops were attacked by Hyder's sepoys 'with as much resolution as was ever seen in Black troops'. 'Journal kept by Lieut-Colonel Henry Cosby of the East India Company's service during campaigns in the Carnatic including the expedition against Tanjore, Bombay and Pondicherry'. B.L. Add. 29898, p. 26. Colonel Macleod, in writing to General Sir Eyre Coote in 1782 about an attack made by Mysorian troops on a Bombay Army detachment admitted that he 'did not expect such from any Black power'. Colonel Macleod to Eyre Coote, 18 December 1782. *Correspondence During the Incapacitation of the Commander-in-Chief in September 1782, With General Orders from the Above Date to April 1783, Collected by Major-General James Stuart*, 1785, p. 72.

[23] Cambridge, *An Account*, p. 31. It is interesting to hear what a French officer in Hyder's service had to say about the above-mentioned attack by Hyder's troops on the English position at Chengama in 1767. He believed that the good conduct of Hyder's troops on that occasion 'must appear surprising to Europeans who are accustomed to entertain a bad opinion of the bravery of the Indians'. M.M.D.L.T., *Hyder Ali*, p. 292.

[24] For a comprehensive discussion of European military stereotypes in the eighteenth century see Christopher Duffy, *The Military Experience*, pp. 3-34.

Their conversation, noted Wilks, 'always assumed a character of contemptuous abuse of a mode of warfare which they stigmatised as unmanly, by excluding the exercise of individual prowess and skill'.[25]

Therefore, although the British harboured a strong prejudice against Indian soldiers it is unwise to put that down to racism in the nineteenth century meaning of the term. European prejudices against Indian soldiers were probably not much different from European perceptions of Muslims as 'indolent' and 'perfidious' rather than a belief in an innate, biologically determined inferiority of Indian soldiers. This is further suggested by the attempts made by European observers to explain Indian military weakness. There were many perceptive Europeans who were quick to attribute the weakness of the Indian military system to causes other than a want of personal bravery in Indian soldiers. As the contemporary French historian Joseph Michaud pointed out, the Indians were 'not inferior to Europeans in valour and in courage, but the courage, the strength and the audacity of a soldier becomes useless before modern tactics'.[26] Likewise, Edward Moor who campaigned in southern India in the 1790's attributed the reluctance of Marathas to charge to their desire to preserve their mounts rather than to a lack of courage.[27] Cambridge also agreed observing that Indian cavalry, 'though not backward to engage with the saber are extremely unwilling to bring their horses within the reach of our guns; so that they do not decline an engagement so much through fear for their lives as for their fortunes which are all laid out in the horse they ride on'.[28]

Another British officer, Captain John Blakiston of the King's 78th regiment came up with an interesting theory to explain Indian military weakness. He rated the Hindu warriors of his acquaintance heads and shoulders above Europeans when it came to bravery in the face of death. But the courage of the Hindu, he claimed 'is of a passive nature, while that of the European is active, the former being inert, has only its own weight to give it power; the latter has activity to increase its momentum'.[29]

[25] Wilks, *Historical Sketches*, vol. 2, p. 391.

[26] Joseph Michaud, *History of Mysore under Hyder Ali and Tippoo Sultan*, trs. V.K. Raman Menon, Delhi: Asian Educational Services, 1985; 1st French edn. 1801-6, 1st English edn. 1926, pp. 68-9.

[27] Moor, *A Narrative*, p. 226.

[28] Cambridge, *An Account*, p. 31. According to Dubois, the concern for their mounts made Indian cavalrymen take to flight at the first order to charge. Dubois, *Hindu Manners*, p. 674. See also Michaud, *History*, p. 68 for a similar view.

[29] Blakiston, *Twelve Years'*, vol. 1, pp. 146-7.

This explanation, ambiguous as it is, is quite clear about one thing; that the European had the edge over the Hindu because of the passive nature of the latter's courage. However, the source of this passive courage is not explained. An interesting feature of the explanation is the use of the term 'Hindu' rather than Indian or 'Black'. Does it suggest that Blakiston is making a connection between the Hindu cultural background and passive courage? It is not very clear but if that is the case, Blakiston may have drawn some inspiration from the contemporary British view of Hinduism as a religion that bred servility and passivity, thereby inviting subjugation. Interestingly, the Abbe' Dubois also made a similar observation; he thought that the 'habits of the Hindus appear more likely to impair their courage than to make them good soldiers'.[30]

There were other explanations as well. Robert Orme in particular, utilized another popular theory of the time—that of climatic influence—to explain the lack of courage in Indians, particularly those from the south: 'The courage of the people depends on the climate. In the northern parts of the kingdom, firmer fibres produce a proportionable degree of resolution; in the southern all is sensuality; and fear must be predominant in such as are infinitely susceptible of the minutest impressions.'[31]

Such views sat comfortably with the contemporary belief that temperate climates produced vigorous, robust and energetic populations. As James Forbes explained, the bravery and the honourable conduct of the Rajputs could be attributed to the rugged country and the bracing climate of Rajasthan, which he compared with Switzerland.[32]

Thus, although the British perceived 'timidity' and 'cowardice' in the Indian soldiers' reluctance to close with the British, enemy, the inclination seems to have been to attribute these characteristics to factors other than innate 'racial' characteristics as happened in the following century. But the fact is that such perceptions, along with the views about Indian artillery, fortifications and the mercenary motives of soldiers, formed the military dimension of the contemporary British representation of India as a backward country, rating below Europe in the scale of civilization. It is this representation of Indian military inferiority that makes the creation of an army of Indian soldiers by the

[30] Dubois, *Hindu Manners*, p. 668.

[31] Orme, *Historical Fragments*, p. 269.

[32] Bayly, ' "Caste" and "Race" ', p. 176.

English East India Company in the second half of the eighteenth century an interesting phenomenon. In the remainder of this chapter we shall trace the origins and expansion of this remarkable institution.

## THE COMPANY'S GARRISONS IN INDIA 1600-1746

Predictably, from the earliest times, the Company's possessions on the subcontinent were protected by garrisons organized around a nucleus of European troops. Their numbers, however, were very small. For example, in 1652, the garrison in Madras numbered barely 70 Europeans and ten years later; Bengal was relying on an even tinier force of 30 Europeans.[33] Even Bombay, which boasted the biggest European garrison, had only 200 men on its rolls in 1668.[34] These numbers gradually increased by early eighteenth century—Madras having 360 Europeans in 1709 and Bengal 280 in 1718.[35] But still these were minuscule forces compared with the armies of the bigger 'country' powers.

The biggest obstacle to maintaining sizeable European garrisons was a combination of a meagre supply and high wastage. Recruits from Europe arrived in a trickle rather than a torrent and even this dried out considerably by the time the ships reached the subcontinent. Wretched living conditions aboard the ships ensured that only a portion on the men embarked in England arrived in India alive. For example, of the 40 recruits sent out from England to Bombay in May 1675, 4 died on the way.[36] And things did not improve much either on land, where an inclement climate and a miserable lifestyle marred by drinking and

[33] Bryant, 'The East India Company', Appendix I, p. 328.

[34] Arthur Edward Mainwaring, *Crown and Company: the Historical Records of the 2nd Battalion Royal Dublin Fusiliers, Formerly the 1st Bombay European Regiment*, 2 vols., London: Arthur and Humphreys, 1911-23, vol. 1, p. 31.

[35] Bryant, 'The East India Company', p. 328. The European force in Bombay had increased to 462 by 1684. Mainwairing, *Crown and Company*, vol. 1, p. 31. The meagreness of the numbers did not deter the authorities at Bombay and Madras from dignifying their European troops with the pompous titles of Madras and Bombay European regiments.

[36] Ibid., p. 58. As the Bengal Council explained to the Court of Directors in 1758, the recruits who arrived in India were very often 'fitter for the hospital than for duty'. J. Long (ed.), *Unpublished Letters of Government for the Years 1748 to 1768 Inclusive Relating Mainly to the Social Condition of Bengal with a Map of Calcutta*, Calcutta: Firma K.L. Mukhopadhyay, 1973; 1st pub. 1869, p. 203.

brawling took its toll on the survivors. As an official of the Bombay Council remarked in 1671, it was not uncommon to see men drunk 'even as they lay on their death beds'.[37] Thus, of the 450 men who arrived from England to take charge of Bombay in 1662, scarcely a 100 remained alive a year later,[38] while in 1756, 87 Europeans are reported to have perished at Fort St. George of drunkenness and 'sickness begun by women'.[39]

In the conditions of the time then, these losses could not be made good by further recruitment from Europe. This left only one expedient, the recruitment of natives. The first choice fell on the Topasses or the descendants of Portuguese. Indeed, Topasses formed a substantial part of most English garrisons from an early time. For example, of the 242 men who formed the Bombay Regiment in 1670, 73 were classed as 'White Portuguese' and 54 as Topasses.[40] while in February 1747, Fort St. David had 100 Europeans accompanied by 200 Topasses.[41] As a part of the regular garrison the Topasses were also subjected to the same discipline 'as the marching Regiments'.[42]

The recruitment of Topasses was largely the result of their European cultural background. As much as their cultural background brought them closer to the English, it also alienated the Topasses from Indian society at large. This made it easier to bind them to the Company's service—making them 'more agreeable to our European soldierie on the place' as one Company official put it in the late seventeenth century.[43] In fact, the English sometimes took an active interest in fostering the European identity among their Topasses. For instance in

[37] Sir Charles Fawcett, *The English Factories in India*, n.s., vols. 1, 3 and 4, Oxford: Clarendon, 1936, vol. 1, p. 28.

[38] Mainwairing, *Crown and Company*, vol. 1, p. 10.

[39] 'Memoirs of an expedition to the East Indies undertaken in the Year 1754, with some Observations on the Climate, People, Customs and Manners'. OIOC Mss. Eur. B. 215, pp. 145-6.

[40] Cadell, *History*, p. 29.

[41] At times, the Topasses seem to have even formed the majority of the regular garrison. Percival Spear, citing Michael Edwardes gives the Bombay garrison in 1737 as 449 European sailors, 299 European soldiers and 817 Topasses. Spear, *The Nabobs*, p. 162, n. 85.

[42] Clement Downing, *A History of the Indian Wars*, with an introduction and notes by William Foster, London: OUP, 1924; 1st pub. 1737, p. 20; Fort St. George Council to Stringer Lawrence, 27 June 1754, *Diary and Consultation Book, Fort St.George, Military Department 1754*, Madras: Government Printers, 1911, pp. 140-1.

[43] Sir William Foster, *English Factories in India*, 13 vols., Oxford: Clarendon, 1906-27, vol. 13, p. 48.

1748 the Topasses in the Madras garrison were being paid a higher wage than those at Fort St. David because they were wearing stockings and shoes![44]

Topasses, however, could not fill all the needs of the Company's garrisons. Therefore, some kind of native recruitment had to be maintained. Thus, as early as 1673, we find the Madras garrison of 225 Europeans and 163 Portuguese being supplemented by 550 Indian 'auxillers'.[45] Around the same time, Bombay was employing two companies of 'Rashpouts'.[46] Native troops are also reported from the English factory at Hughli in 1681,[47] indicating that the employment of native personnel was a common practice at all presidencies from a very early time.

The titles of these troops varied at the three presidencies. On the east coast, the term 'peon' seems to have been predominant,[48] although in Bengal native troops were often called 'Bakserrys'—an obvious reference to the place of their recruitment.[49] But interestingly, we do not hear of 'sepoys' being employed in any of the Company's settlements until well into the eighteenth century and that, too, only on the west coast of India. The earliest manuscript reference occurs in 1717 when several hundred of them were used in an expedition against the Raja of Karwar.[50] Further references occur later. For instance, when the Bombay presidency agreed to assist the Portuguese against the Marathas in 1730, 100 sepoys were employed in the vessels that were sent into battle against the Maratha naval forces.[51]

[44] FSD Cons. 5 May 1748. OIOC FR G/18/6, p. 181.

[45] Sue Pyatt Peeler, 'Land Forces of the East India Company in the Seventeenth Century', *Journal of Indian History Golden Jubilee Volume*, 1973, p. 552.

[46] Cadell, *History*, p. 29.

[47] Kolff, *Naukar*, p. 177.

[48] For instance, we hear of the Madras Council despatching 150 Europeans and 120 peons to despute some villages with the Nawab of the Carnatic in 1717. H.D. Love, *Vestiges of Old Madras*, 3 vols., London: John Murray, 1913, vol. 1, pp. 153-4.

[49] For example, in January 1743 the Bengal Council recruited 200 such Baksaris 'to man the Choukeys and patrol at nights on skirts of the Town'. C.R. Wilson (ed.), *Old Fort William in Bengal: a Selection of Official Documents dealing with its History*, 2 vols., London: John Murray, 1906, vol. 1, 169.

[50] 'The Journal of the Siege of Karwar', OIOC FR G/22/1. But Patrick Cadell refers to the native troops in Bombay in 1710 as sepoys. But it is not certain whether this term is employed by Cadell with later developments in mind or whether it is taken from a manuscript source. Cadell is not clear about this. Cadell, *History*, p. 40.

[51] Desai, *Bombay*, p. 83.

We do not have exact details of the numbers of native troops employed by the English East India Company in the seventeenth and early eighteenth centuries but they could not have been very high. Moreover, it appears that they were usually raised in response to emergencies. For instance, when the threat of a Maratha incursion loomed in January 1740, Fort St. David resolved to enlist 30 Topasses and 70 peons as a precautionary measure.[52] Many of them were discharged when the Maratha threat receded in the following year.[53] In Bengal, too, Maratha raids produced similar responses, the Fort William Council resolving to raise 300 Baksaris in May 1745 to help ward off the imminent intrusions and disbanding them when things settled down two months later.[54]

These modest garrisons of Europeans and Topasses supported by their Indian 'auxiliaries' were satisfactory as long as the Company was not required to undertake military operations of any intensity. This however, changed in the middle of the eighteenth century when the Company found itself drawn into a steadily escalating series of military confrontations.

## WAR IN INDIA AND THE DEMAND FOR TROOPS

The English Company's forces on the subcontinent received their baptism of fire with the outbreak of hostilities against the French in south India in 1746. The first Anglo-French confrontation in the Carnatic was limited to feeble attempts to capture the others' forts, but in the 1750s the conflict expanded into a wider war involving the English and the French East India Companies as allies of warring 'country' powers. This escalation of violence created an unprecedented demand for troops, not merely to fight the battles but also to safeguard the spoils. The first phase of the Carnatic War brought the Nawab Mohamed Ali firmly under the control of the Company, dependent as he was on English military support. This also resulted in the Nawab offering the Company the control of the revenue from territories north of the Paliar river to defray the costs the Company had incurred on his behalf. To maintain control over this revenue the Company had to

[52] James Hubbard to the Court of Directors, 8 January 1740. Henry H. Dodwell (ed.), *A Calendar of Madras Despatches 1740-44*, Madras: Government Printers, 1920, p. 10.

[53] Letter from James Hubbard to the Court of Directors, 9 June 1741. Ibid., p. 175.

[54] Wilson, *Old Fort William*, vol. 1, p. 183.

garrison outposts at places like Chingleput, Trivatore, Covelong and Chittapet. Propping up the Nawab also involved the Company in further military campaigns. For example, in 1755 and 1756 two expeditions were sent to bring Madura under control. But this was not all. In 1756, the Seven Years' War broke out in Europe and the Company was embroiled in a fresh—and even more serious—conflict with their arch rival. Then, to add to their woes, the headstrong Nawab of Bengal, Siraj-ud-Daulah attacked and captured Fort William (Calcutta) in June 1756. The Company was now caught up in a war on two fronts.

The wars in the Carnatic and Bengal ended, however, with resounding successes for the Company. The French were defeated at Wandiwash in 1760 and in the following year Pondicherry was captured. In Bengal, the Battle of Plassey broke the Nawab's power and delivered the de facto control of the province to the Company. Mughal attempts to dislodge the Company from Bengal were effectively thwarted at Baksar in 1764. But the Company's emergence as a key player in the Carnatic and Bengal meant that they were now in direct competition with the other major powers on the subcontinent like the Marathas and Mysore. Between 1767 and 1805, the Company had to fight four major wars with Mysore and three with the Marathas before its paramountcy on the subcontinent was assured.

These growing military commitments called for a substantial expansion in the Company's manpower resources. The emergence of the Company's native army has to be viewed in this context. The initial escalation of violence in the Carnatic found the Company struggling desperately to increase its meagre garrisons of European soldiers, but with little success. To be sure, the British government, conscious of the importance of the Anglo-French struggle in India, did despatch two large contingents of European troops to India in 1748 and 1754, the latter contingent a regular British army unit—the King's 39th regiment.[55] This was in addition to sending Major Stringer Lawrence, a British army officer, to take command over the Company's forces in 1748.[56] Yet such aid, though welcome, was not quite sufficient. Events on the subcontinent moved with a fluidity hardly anticipated in

[55] The first contingent consisted of twelve companies of infantry numbering 1,200 men. Half of this number was drawn from British army units in Ireland while the remainder came from units based in England. J.A. Macaulay, 'The Dublin Fusiliers', *Irish Sword*, vol. 6, no. 25, 1964, p. 257.

[56] Charles Floyer to the Court of Directors, Fort St. David, 13 February 1748, Dodwell, *Calendar*, p. 50.

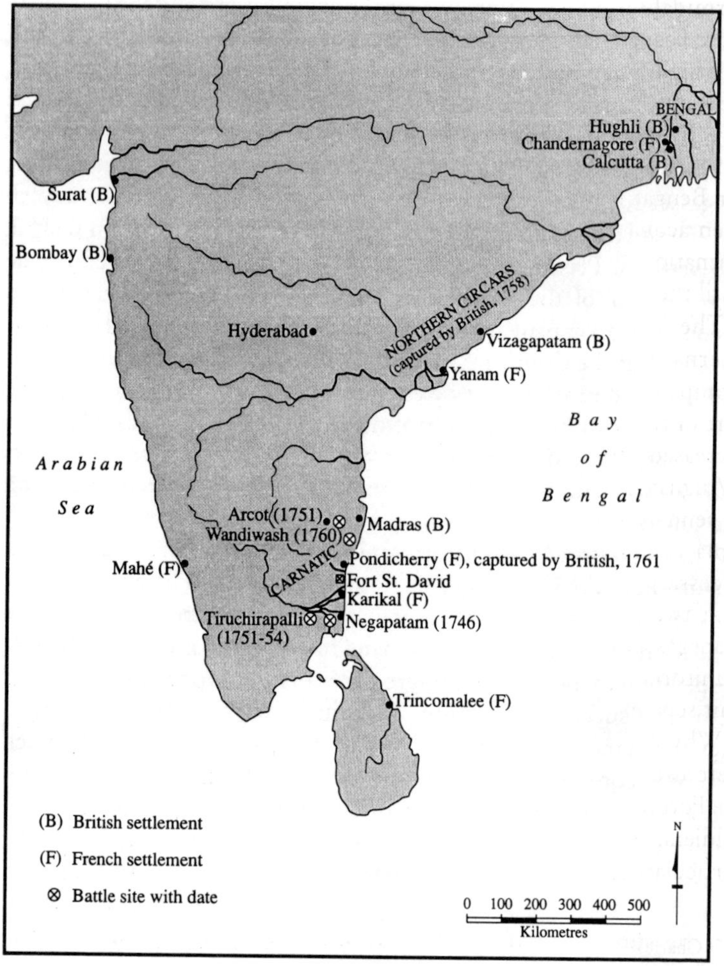


Map 2: Anglo-French Conflict in the Carnatic, 1746-61.

London, forcing the Company to confront substantial odds in their military campaigns. For example, the Company's Europeans at Madras amounted to only 797 in October 1749, while the European forces available to the French at Pondicherry were calculated at a comparatively formidable 1,800.[57] Such desperate situations called for desperate remedies, and the Fort St. David Council was sometimes driven to defying London in their search for European troops. For instance, they were quick to pounce on recruits meant for other presidencies despite directives from London to the contrary. On one such occasion, in May 1751, the Council defended its decision to detain 22 recruits meant for Bengal on the basis that the Court of Directors could not have been acquainted with the necessity for a large military force in the Carnatic. They also resolved to 'keep recruits on other similar ships, until the emergency at the presidency is over'.[58]

The lack of European troops triggered a desperate search for alternatives. Interestingly, one of the early choices made by the Company involved 'Coffrees' or African slaves. Africans had formed a part of the Bombay garrison as early as 1710,[59] but demand for them increased after the outbreak of hostilities in the Carnatic. Thus, on 8 August 1750, the Fort St. David Council ordered one Captain Bell to send ashore one hundred of his slaves to be trained in the use of arms 'as the present situation in the country render [*sic*] it absolutely necessary to keep up as large a military force as possible'.[60] Within the next two years several more batches of African slaves arrived from Madagascar at Fort St. David. They were disciplined and provided with a uniform as well as a living allowance but they were maintained as a unit separate from the Europeans and Topasses.[61]

Why 'Coffrees'? For one, being slaves, they were cheap. But there were also other reasons that made them 'serviceable'. In February 1752 the Fort St. David Council assured London that 'Coffrees made good soldiers. They are dreaded by the Moors.' They were also considered particularly useful in performing duties that required great physical

[57] Charles Floyer to the Court of Directors, Fort St. David, 30 October 1749, ibid., p. 83.

[58] FSD Cons., 5 December 1751. OIOC FR G/18/7.

[59] Cadell, *History*, p. 33.

[60] FSD Cons. 28 August 1750, OIOC FR G/18/7, p. 317.

[61] In April 1761 the two existing African companies were attached to the two battalions of the Madras European Regiment. Madras Mil. and Sec. Cons. 28 April 1761, OIOC P/D/45, p. 366.

exertion, which gained them a reputation as 'excellent pioneers'.[62] There was also the question of loyalty. The fact that they were slaves and alienated from the society of the subcontinent and, as a result, largely dependent on the English, would also have made the Africans ideally suited for employment as soldiers. But, unlike the Topasses, the Africans had no cultural ties with Europeans. This is probably why they were not incorporated into the European units like the Topasses.

But the problem with Africans was that they were no less a scarce resource than Europeans. They had to be shipped from Madagascar—not a very encouraging circumstance for an army pressed for manpower. Besides, the military situation on the subcontinent was escalating rapidly. Therefore, other alternatives had to be sought—and the only effective choice left was the recruitment of more Indian troops.

## THE EMERGENCE OF THE SEPOY ARMY 1746-1805

The growing demand for troops in the late 1740s and 1750s set the stage for a substantial increase in the number of native troops employed by the Company. Thus, in January 1747, soon after the fall of Madras to French, Fort St. David decided to recruit 500 more peons to augment the 200 Europeans and Topasses they had left.[63] By February 1747 such recruitment—and possibly the arrival of some of the fugitives from Madras—had raised the number of peons at Fort St. David to about 3,000.[64] On the west coast, Bombay took similar measures, raising 2,000 sepoys at Surat.[65] In May 1747 they also sent a reinforcement of

[62] For example, in December 1761 Colonel John Caillaud requested the Coffree company to assist him in siege work because they were 'excellent pioneers'. Madras Mil. and Sec. Cons. 7 December, OIOC P/D/45. Nearly a decade earlier the Fort St. George Council wrote to the Court of Directors that the Coffrees were 'of infinite service in the [artillery] train'. T. Saunders to London, 3 November 1752. Dodwell, *Calendar*, p. 174. As late as the 1830s some British military writers were stereotyping Africans as ideal for heavy labour due to their renown for physical strength. Peers, 'Habitual Nobility', p. 566. Interestingly, the French also used Africans in their artillery. The French army at Cuddalore in 1783 is said to have included 800 Africans, 'strong and active assistants to their artillery'. Burrish Crisp (trs.), *British India Analysed: the Provincial and Revenue Establishments of Tippoo Sultaun and of Mahomedan and British Conquerors in Hindustan, Stated and Considered in Three Parts*, 3 vols., Delhi: Crown Publications, 1988; 1st pub. 1793, vol. 3, p. 814.

[63] FSD Cons. 1 January 1747. OIOC FR G/18/6, p. 3.

[64] FSD Cons. 27 February 1747. OIOC FR G/18/6, pp. 30-1.

[65] Cadell, *History*, p. 49.

,100 sepoys to Madras[66] followed in June by a further 225 sepoys dispatched from Tellicherry.

The arrival of the Bombay and Tellicherry sepoys in the east led to an interesting development in the Company's Indian army in the east coast. This was because, after their arrival, the Company began to use the term 'sepoy' for native troops raised on the east coast as well. According to Clive about 1,000 'sepoys' accompanied Boscawen to the siege of Pondicherry[67] and 1,000 'sepoys' are also mentioned as having taken part in the first expedition to Tanjavur in April 1749.[68] It can safely be assumed that at least a few hundred of these would have been raised on the east coast as the Bombay and Tellicherry sepoys did not number more than a few hundred. But the first direct reference to raising sepoys on the east coast occurs in September 1749 when the Fort St. David Council informed Nawab Mohamed Ali that they had collected for him a force of 500.[69] In the event the Council sent the Nawab 663 'sepoys' together with 30 Europeans under Lieutenant Phillip Bulkley. The fact that they were discharged from service soon after is a clear indication that they were definitely raised in the east because the Bombay sepoys, we are told, were still on the east coast in 1751.[70]

We shall discuss this replacement of 'peons' by 'sepoys' later. But it suffices to say here that sepoy numbers on the east coast continued to grow during the 1750s. This growth, however, was steady rather than spectacular. As suggested by the dismissal of the sepoys sent to Mohamed Ali, sepoy recruitment was still seen as a temporary measure taken to meet military demands as they arose. In November 1752, the Madras Council decided that a permanent force of 1,300 sepoys was sufficient for their needs. Of these, Fort St. David and Fort St. George were to have 600 sepoys each while 100 were allocated for Devicottai. But the demand for sepoys continued to increase with the renewal of hostilities during 1753-4 and in March 1754 the Fort St. George Council gave Stringer Lawrence permission to raise as many sepoys as he liked.[71]

[66] FSD Cons. 5 May and 7 July 1747, OIOC FR G/18/6, pp. 156, 217.

[67] OIOC Orme India I, pp. 219-20.

[68] OIOC Orme India I, pp. 219-20.

[69] *Country Correspondence, Fort St. George, Military Department, 1749*, Madras: Government Printers, 1910, p. 36.

[70] Madras Pub. Cons., 20 May 1751, OIOC P/240/8, p. 82.

[71] Madras Mil. Cons., 8 April 1754. *Diary and Consultation Book, 1754*, p. 81.

By mid 1756 there were nearly 2,000 Europeans and as many as 10,000 sepoys employed by the Company in the Carnatic.[72]

Significantly, by this time, 'sepoys' were also being raised in Bengal. When Siraj-ud-Daulah attacked Fort William in June 1756 there were several hundred Baksaris in the garrison[73] and following the re-establishment of English control; Clive hastened to raise 'sepoys' for service in the Bengal presidency as well. By April 1757, he had raised 448,[74] and by June, when he marched out to take on Siraj-ud-Daulah at Plassey, his small force included about 2,100 sepoys—nearly 1,400 of them raised in Bengal. By the end of 1758, the sepoy force in Bengal had grown so substantially as to enable Colonel Francis Ford to bring nearly 2,000 sepoys with him on the expedition to the northern Circars in October 1758.

However, this was nothing compared to the growth of the sepoy army after 1760 in the wake of the Company's campaigns against Mysore and the Marathas. By 1782, Bengal had 52,000 native troops on its rolls, Madras and Bombay 48,000 and 15,000 respectively. By 1805 the total for Bengal and Madras were 64,000 respectively and 26,000 for the less embattled Bombay presidency.[75] These large infantry forces were supplemented by much smaller contingents of cavalry and artillery.[76] To be sure, growth occurred in fits and starts, than in a steady linear fashion. Large numbers of sepoys were usually raised before and during major campaigns and substantial reductions were carried out after the fighting. Nevertheless, each new campaign saw more sepoys recruited and retained than the previous one, leading to the steady expansion of the army.

Thus, it would be fair to say that the emergence and expansion of the English East India Company's native army in the eighteenth century

[72] Orme, *History*, vol. 2, p. 85.The biggest concentration of sepoys was at Fort St. George. In December 1758, its garrison included 2,220 sepoys, besides 1,605 Europeans, 64 Topasses and 89 'Coffrees'. Ibid., pp. 388-9.

[73] Wilson, *Old Fort William*, vol. 2, p. 62.

[74] OIOC Home Misc. 805, p. 727.

[75] Figures are taken from Raymond Callahan, *The East India Company and Army Reform*, Cambridge, Massachussetts: Harvard University Press, 1972, p. 6.

[76] For much of the eighteenth century, the Company depended on its native allies like the Nawab of the Carnatic for cavalry support. Although the dire need for a regular force of cavalry was felt on many occasions it was not until late in the century that the Company began forming a substantial Indian cavalry force. The real expansion of the Company's Indian cavalry took place in the following century.

was favoured by the lack of European troops and the steadily escalating military commitments of the Company. This expansion of the sepoy army was also aided by the relative cheapness of native soldiers. In 1755 a company of European soldiers—about 50-60 men—cost about 2,000 pounds sterling per year while the same number of sepoys cost only 850 pounds.[77] The situation had barely changed by the beginning of the nineteenth century; a thousand sepoys costing much less than what some individual European employees cost the Company.[78]

However, even if they were cheap, no self-respecting commercial organization would have employed thousands of soldiers had they not been useful and the steady growth of the sepoy army suggests that the native troops were also useful. As Lord Cornwallis declared in 1789, a battalion of British sepoys had the potential to make 'make anybody emperor in Hindustan',[79] a clear indication of the value placed on sepoys. But the question is, how did the British make useful soldiers out of men, whose military traditions seemed to be the antithesis of European military practices and therefore perceived to be inferior to the European model. And how useful were they? In the next chapter I shall begin to answer these questions by looking at the recruitment and organization of the sepoy army.

[77] Bryant, 'The East India Company', p. 53.

[78] Rev. William Tennant, *Indian Recreations, Consisting Chiefly of Strictures on the Domestic and Rural Economy of the Mahomedans and Hindoos*, 2 vols., London, 1804, vol. 1, p. 393.

[79] Quoted in K.M. Saxena, *The Military System of India 1850-1900*, Delhi: Sterling, 1974, p. 5.

*Three*

# The Sepoy Army in the Making: Recruitment, Command and Discipline, 1746-1800

THE PREVIOUS CHAPTER examined how the British perceived Indian soldiers as timid and undisciplined and yet proceeded to raise an army of Indian soldiers for themselves. The purpose of this chapter is to delve deeper into the creation of the sepoy army by examining its formation with relation to the areas of recruitment, command structure and discipline. I shall begin by focussing on the strategies adopted by the Company to recruit its sepoys.

## RECRUITING THE SEPOY

In recruiting their peons and sepoys, the English logically turned to the contractors who controlled the Indian military labour market. A 'list of peons sepoys and Arabs' dated January 1749 shows sepoys and peons organized in companies under *jamadars*, suggesting that this was probably the system whereby native troops had been recruited for many years. Sometimes, however, officers called *subedars* were placed over several *jamadars*. In the list mentioned above, we find the company under the *subedar* called Mohamed Usanbech having 7 *jamadars*, 10 *havildars*, 12 *naiks* and 179 sepoys.[1] The *jamadars* in this case may have been in charge of small numbers within the company. Likewise, in 1753, the Bombay sepoys were said to be under the command of a *subedar* named Hadjee Amol.[2] Below the *jamadars* were ranked other inferior officers, namely *havildars* and *naiks*. Modern historians are fond of defining these positions with relation to positions in European

[1] Abstract of the list of peons, seapoys and Arabians and horsemen in Fort St. David, FSD Cons., 31 January 1749, OIOC FR G/18/10.

[2] Madras Pub. Cons., 12 April 1753, OIOC P/240/11, pp. 152-3.

armies like sergeant and corporal,[3] but whether the *havildars* and *naiks* had military functions similar to the European offices related to them is doubtful. Rather, they probably held positions of trust within the companies, in charge of smaller numbers of men whom they may have helped the *jamadars* to raise.[4]

During the latter half of the eighteenth century, the British incorporated these sepoy officers into a regular command structure. This will be discussed in detail in the next chapter but for our present purposes it is sufficient to say that even in the latter decades of the eighteenth century the English continued to depend largely on native agents for recruitment, sometimes offering military rank as an inducement. In 1767 we hear of the Commander of EIC forces in Madras offering anybody who brought in 50 recruits the rank of *jamadar* and the rank of *havildar* to one who brought in 30 and to one who brought in 20 the rank of *naik*.[5] But this was a measure frowned up on by the Madràs government as causing 'great irregularities and confusion in the establishment by making many supernumerary officers'. Wood's actions seem to have been sanctioned only due to the urgency for a large number of recruits during the First Mysore War.[6] The practice, however, did not die out and appears to have been in full swing during the Second Mysore War when commissions as sepoy officers were promised to those who brought in a specified number of troops.[7]

Apart from using their officers as recruiting agents, the Madras

[3] See for example the explanation of these terms in Amiya Barat, *The Bengal Native Infantry: its Organisation and Discipline*, Calcutta: Firma K.L. Mukhopadhyay, 1962, p. 7, fns. a, b, c and d. See also Eric Swift, *The Brave and the Prejudiced*, Chelmsford, Essex: Springfield, 1982, p. 34.

[4] According to a Colonel Caillaud, their functions were 'imperfectly ascertained, and as little observed, but they are nominally kept up as their pay, which is something better puts so much more in the jemadars pocket when he makes up his account with the government'. OIOC Orme India XIII, p. 3749. In the Maratha army under Shivaji, a *naik* is said to have commanded 10 men while a *havildar* had the control over 50. Egerton, *Indian and Oriental Armour*, p. 26.

[5] H.H. Dodwell, *Sepoy Recruitment in the Old Madras Army*, Calcutta: Superintendant, Govt. Printing, 1922, p. 49.

[6] Madras Mil. Cons., 1768. OIOC P/251/63, pp. 1510-11.

[7] Dodwell, *Sepoy Recruitment*, p. 19. Apparently this practice continued beyond the Second Mysore War. When additional sepoys were recruited in 1790, officers' ranks were promised to sepoys who brought in considerable numbers of sepoys. For instance, *jamadars* were promoted to *subedars* if they presented 38 recruits. Wilson, *History*, 2, p. 237.

government also encouraged the children of sepoys wounded or killed in action to join the service. In 1785 each sepoy company was authorized to take on its rolls two such boys.[8] These boys grew up within their units and were greatly valued as prospective sepoys. So too were the young boys who were attached to European units as cook-boys. As Innes Munro explains: 'Those cook-boys are amazingly attached to their masters, and will keep close to their heels in the midst of the greatest dangers. When they grow up they make the best sepoys, for all of them speak English well.'[9]

Dependence upon sepoys themselves for recruitment often led to the sepoy companies being filled with men who were from the same village or related to each other. Thus, when in 1795 a Madras sepoy unit mutinied in Colombo and their native officers tried to distance themselves from this act of insubordination, their explanation that they were unaware of the sepoys intentions was dismissed as being unlikely because they were 'closely connected with, and often nearly related to the sepoys'.[10]

In Bombay too, the Company relied largely on the sepoy officers for recruitment. When they resolved to raise 1,000 sepoys in 1768, the authorities at Surat decided to send their *jamadars* and *havildars* to raise the required number of men with the promise of a gratuity of Rs. 5 for every man enlisted.[11] And the general order issued by the Bombay Army on 5 October 1797 shows that this practice continued till later times. It authorized each battalion to send parties comprising one native officer, six non-commissioned officers and twenty privates on recruiting service. Sepoy officers were also encouraged to procure recruits in exchange for promotion. For instance, a *havildar* raising

[8] Dodwell, *Sepoy Recruitment*, pp. 29-30. By this time however, this practice seems to have been quite common. For example we hear Colonel William Fullerton recommending in 1784 the continuation of the 'institution of admitting the children of wounded or deserving sepoys'. William Fullerton, *A View of the English Interests in India and an Account of the Military Operations in the Southern Part of the Peninsula During the Campaigns of 1782, 1783 and 1784. In Two Letters addressed to the Right Honourable the Earl of . . . and to Lord Macartney and the Select Committee*. At Fort St. George, London, 1788, p. 222. By mid-1790s this mode of recruitment had become a major source of military manpower. See *Fort St. George General Orders July 12, 1796*, Madras, 1796, p. 28.

[9] Munro, *A Narrative*, p. 197.

[10] The opinion was expressed by colonel Stuart, quoted in S.C. Hill, 'The Old Sepoy Officer', *English Historical Review*, vol. 28, no. 111, 1913, p. 514.

[11] Bombay Pub. Cons., 12 December 1768, OIOC P/341/31, p. 698.

20 grenadier or 25 battalion recruits was to be promoted to *jamadar* while a *jamadar* raising 40 grenadier recruits or 40-5 battalion recruits was promoted to *subedar*.[12]

The Bengal Army also sent out its *jamadars* and *havildars* in search of prospective recruits.[13] And during the Governor-Generalship of Lord Cornwallis, recruitment was made more methodical by the despatch of recruiting parties into the *mofussil*. Comprising a European officer, a native officer and a doctor, these recruiting parties went into villages and signed up the young men who approached them with a view to enlistment. The recruiting officers were charged with the task of keeping detailed records of all the men they recruited.[14] Alternatively, serving sepoys were also encouraged to bring their friends and relatives; it was a *jamadar* uncle who first introduced Sita Ram Pandey to the Company's army.[15]

The Company employed a number of criteria in selecting prospective sepoys. One was physical fitness, 'a Prussian passion for tall men' as Amiya Barat describes it.[16] This was reflected in the physical criterion employed to recruit sepoys. Recruiting instructions issued to one Lieutenant Holland by the Bengal government in 1762 advised him to entertain 'no men but such as are of good stature, strong limbed and free from any bodily imperfections nor any under sixteen years of age or above thirty five'.[17] In the Bengal Army 'good stature' meant a minimum height of 5'7".[18] In the Bombay and Madras Armies, standards were considerably lowered. At Bombay, the minimum height was 5'2" while at Madras it was 5'4".[19] These criteria compared favourably with those employed in selecting recruits for the Company's European units

[12] Edward Moor (ed.), *A Compilation of all the Government, General, Brigade and Garrison Orders of the Bombay Army 1750-1800*, Bombay, 1801, Chapter XXXIX.

[13] Barat, *Bengal Native Infantry*, p. 49.

[14] Alavi, *The Sepoys*, p. 47.

[15] Sita Ram Pandey, *From Sepoy to Subedar, Being the Life and Adventures of Subedar Sita Ram, a Native Officer of the Bengal Army, Writen by Himself*, ed. James Lunt, London: Routeledge and Kegan Paul, 1973, pp. 4-6.

[16] Barat, *Bengal Native Infantry*, p. 49.

[17] Recruiting instructions issued to Lieutenant Holland, 29 October 1762. Carnac Papers, OIOC Mss. Eur. F. 128/4.

[18] Bengal Mil. Cons., 16 June 1785, OIOC MR L/MIL/17/2/438, p. 377. Also Bengal Mil. Cons., 8 August 1796, OIOC P/19/19, p. 12.

[19] For Bombay see Moor, *A Compilation*, Chapter XXXIX. For Madras see Major Madan Paul Singh, *Indian Army Under the East India Company*, New Delhi: Sterling, 1976, p. 150.

and the regular British army. Troops recruited for the Company's European regiments fitted a height requirement of 5'1" to 5'5".[20] The King's troops had the potential to be slightly taller mainly because the Company's recruiting agents were keen to avoid competition with the British army regiments, but even then, the standards were not markedly different. For instance, the King's 44th which was recruiting in 1786, required a minimum height ranging from 5'5" to 5'7".[21]

In recruiting their sepoys the Company also showed a marked preference for Indians of particular social and ethnic backgrounds. When Clive started recruiting sepoys for the Bengal presidency in 1757 the men were drawn mostly from the high caste Rajput peasantry in north India.[22] This practice continued with the expansion of the Bengal Army during the rest of the century, with Warren Hastings in particular showing a keen interest in filling the sepoy ranks with the indigenous social elite.[23] Thanks to such predilections, the Bengal Army had already established itself as a predominantly Hindu army towards the end of the eighteenth century, most of its sepoys being drawn from the 'Bramins [*sic*] and many other of their higher casts' as Lord Cornwallis informed London in 1789.[24]

[20] For example, an advertisement in 'The Gazeteer and New Daily Advertiser' of 31 August 1781 calls for 'lads five foot one' to enlist for service in India in the Company's army. Cited in H.C. Wylly, *Life of Lieutenant-General Sir Eyre Coote, K.B.*, Oxford: Clarendon, 1922, p. 202. A general order for the Bombay Army dated 5 September 1790 speaks of a minimum height of 5'2" for 'lads under 20 years' and 5'5" for those between 20 and 30 years of age. Moor, *A Compilation*, Chapter XXXIX. In October 1768, the committee of shipping even called for 'healthy lads of about fourteen or fifteen years of age', and of 'five feet in stature or upwards'. H.V. Bowen, 'The East India Company and Military Recruitment in Britain, 1763-1771', *Bulletin of the Institute of Historical Research*, vol. 59, no. 139, 1986, p. 81. See also G.O. Rickword, 'Note on an Announcement in Ipswich Journal 15/11/1766', *Journal of the Society for Army Historical Research*, vol. 32, no. 83, 1954, p. 149.

[21] Rickword, 'Note'.

[22] Barat, *Bengal*, p. 48. When Clive raised the 3rd Bengal sepoy battalion in January 1758, the men were drawn from the Bhojpur district in Bihar. Clive to Bengal, 30 January 1758, Bengal Sel. Comm. Cons., OIOC P/A/2, p. 28.

[23] Alavi, *Sepoys*, p. 39. The names of sepoy recruits clearly demonstrate the emphasis on high-caste background. For example, the descriptive roll of sepoy recruits sent by Colonel James Morgan at Burhanpur to Captain Thomas Adderly provides names of 37 recruits. Of these, 33 are Hindus, 26 of them bearing the high caste name Singh. Bengal Mil. Cons., 17 March 1779, OIOC P/18/47, pp. 449-50.

[24] Cornwallis to London, 6 November 1789. B. Prasad (ed.), *Fort William India House Correspondence and Other Papers Relating Thereto*, 21 vols., Delhi: National Archives, 1975, vol. 19, pp. 363-4. An officer of the Bengal Army made a similar

In geographical terms, sepoy recruits for the Bengal Army were initially drawn from the rural areas in Bengal but under the Governor-Generalship of Warren Hastings recruitment moved westward beyond the territory under the Company's control. Bihar, Benares and Awadh became major sources of recruits with permanent recruiting centres established in Bhojpur, Patna, and Buxar in Bihar and Jaunpur and Ghazipur in Benares.[25] However, Awadh soon proved an unsatisfactory source of recruits, largely due to their high desertion rate, forcing the Bengal Army to withdraw its recruiting parties from that province towards the end of the eighteenth century.[26]

The recruitment policy of the other presidencies differed somewhat from that of Bengal. In 1747 when the Fort St. David Council requested help from Bombay their first choice was—typically—for Europeans 'without whom it would be impossible to maintain this settlement'. But, failing that, Bombay was requested to send 'five or six hundred of the best northern people'.[27] Who were these northern people? They were not, as Kolff suggests, Rajputs,[28] rather, people of Arabian descent. In a letter to London dated 2 May 1747, the Fort St. David Council clearly speaks of a request for 600 Arabs from Bombay,[29] and in a list of native troops serving at Fort St. David dated January 1749, the majority of the sepoys have Muslim names with 279 classified as Arabs.[30] Likewise, of the fourteen companies of Madras sepoys that

---

observation early in the following century, writing that the Bengal Army was 'chiefly composed of Bramins [*sic*] and Rajputs'. *Observations and Remarks on the Dress, Discipline & ca of the Military by a Bengal Officer*, Calcutta, 1809, p. 105.

[25] Alavi, *Sepoys*, p. 41. Also see Cornwallis to London, 6 November 1789. Prasad (ed.), *Fort William Correspondence*, p. 364.

[26] A general order issued on 29 June 1790 speaks of a large number of desertions among sepoys recruited from Awadh and 'the countries beyond Benares', and goes on to advise that 'whatever advantage such men may possess, in point of height and appearance, they are by no means fit for soldiers in the Company's service, as the natives of our own provinces'. OIOC MR L/MIL/17/2/438, p. 377.

[27] FSD Cons., 16 March 1747, OIOC FR G/18/6, pp. 46-7.

[28] Kolff, *Naukar*, p. 174

[29] Dodwell, *Calendar*, p. 40.

[30] FSD Cons., 31 January 1749, OIOC FR G/18/6. The native military forces of both French and English seem to have been dominated by Arabians and Turks at this time. The commanders of contemporary French sepoys all bear Turkish or Arabian names. See V.G. Hatalkar (ed. and trs.), *French Records Relating to the History of the Marathas*, 9 vols., Bombay: Maharashtra State Board for Literature and Culture, 1980-5, vol. 8, pp. 303-5. The translator of the *Seir Mutaqherin* also claims that the first sepoys, both French and British, were commanded by Arabians. Seid Gholam

accompanied Clive to Bengal in 1756, only six were commanded by Hindus.[31]

Arab recruitment seems to have dropped off in the latter decades of the century, probably because there were not enough of them to fill the ranks of a rapidly expanding army. But Madras continued to recruit Muslims in large numbers. Of 89 sepoys presented before an invaliding committee in April 1775, 39 were Muslims and 38 Hindus while the roll of the 30th battalion in 1791 shows 45 per cent of the men to have been Muslims.[32] Thus, contrary to general belief, during the eighteenth century, the Madras Army seems to have been composed of almost equal numbers of Muslims and Hindus. Here it stood in sharp contrast to the army of Bengal.

However, when it came to recruiting Hindus the Madras Army also showed a preference for the higher castes. Charged with raising 1,000 men to serve with the King's 39th regiment in 1754, Stringer Lawrence was urged by the Fort St. George Council to recruit from the areas of Tanjore and Tiruchchirapalli for 'the people that can be enlisted this way at Fort St. David are not to be depended on many of them having been menial servants and never bore arms in their life'.[33] And similar indications of a preference for higher castes can be found in the records from the latter part of the century too.[34] The Madras Military Regulations of 1766 recommended recruitment from the 'casts' of 'Rajpoot, Mussulmen, Camawar, Rachwar Yelmawar and Buckserry',[35] while in the above-mentioned list of invalid sepoys dated April 1775 there are 16 'gentues' (Telugus), 22 'Malabars' (Tamils), 3 Rajputs and 7 Pariahs.[36] A similar composition is alluded to by James

---

Hussain Khan, *The Seir Mutaqherin or Review of Modern Times Being a History of India as Far Down as the Year 1783*, 4 vols., Lahore: Sheikh Mubarak Ali, 1975; rpt. of 1902 edn., 1st pub. 1789, vol. 2, p. 534. Ananda Ranga Pillai, the interpreter to the French Governor Francois Dupleix, also mentions a French officer speaking of 'Tamil and Muhammedan sepoys' in August 1752. Ananda Ranga Pillai, *The Private Diary of Ananda Ranga Pillai, Dubash to Joseph Francois Dupleix, Governor of Pondicherry*, ed. H. Dodwell, 13 vols., Delhi: Asian Educational Services, 1985; 1st pub. 1922, vol. 8, pp. 152 and p. 162.

[31] OIOC Home Misc., 805, p. 727.

[32] Dodwell, *Sepoy Recruitment*, p. 44.

[33] *Diary and Consultation Book 1754*, pp. 229-30.

[34] For example Captain James Oliver who commanded the 7th battalion of Madras native infantry in 1783, claimed to have recruited 'a number of good men and of superior cast'. 'Memoir of James Oliver', OIOC Mss. Eur. D. 799, p. 17.

[35] Wilson, *Madras Army*, vol. 1, p. 227.

[36] Dodwell, *Sepoy Recruitment*, p. 42.

Welsh who was writing at the beginning of the century. According to Welsh, five major 'casts' made up the Madras Army. One-third comprised Muslims, while the rest consisted of Rajputs, Telugus, Tamils and Pariahs. The inclusion of Pariahs indicates that the Madras Army was far less exclusive than the army in Bengal, but still, their recruitment seems to have been met with strong resistance from the upper castes. Welsh writes that by beginning of the nineteenth century, the untouchables were being gradually excluded and relegated to the ranks of the pioneers and gun lascars 'in order more fully to conciliate the higher classes'.[37]

The preponderance of southern ethnic groups like Telugus and Tamils also shows that the eighteenth century Madras Army was in the main recruited locally. But in that respect, things were to change. By the 1790s, the ravages of two wars with Mysore had denuded large parts of the south of good recruits—so much so that the 35th battalion which was sent to Ceylon in 1795 is said to have consisted mainly of boys.[38] Faced with a crisis, the Madras government seized on a proposal from Captain Henry White for a permanent recruitment program in Bengal for the Madras Army. The idea was for a nursery of 2,000 recruits always kept in readiness to supply the Madras Army when the need arose.[39] In the event however, just 350 sepoys and 150 gun lascars made it to Madras by the end of 1795, followed by another small batch in the following March. And they did not last. Within a year of their arrival, the majority of the Bengal recruits had deserted, leaving the council to admit the complete failure of the plan.[40]

[37] James Welsh, *Military Reminiscences Extracted from a Journal of Nearly Forty Years' Active Service in the East Indies*, 2 vols., London: Smith, Elder & Co., 1830, vol. 1, pp. 14-15. William Fullerton, who was writing in the 1780s also speaks of the Madras sepoys as being drawn from 'moormen, Rajahpoots, Gentoos and Malabars'. He also doubts whether 'it is judicious to admit Pariahs into battalions with men of reputable casts'. Fullerton, *A View*, p. 223. According to an early nineteenth century Bengal Army officer, high caste Hindus from northern India 'generally refused to enlist to enlist in the coast battalions' owing to the 'very mixed nature of those battalions'. *Observations and Remarks*, 1809, p. 129.

[38] Hill, 'The Old Sepoy Officer', p. 510. In the same year, we find one Captain Floyd of the Madras Army lamenting the lack of proper recruits south of the Coleroon, saying that 'even the best battalions have many sepoys too small and much too slender for the service'. Dodwell, *Sepoy Recruitment*, p. 34.

[39] Captain Henry White to Madras Government, 24 February 1795, Madras Mil. and Pol. Cons., OIOC P/253/43, pp. 678-9.

[40] Dodwell, *Sepoy Recruitment*, pp. 36-7.

Of the three presidency armies, the native army of the Bombay presidency was the most heterogeneous. When Bombay decided to recruit 2,000 Indian troops in 1745 they also showed a preference for people of Turkish or Arabic descent.[41] The sepoys sent to reinforce Fort St. David in 1747 also seem to have been largely Muslims. But by the late 1750s Hindu recruitment had been stepped up and a list of invalid sepoys dated June 1759 shows the overwhelming majority to be Hindus and, interestingly, Marathas.[42] Moreover, by the end of the eighteenth century, the Bombay government, too, had been lured into the northern military labour market. In 1797, the Commander-in-Chief recommended that, henceforward, the sepoys for the Bombay Army be recruited from the 'the countries extending without limitation to the northward' from Carwar[43]—even though this meant entering into competition with the Marathas, who were also entering the market in full force at this time.[44] But this competition the Bombay government appears to have handled successfully as we hear them claiming in 1795 that their sepoy battalions are chiefly composed of men from 'Bengal and other countries not subjected to this [Bombay] government'.[45]

But again, in choosing northerners, the Bombay government stipulated that they should, as much as possible, come from the ranks of the higher castes. Indeed the general orders of 5 October 1797 mentioned earlier strictly forbade commanding officers of sepoy battalions from enlisting men who had 'lost their cast, who are of a mean and disgraceful cast or who may be of depraved characters'.[46] Still, this tendency towards a high caste and northward bias did not make the Bombay Army quite as rigidly exclusive as the Bengal Army. For instance, they did not hesitate to recruit Jews settled along the Malabar coast.[47]

[41] Cadell, *History*, p. 49.

[42] Bombay Pub. Cons., 19 June 1759, OIOC P/341/22, p. 420.

[43] Moor, *A Compilation*, Chapter XXXIX. A general order of 16 May 1798 permitted the battalions serving in Malabar to enlist 'a few Carnatic men' but never more than 50 per battalion. Ibid.

[44] For example, the Maratha State of Gwalior recruited heavily from the Rajput peasantry in Awadh, the Doab and the Rohilkand. John Pemble, 'Techniques and Resources', p. 392. Mountstuart Elphinstone, the aid-de-camp to Arthur Wellesley during the Second Maratha War (1803-5) was informed by an officer that the Maratha dead lying on the battlefield of Assaye were 'all stout Bengalees—meaning, I suppose, people like our Bengal sepoys'. Colebrooke, *The Life*, vol. 1, p. 69.

[45] Madras Mil. and Pol. Cons., 15 September 1795, OIOC P/253/47, p. 3154.

[46] Moor, *A Compilation*, Chapter XXXIX.

[47] Captain Henry White describes the Bombay native army in 1795 as being

The recruitment policies in the three presidencies then, varied quite considerably. But in general it would be fair to say that they all worked mainly within the indigenous recruiting system and showed a preference for high caste recruits. But recruitment was only the first step in the making of a sepoy. The recruits also had to be moulded into European-style soldiers and in the rest of this chapter, we shall explore the strategies adopted by the Company to organize the native army as a military force. Attention will be focussed on two major aspects of the native army's military organization, its command structure and its training. I shall start by looking at the organization of the sepoys employed in the first military campaigns waged by the Company in the Carnatic and Bengal.

## TACTICAL ORGANIZATION OF THE EARLY SEPOY

In the previous chapter it was noted that in recruiting the sepoys, the Company operated largely within the indigenous military tradition, using sepoy officers as recruiting agents. Likewise, the sepoys in the early period were controlled by a command structure that had more to do with the native system than the European. Like all *jamadari* contingents, the early sepoy companies had highly irregular numbers; giving them the character of war-bands rather than military units in the European sense of the word 'company'. For instance, the seven sepoy companies in the 'list of peons and sepoys' dated January 1749 mentioned in the previous chapter had strengths ranging from 22 to 247,[48] while in another document of 1752 listing the strengths of seven sepoy companies, one is recorded as having 116 men and another just 2![49] These lists also show glaring discrepancies from company to company in the matter of pay suggesting that each company was raised and contracted through a separate process of negotiation. For example, in the company under 'Malrauze' two *jamadars* were paid Rs. 12 each and the sepoys Rs. 6 each while in Abdul Cawder's company,

---

'principally composed of men from the neighbouring Maratha districts and of Jews, the descendants of those people on the Malabar coast'. Madras Mil. and Pol. Cons., 26 March 1795, OIOC P/253/43, p. 950. See also Peers, 'Habitual Nobility', p. 550.

[48] FSD Cons., 31 January 1749, OIOC FR G/18/10.

[49] Account of allowances paid to sepoys from 5 May to 10 June 1752. OIOC O.V. 287, p. 392. Another breakdown of sepoys companies in Bombay dated 5 June 1759 also shows a similar disparity. The numbers in the 20 sepoy companies range from 29 to 96. Bombay Pub. Cons., 5 June 1759, OIOC P/341/22, p. 397.

the *jamadar* Abdul Cawder was paid Rs. 20 and the sepoys Rs. 6 each.[50]

The first serious attempt to regularize the organization of the sepoy companies occurred in November 1755 when the Company laid down regulations for the number of the numbers of officers and sepoys in a company. The strength of a sepoy company was now prescribed as 1 *subedar*, 4 *jamadars*, 8 *havildars*, 8 *naiks* and 84 sepoys.[51] This brought the *jamadari* war bands closer to the European ideal of a 'company' and also seems to have led to an evening-out of numbers as between companies, a muster taken of the Madras sepoys in April 1757 showing the strength of the companies in that presidency varying only between 71 and 83.[52]

To some extent, the Company relied on European personnel to maintain its authority over these companies of mercenary soldiers. Clive tells us that soon after the abortive siege of Pondicherry Lieutenant Bulkley was appointed 'commander of sepoys'.[53] This probably meant that Bulkley had overall supervision but it is not clear whether the individual companies of sepoys were also under European officers. When a large sepoy force was sent under Bulkley to support Mohamed Ali in 1749, it was accompanied by a small European contingent of 30 men 'to keep them [sepoys] together' as the Company explained to the court of Directors. Again, though, we do not know whether any of these men held any command over any of the sepoy companies that formed the detachment. On the other hand a document of January 1749 speaks of payments made to 2 European officers, W. Ralph Wardlow and W.A. Noles, for the service of 'commanding a sett of peons' during the siege of Pondicherry in 1748.[54] And another officer, Lauchlin Maclean, claims that he was appointed a sergeant of the sepoys sometime prior to 1753.[55] Thus it would seem that by the 1750s the practice of appointing Europeans to command individual sepoy companies had become commonplace at least in the Madras presidency. All nineteen companies of sepoys at Tiruchchirapalli in 1755 were under Europeans and sixteen of these were sergeants, the other three being

[50] FSD Cons., 31 January 1749, OIOC FR G/18/10.

[51] OIOC O.V. 288, pp. 213-15.

[52] OIOC Home Misc., 805, p. 727.

[53] Robert Clive to the Company, 8 March 1755, OIOC Misc. Ltrs. Recd., E/I/38, no. 120.

[54] OIOC FR G/18/10, p. 417.

[55] Lauchlin Maclean to Robert James, 1 January 1761, OIOC Misc. Ltrs. Recd. E/1/43, no. 4.

under a corporal and two privates.[56] The appointment of a corporal and a private—obviously the result of a want of sergeants—shows that some kind of European leadership was considered better than nothing. This is probably why one hears of two companies of sepoys being sent as reinforcements to Chinglepet in June 1753 under the command of a European corporal and six matrosses.[57]

The European officer was the simple mechanism by which the Company's authority and control was maintained over the military communities that comprised the sepoy companies. Yet we do not know much about the operation of this command mechanism. For instance, how did the officers communicate with the men? Not all by any means were fluent in the vernacular. Did they use interpreters? Or (more likely) did the sepoy officers function as the main link between the European officers and the men, making the position of the *subedars* as commanders of independent companies a powerful and pivotal position? One important piece of evidence pointing to this conclusion is the fact that sepoy companies were invariably identified by the name of their *subedars*, a practice which persisted even after the regularization of sepoy companies in 1755.[58] The pivotal position of the native officers also meant that there was scope for talented individual sepoy officers to gain recognition as leaders, and some achieved positions of considerable independence from European control. For instance, we hear of one Keser Singh leading the Madras sepoys in an overland march during Clive's expedition to Bengal in 1756,[59] and a *subedar* named Jemal Sahib commanding the sepoys at Fort St. George during its investment by the French in 1758-9. Indeed, Jemal is recorded as having led several hundred sepoys in a sortie against enemy positions.[60]

But the best example of the kind is that of Yusuf Khan, the *subedar* who was endowed with the position of commandant over all the sepoys employed by the Company. The 'honour' rings hollow when we consider that the operations entrusted to the likes of Keser Singh and Jemal Sahib hardly required his directions, but it cannot be denied that

[56] Captain Caillaud to Council, 3 July 1755, *Diary and Consultation Book, Fort St. George, Military Department 1755*, Madras: Government Printers, 1912, pp. 113-14.

[57] Madras Mil. Cons., 25 June 1755, *Diary and Consultation Book, Fort St. George, Military Department 1753*, Madras: Government Printers, 1910, pp. 107-8.

[58] The muster of troops in Bengal mentioned above (see fn. 52 of this chapter) shows sepoy companies still identified by their *subedars*.

[59] Wilson, *History*, vol. 1, pp. 78-9; OIOC Mss. Eur. B. 215. p. 236.

[60] Love, *Vestiges*, 3, pp. 542-3.

Yusuf Khan enjoyed extraordinary independence. In 1756 he was entrusted with a major expedition to bring Madura under the Company's control. While in the field, he was given specific instructions to consult with the European sergeants in charge of the artillery and defer to their opinion but the fact that the Company's authorities corresponded with Yusuf Khan regarding the progress of the expedition shows that they treated the 'Nellore Subedar' as the leader of the expedition.[61] Moreover, Yusuf Khan himself would have hardly stood for an inferior position. In the previous year he had accompanied Colonel Alexander Heron on a similar expedition. The two clashed often and Heron was quite openly resentful of or hostile to the Nellore Subedar's independent attitude, calling him 'a brave man but by no means fit for an independent command'.[62] Heron was soon to be disgraced but the Company's confidence in Yusuf Khan was obviously enhanced by the expedition as is evident from the commands entrusted to him in the following years. For instance, when Lally set siege to Madras in 1758-9, Yusuf Khan was entrusted with the task of creating a diversion behind enemy lines, and in carrying out this mission he was allowed to have direct command over the European sergeants and artillerymen in his detachment. Indeed Captain Joseph Smith, who was to oversee the operations from Tiruchirapalli, was given very clear instructions to this effect.[63] But the apogee of Yusuf Khan's brilliant career came in 1759 when he was appointed the Governor of Madura, a town he himself had helped the Company to conquer.[64]

Yusuf Khan's meteoric rise is a telling example of what a native officer could achieve in the Company's service during this early period. Because the Company had left the pivotal role of the native officers

[61] For example, the Company advised Captain John Caillaud at Tiruchirapalli: 'We have advised Usof Cawn to correspond constantly with you on what passed and to follow your orders and advice on all occasions you will therefore continually give him such advice as you think will be useful to the service and communicate to us the news you may receive from him.' Madras Mil. Cons., 10 March 1756, *Diary and Consultation Book, Fort St. George, Military Department, 1756*, Madras: Government Printers, 1913, p. 116.

[62] Quoted in S.C. Hill, *Yusuf Khan, the Rebel Commandant*, London: Longmans Green, 1914, p. 28.

[63] The council ordered that, 'the gunners and sergeants that command the sepoy companies must be strictly enjoined to yield entire obedience to the orders of Yusuf Khan', adding that they shall 'severely resent a contrary behaviour'. Madras Sel. Com. Cons., 9 November 1758, OIOC P/C/53, p. 461.

[64] Hill, *Yusuf Khan*, pp. 89-90.

largely undisturbed, ambitious and enterprising leaders like Yusuf Khan could win the confidence of their employers or overlords and consequently expand their command and authority. In the case of Yusuf Khan, the Company's decision to put Europeans under his direction and his appointment as the Governor of Madura were the supreme expressions of the confidence they had come to repose in his ability and loyalty. But the Nellore Subedar's career was cut short in 1764 when he took the rash step of declaring political independence. The Company responded the way any self-respecting overlord was expected to do in the circumstances and sent its army to bring Yusuf Khan to heel. The Company captured Madura—albeit after a costly campaign—and hanged Yusuf for treason.

But a few years before Yusuf Khan's ambition took a tragic turn the Company had decided to overhaul the system of command and control over the sepoys. In 1758 and 1759 both the Bengal and Madras governments moved towards forming their sepoys into regular, European-style, battalions. Bombay followed ten years later in 1768. As shall be seen below, this reorganization was to lay the foundation for the emergence of the Company's native army as a regular military force.

## THE FORMATION OF SEPOY BATTALIONS

The formation of sepoy battalions was initiated by Clive in Bengal. As has been noted in the previous chapter, Bengal remained untouched by the developments in the south until 1757 when sepoys began to be raised in considerable numbers following Clive's expedition to recapture the British possessions lost to the Nawab of Bengal. The two oldest authorities on the Bengal Army, Broome and Williams, and the modern historian Amiya Barat maintain that the first Bengal sepoys were raised in January 1757 as a battalion.[65] But as W.J. Wilson correctly points out there is no specific general order pertaining to this reform. The sketchy information we have suggests a very gradual or staggered recruitment pattern starting perhaps early in 1757. For instance, a letter written by a European in Calcutta dated 30 January 1757, claims that of the 1,400 sepoys then in Bengal, only 200 were raised locally, at

[65] Captain A. Broome, *History of the Rise and Progress of the Bengal Army*, Calcutta, 1850, p. 92; Captain John Williams, *An Historical Account of the Rise and Progress of the Bengal Infantry from its Formation in 1757 to 1796*, London, 1810, p. 3; Barat, *The Bengal Native Infantry*, p. 4.

Ballisore.[66] Likewise, musters taken in April and 7 June of the same year show the sepoy forces still organized as independent companies.[67] Again, Williams and Broome speak of three 'battalions' being in service by the end of 1758—a second battalion being raised in August 1757 and a third in January 1758. The latter was no doubt the thousand sepoys Clive ordered to be raised at the time. But contemporary sources maintain their silence about a battalion-style organization until October 1758, when the 'first and second battalions' accompanied Colonel Francis Forde on the expedition to the northern Circars. This suggests that Bengal sepoys had been in battalion-type formations for some time by then though certainly not from before Plassey. Therefore, we may take it that the organization of sepoys into battalions was something which happened after Plassey but well prior to Forde's expedition of 1758.

Madras soon followed in the footsteps of Bengal. On 4 December 1758, the Madras Select Committee resolved to form their sepoys into four battalions, each under the command of a subaltern and the whole force commanded by a captain.[68] The plan was interrupted by Lally's siege of Fort St. George later that month but it was taken up after the siege was raised and finally implemented in September 1759. In the event, the Madras government formed seven sepoy battalions.

And Bombay too, was not far behind. In 1759 Major William Fraser, who commanded the Company's forces in Bombay, proposed the 'establishment of 1500 sepoys, complete, regulated disciplined and paid in the same manner as they are upon the Coast [Madras] and in Bengal'. As a result of this proposal, in October 1759, the Bombay authorities approved the formation of a regular force of 500 sepoys who were to be selected from the best sepoys and separated from those performing police and revenue collecting duties. These sepoys were, however, not at first organized in battalions.[69] That move came in nearly a decade later in 1768 when two sepoy battalions were formed.[70]

The early Bengal battalions had a permanent complement of European officers. According to Williams, each battalion had a

[66] H.C. Hill, *Bengal in 1756-57*, vol. 3, pp. 91-2.

[67] The muster taken in April shows 448 Bengal sepoys while the number for June is 550. OIOC Home Misc. 805, pp. 727-9.

[68] Madras Sel. Com. Cons., 4 December 1758, OIOC P/C/52, p. 493.

[69] Cadell, *History*, p. 67.

[70] 'An unpublished account of the Bombay Army by Edward Sambrooke John Anderson', 2 vols., OIOC Mss. Eur. C. 155, vol. 1, pp. 56-7.

European captain, lieutenant and ensign assisted by a sergeant major and a few sergeants—all Europeans. The sepoys in each battalion were divided into ten companies that comprised 1 *subedar*, 3 *jamadars*, 5 *havildars*, 4 *naiks*, 2 drummers, 1 trumpeter and 70 sepoys. Each battalion also had a 'black commandant' who was to take post in front of the battalion.[71] The organization in Madras was somewhat similar. Each of the seven battalions consisted of nine companies, one of which was to be a grenadier company. Each company had 100 men in the following order: 1 *subedar*, 2 *jamadars*, 6 *havildars*, 6 *naiks*, 2 colourmen, 2 tom-tom beaters, 1 trumpeter and 78 sepoys.[72]

In addition, two linguists and five armourers were attached to each battalion. Two European subalterns and three sergeant majors were also assigned to each battalion while two European captains were to have overall command over all seven battalions. As in Bengal, Madras also appointed a 'black commandant' who was to be subordinate to the commissioned European officers. Of the seven battalions, two each were to be allocated to the dependencies of Tiruchirapalli, Madras and Conjeevaram while Chinglepet and its dependencies were to be covered by the remaining battalion. In Bombay, each battalion had 1 captain, 1 lieutenant, 1 ensign, 10 sergeants, 10 *subedars*, 20 *jamadars*, 60 *havildars*, 60 *naiks* and 800 sepoys, a total of 963 men.[73]

The formation of sepoys into regular battalions—first undertaken in Bengal and later emulated in Madras and Bombay—represented the first serious attempt to introduce a European-style organization to the sepoy army. But this was not the only interesting thing about this development. The formation of sepoy battalions also diluted the authority of the sepoy leaders, for the *subedar* was now subject to the command structure of the battalion. In other words, whereas earlier the *subedar* had commanded an independent company, now his company became one among nine or ten that made up a battalion. Moreover, the company's importance was reduced by the fact that the battalion now became the basic tactical unit. But this was not all. The battalions also increased European control over the sepoys; unlike independent companies where the *subedars* had only a single European officer above them, in the battalions they now had several officers to supervise them. As the Madras Council stipulated:

[71] Williams, *An Historical Account*, pp. 4-5.

[72] Wilson, *History*, vol. 1, p. 142.

[73] There were also 30 tom-tom beaters, 10 interpreters and 10 water-carriers. OIOC Mss. Eur. C. 155, vol. 1, pp. 56-7.

As it is proposed to have three sergeants majors to each battalion, three companies to each arc to be given, over whom they are to have the more immediate direction, and the care of their discipline, and when any detachment is made of that number of companies from a battalion, a sergeant-major is to go with them; if the detachment is of half the battalion, a subaltern.[74]

Here is a very basic chain of command: captain–subaltern sergeant major–*subedar*. There is no mention of the mechanism of control over detachments smaller than three companies—the sergeants were probably placed in charge of them. But the fact that small detachments were now 'officially' entrusted to European officers meant that such operations as had been entrusted to Keser Singh and Jemal Sahib were things of the past. But as shall be seen later, the formation of battalions was only the first step in a series of developments that were to bring the sepoys under greater control of their European officers.

## THE EXPANSION OF EUROPEAN CONTROL

Predictably, the number of European officers in each sepoy unit steadily increased after the formation of the first sepoy battalions. Again, Bengal seems to have taken the lead. In 1765, Robert Clive initiated a major reorganization of the Bengal Army by dividing it, Europeans and sepoys, into three 'brigades', each containing six sepoy battalions, one European regiment, one troop of European cavalry and one company of artillery. To each sepoy battalion were assigned 11 European officers, comprising 1 captain, 2 lieutenants, 2 ensigns, 3 sergeants and 3 drummers.[75] Similar changes were effected in the Madras Army in 1766. The European officers now comprised 1 captain, 2 subalterns and 5 sergeant majors with a provision for the addition of more occasional sergeants as required.

The reorganizations in both Bengal and Madras retained the position of the 'Black commandant'; but not for long. The Madras Army abolished the post in 1781, followed by the other two presidencies three years later. This took away at one stroke the highest office available to a native officer in the Company's service. On the other hand, the European presence in sepoy battalions continued to grow. By 1780, a European subaltern was commanding each sepoy company

[74] Wilson, *History*, vol. 1, pp. 146-7.

[75] Barat, *Bengal Native Infantry*, pp. 25-7.

Plate 3: Subedar, Bengal Army. Inscribed: 'Subidar'. OIOC Add. Or. 1179.

in all three presidencies.[76] In 1785 a major reorganization brought the sepoy armies in all three presidencies within a uniform command structure. All sepoy battalions were now required to have eight companies, each commanded by a European subaltern and a sergeant. The Indian component of each company consisted of 1 *subedar*, 1 *jamadar*, 4 *havildars*, 4 *naiks* and 68 sepoys. A permanent European presence was thus guaranteed even at the company level. European control over the sepoys was further strengthened by another major reorganization in 1796, which brought sepoys in all three presidencies under a regimental system of organization. Each regiment was to consist of two battalions, each of ten companies. Each regiment now had a complement of 48 European officers: 1 colonel, 2 lieutenant-colonels, 2 majors, 7 captains, 1 captain-lieutenant, 22 lieutenants and 10 ensigns.[77]

What this gradual infusion of European officers did was to create gradually an exclusively European chain of command for the sepoy units. The appointment of European officers to sepoy companies meant that by the 1780s Europeans were in charge of sepoys even at the lowest possible level of organization. This reduced the *subedars* to mere figureheads as far as command over their companies was concerned. Now, on campaign or in camp, sepoy officers were never entrusted with the independent command of more than 2 or 3 dozen sepoys. A *naik* usually commanded 6 sepoys, a *havildar* 12 and a *jamadar* and *subedar* anything between 20 and 40, but anything more than this was invariably presided over by a European officer.[78] As a general order of the Bengal Army stated in May 1789, when a detachment of native troops exceeding 50 men was sent out 'with a probability of using their arms', the command was always to be entrusted to a European.[79]

[76] For example, in 1781, each company of Bengal sepoys was usually commanded by a European lieutenant. Barat, *Bengal Native Infantry*, p. 37. In the Madras Army, a native company was headed by a lieutenant or an ensign. Wilson, *History*, vol. 1, p. 363. Around the same time, Bombay employed a lieutenant and a sergeant over each of their sepoy companies. OIOC Mss. Eur. C. 155, 1, p. 79.

[77] Wilson, *History*, vol. 1, p. 290.

[78] The numerous surviving journals of marches and orderly books provide an abundance of evidence on this aspect of the sepoy officers' responsibilities. See for example 'The orderly book of a detachment of the Madras Army commanded by Colonel Sir Henry Cosby in 1785-6', Pasley Papers, BM. Add. 29900 and the brigade orders for the 2nd brigade, Bengal Army, OIOC Mss. Eur. D. 459.

[79] OIOC MR L/MIL/17/2/438, p. 55.

Moreover, although the *subedars* and *jamadars* were commissioned officers, even the lowest ranking European non-commissioned officer could command them. Captain Innes Munro who was in south India in the early 1780s, explained this clearly:

> These Black Corps have attached to them a full compliment of native as well as European officers. The former rise according to their merit from private sepoys; and before most of them arrive at the rank of subedars or captains (for higher they do not go) they have become quite bald and grey in the service.... Their rank gives them no authority except over their own countrymen; for an European sergeant would command any of the native officers upon duty....[80]

Yet the changes mentioned earlier did not render the native officer completely powerless. He still had a significant liaison role to perform. At one level, this consisted of ensuring that the orders of the Europeans were passed on in the vernacular. Thus, during the expedition to Nepal in 1767 we find Captain George Kinlock requesting the 'Black officers' prior to an attack on a fort, to 'acquaint their men that any man who fir'd a piece would be immediately put to death'.[81] At another level, though, it meant inspiring the sepoys to follow their orders in the spirit as well as in the letter, Colonel Fitzgerald instructing the 'Black Commandants' on the eve of the Battle of Chengama in 1767 to 'influence the sepoys to behave with steadiness and resolution'.[82]

Moreover, the British looked to the subedars to contain dissent in the ranks before it got out of hand. When the 35th regiment of Bengal native infantry broke out in mutiny in early 1782, a clearly distraught Captain Sparkes wrote to Major Popham that 'the subedars and

[80] Munro, *A Narrative*, pp. 23-4. Another English visitor, Mrs. Kindersley made a similar observation with regard to the Bengal Army in 1767. She wrote from Allahabad in September 1767 that she had heard of no instance 'of an European soldier being under a black man, for the sergeants are superior in command to even the first black officer of the army; the natives are most numerous, but the power and command is vested entirely in the Europeans'. Mrs. Kindersley, *Letters from the Island of Teneriffe, Brazil, the Cape of Good Hope and the East Indies*, London, 1777, p. 209. In late eighteenth century, an officer of the Bengal army made an interesting plea for greater sympathy for the native officer. He did not seem to have a problem in understanding the necessity for giving a sergeant the command over a subedar. But he proposed that a subedar not be harshly treated 'if the subedar were to demur, or refuse obedience'. *Observations and Remarks on the Dress, Discipline & ca of the Military by a Bengal Officer*, Calcutta, 1798, pp. 34-5.

[81] 'Journal of Captain George Kinlock on the expedition to Nepal begun on the 26th August 1767.' OIOC Mss. Eur. F. 128/40, pp. 31-2.

[82] OIOC O.V. 215, p. 30.

jamadars seem to have lost all authority',[83] and when the 35th battalion of Madras native infantry mutinied in Colombo in March 1795 all the officers were cashiered, except for those who had helped actively in restoring order.[84] The Company may have been reluctant to admit sepoy officers to the higher echelons of command but they certainly found them useful.

Effective communication was essential for the smooth functioning of the relationship between the European and their native subordinates. To this end, the Company encouraged their European officers to acquire a competence in native languages. In 1767, the Directors ordered that no officer be given the command of a sepoy battalion 'until he has made himself sufficiently master of the language to acquit himself in his duty without the assistance of an interpreter'[85] and in 1770 the Madras Army informed prospective officers of the sepoy units that a knowledge of the 'Moorish language' was 'deemed to be an essential and indispensable qualification for such a command'.[86] Besides facilitating military operations such requirements also helped training by enabling the European officers to communicate their instructions effectively.

Thus, by the close of the eighteenth century, the segmented organization of the early sepoy army had been superseded by a regular battalions dominated by European officers. The formation of battalions

[83] Captain Sparke to Major Popham, 8 March 1782, Bengal Sec. Cons., 11 March 1782. OIOC P/A/63, p. 569. Again, when sepoys began to desert in considerable numbers during the Siege of Mangalore by Mysorian troops in May 1783, the Commanding Officer Colonel Campbell ordered the European officers commanding the sepoy battalions 'to assemble all the sepoys under their command to hear what they have to say, and to take the opinions of the Black officers and non-commissioned officers respecting it, that if there are any real grievances they may be instantly redressed', *An Account of the Gallant Defence of Mangalore in 1783*, London, 1786, pp. 155-6.

[84] Madras government to General Stuart, 12 April 1795, Madras Mil. and Sec. Cons., 12 April 1795, OIOC, P/253/60, p. 1538.

[85] Quoted in Bruce Lenman, 'The Transition to European Military Ascendancy in India 1600-1800', in John Lynn (ed.), *Tools of War: Instruments, Ideas and Institutions of Warfare, 1445-1871*, Chicago: University of Illinois Press, 1990, p. 122, n. 51.

[86] Wilson, *History*, vol. 1, p. 333. 'Moorish language' and 'Hindustani' both referred to Urdu. See C.A. Bayly, *Empire and Information*, p. 284. In August 1806, the commander-in-chief issued a general order announcing that 'means of distinct communication with the native army' was to be treated as a 'basic requirement for all regimental staff officers'. James Mill, *History of British India*, vol. 8, p. 125, n. 1. See also Welsh, *Military Reminiscences*, 1, p. 16.

heralded another important change to the organization of the sepoy army: the introduction of regular training.

## TRAINING THE SEPOY

Until the mid-1740s, the native troops in the English East India Company's pay were armed with a variety of weapons, including firearms. However, of 2,000 peons who were at Fort St. David in 1747, only about 900 are said to have carried guns.[87] The rest were armed with 'traditional' weapons such as swords and spears.[88] In the French camp however, interesting developments were taking place. The French had taken to drilling their native troops in the European manner at their settlements on the west coast in the late 1730s and early 1740s and this was emulated at Pondicherry by Dumas, the predecessor of Francois Dupleix. In 1742 he formed two companies amounting to about 200 men. They were disbanded at the end of that year but, faced as he was with the prospect of hostilities with the English, Dupleix soon revived the practice by training another batch of native troops in 1746.[89]

The French example inspired the English. In February 1747 the Fort St. David Council pointed out that 'care has not been wanting to put their chiefs in mind to exercise them often and make them fitt [*sic*] for service in our way of engaging and the manner shown them how to behave in time of action'.[90] The sepoys sent to Mohamed Ali in September 1749 were also described as being 'well trained in the exercise of firelocks after the European Manner'.[91] Similar measures seem to have been taken in Bombay as well, because the sepoys sent to Fort St. David in 1747 were described as being 'well trained'.

[87] Orme, *History*, vol. 1, p. 82.

[88] Lieutenant-Colonel E.G. Pythian-Adams, *The Madras Regiment 1758-1958*, Wellington: Defence Services Staff College Press, 1958, pp. 1-2. According to Henry Grose, the 'Buckserries' were armed only with 'sword and target'. Grose, *Voyages*, cited in Hobson-Jobson, *A Glossary*, p. 136. Broome probably has a similar situation in mind when he speaks of the Baksaris in Bengal prior to the formation of the first sepoy units as having been armed 'in the usual native manner'. Cited in ibid., p. 136.

[89] Dodwell, *Sepoy Recruitment*, pp. 3-5; Orme says that the French raised four or five companies of sepoys at Pondicherry but does not mention a date. Orme, *History*, vol. 1, p. 82.

[90] FSD Cons., 27 February 1747, OIOC FR G/18/6, pp. 30-1.

[91] *Country Correspondence 1749*, p. 36.

What did this training consist of? To understand this I shall now look at the training of contemporary European infantrymen. The contemporary European training regimens introduced their recruits to the complexities of eighteenth century warfare through a number of stages. The first stage involved training the recruit to march in step without arms which then led to the second stage, the 'manual exercises'. This introduced the recruit to his weapon and the process of loading and firing it at the word of command. Following this the fledgling soldier was taken through the paces of 'platoon' exercises which consisted of training the troops to fire as part of a tactical unit—the platoon. After this came training in the more complex manoeuvers like forming line from column and square which completed the transformation of the recruit.[92]

All these aspects of training were encapsulated in the terms 'exercising' and 'discipline'. But it is very doubtful whether in India such terms had the same range of meanings when used in the context of the sepoys' training during the early stages. One does not hear of sepoys performing any complex manoeuvers like forming squares or columns at this early stage. What the Fort St. David Council most probably meant when they spoke of sepoys 'well trained in the exercise of firelocks after the European manner' was the teaching of the basic manual exercises. The little that was invested in the training of these sepoys is evident from the summary dismissal of the nearly 700 of the 'regularly trained' sepoys soon after they were sent to Nasir Jang.[93] Richard Cambridge also describes the early sepoys as 'having familiarised themselves to firearms'[94] and according to Broome, those sepoys who went to Bengal with Clive in 1756 were subject to 'very little discipline or drill'.[95]

Accordingly, providing their native troops with muskets became a prime concern for the English. According to Orme, the Company had provided about 900 of the 2,000 peons at Fort St. David in early 1747 with muskets and it was most probably these men that received training at this time.[96] When a large number of Chanda Sahib's sepoys joined

[92] For a comprehensive description of the drill practiced in contemporary European armies in general and the British army in particular, see, J.A. Houlding, *Fit for Service: the Training of the British Army, 1715-1795*, Oxford: Clarendon, 1981, pp. 160-1.

[93] Charles Floyer to Court, 2 November 1749, OIOC FR G/18/10, pp. 616-17.

[94] Cambridge, *Account*, p. xxxiii.

[95] Broome, *History*, p. 92.

[96] Orme, *History*, vol. 1, p. 82.

Plate 4: Grenadier sepoy, Bengal Army. OIOC Arms and Armour Series 5346.

Clive's force after the Battle of Arni in 1751, only those who carried muskets were admitted to service.[97] Likewise, when Lawrence decided to raise more sepoys in March 1754 he requested 'as many stand as will Arm the Number of additional sepoys'.[98]

By a 'stand of arms' what was meant was a musket with a bayonet[99] but it is doubtful whether the Company was very particular about the type of firelock provided for the early sepoys. When Lawrence made the earlier-mentioned request for arms, Fort St. George Council authorized 500 buccaneer and trading guns to be sent to him.[100] Buccaneer guns seem to have been common among sepoys at this time because in January 1756, Major Kilpatrick mentions that among the weapons of the sepoys at Tiruchirapalli were 'many Buccaneer and French pieces'.[101] Buccaneer trading pieces were a species of long-barrelled hunting musket[102] and were often used as a medium of exchange in trade with African peoples.[103] Both varieties took longer to reload than the military muskets but were also cheaper, lighter in

[97] OIOC Orme India III, p. 291. Fort St. David authorities also advised Clive to employ only those who had firearms. Richard Prince to Robert Clive, 11 November 1751. Clive. Coll. OIOC Mss. Eur. G. 37, Box 20.

[98] Lawrence to Council, 23 March 1754, *Diary and Consultation Book, 1754*, p. 81. By 'stand' Lawrence means 'stand of arms', commonly meaning firearms. On the west coast however, the sepoys' training seems to have been gradually neglected by the Company towards the latter end of the 1750s, possibly due to the lack of a military incentive as in Madras or Bengal. According to Grose who was in western India in the mid-1750s, only some of the 'sepays' in Bombay were armed with muskets, 'at which they are indifferently expert'. The rest were armed 'in the country manner with sword and target'. Grose, *A Voyage*, p. 61.

[99] Houlding, *Fit for Service*, p. 142, n. 88.

[100] Lawrence to Council, 23 March 1754, *Diary and Consultation Book, 1754*, p. 81.

[101] Major Kilpatrick to Council, 17 January 1756, *Diary and Consultation Book, 1756*, p. 21.

[102] *Oxford English Dictionary*, Oxford: Clarendon, 1989, vol. 1, p. 1148.

[103] Gavin White, 'Firearms in Africa: an Introduction', *Journal of African History*, vol. 12, no. 2, 1971, p. 179; Buccaneer and Trading guns were among a number of such firearm types used in the African trade. These included Tower Guns, Round Muskets, Bonny Muskets and Angola Muskets. See J.E. Inikori, 'The Import of Firearms into West Africa 1750-1807: a Quantitative Analysis', *Journal of African History*, vol. 18, no. 3, 1977, pp. 339-68. The EIC itself used Buccaneer pieces as a medium of exchange in their dealings with African peoples. For instance, in April 1761, the Fort St. George Council ordered that, '20 Buccaneer pieces, 1000 flints and 2 barrels of indifferent gunpowder be put on board the *Plassey* for purchasing fresh provisions at Madagascar or any other place he may touch at where that custom is established'. Madras Mil. and Sec. Cons., 23 April 1761, OIOC P/D/45, p. 297.

weight, and easier to repair than military guns.[104] They were also less reliable than military muskets made for European markets.[105] Both varieties could not be fitted with bayonets, an essential part of a contemporary European soldier's armaments. Although we do hear of other types of firearms, including bayonet pieces being in the possession of sepoys, what the frequent issue of buccaneer pieces in large quantities suggests is that the sepoy was primarily meant to provide little more than a disciplined volume of fire.

Thus, the early sepoy was little more than a poor imitation of a drilled infantryman in a contemporary European sense of the term. But how better trained were the Company's Europeans? Robert Clive has gone on record as saying: 'If there be any officers or soldiers in India remaining of those who were at the siege of Pondicherry 12 or 13 years experience must have convinced them how very ignorant we were of the art of war in those days.'[106] Here Clive was clearly making a contrast between the Company's European troops of the 1760s and those of the late 1740s and his point seems well taken. But the Anglo-French War also saw an improvement in the training of the Company's European troops and the transition was already apparent in the 1750s. We have at least one instance—at the Battle of the Sugar Loaf Rock before Tiruchirapalli in 1754—where the English successfully manoeuvered from a column of three divisions into line. According to Lawrence, the European battalion which comprised about 600 men marched in a column of three divisions 'just at a proper distance to form the line when it was ordered' and manoeuvered into line when within musket range of the French.[107] According to Orme, after forming the line, the grenadiers who formed the right of it executed a further manoeuver. They now wheeled around to face the left flank of the French battalion.[108] This was indeed a very complex manoeuver to carry out in the face of an enemy and could have been possible only if such evolutions had been regularly practised.[109]

[104] Gavin White, 'Firearms in Africa', p. 179.

[105] Inikori, 'The Import', pp. 358-9; Also, Parker, *The Military Revolution*, p. 131. Buccaneer guns however, were at the upper end of the scale of quality as far as trading guns were concerned. W.A. Richards, 'The Import of Firearms into West Africa in the Eighteenth Century', *Journal of African History*, vol. 21, no. 1, 1980, p. 53.

[106] OIOC Home Misc., 806, p. 104.

[107] Stringer Lawrence's Journal, OIOC O.V. 13, pp. 62-4.

[108] Orme, *History*, vol. 1, p. 316.

[109] There is however, some reference to the training of manoeuvers at Fort St. George in 1741. In June 1741, the military officers were instructed to begin the training with

The Company's Europeans then, were fairly well instructed compared to the sepoys. But their basic drill and discipline set the sepoys apart from the peons who were undisciplined and armed in the 'country style'.[110] The sepoys from the west coast probably brought with them a higher standard of training that led the authorities in Madras to emulate them and call similarly trained troops. The esteem in which the Bombay sepoys were held can be understood by the fact that it was only in 1755 that Madras authorities allowed them to return to Bombay, explaining that the Madras sepoys and the Bombay sepoys were now 'equally serviceable'.[111]

But it was not long before the sepoys' training was upgraded. The Madras Regulations of 1759 stipulated the introduction of a 'a form of exercise the most simple and easy, as likewise evolutions such as will be best adapted to the nature of these troops and the intended use of them'.[112] Clearly the training was still of a rudimentary nature, but the reference to 'evolutions' suggests that the sepoys are beginning to learn to manoeuver,[113] an essential tactical requirement for battalion-style units. By the mid-1760s the sepoys were all armed with regular military firearms and there are also indications that the sepoys are becoming quite familiar with manoeuvering in large bodies. For example, at Buxar in October 1764, the Bengal sepoys successfully negotiated a morass in their front by moving to their right and facing the front again. A similar proficiency is suggested by the movement of a few battalions

---

manual exercises and then to proceed 'to the evolutions and platoons and any other different firing'. However, it is likely that this training was nothing more than going through the motions, aimed at maintaining a semblance of discipline rather than as a military preparation. Madras Public Consultations, 6 June 1741. *Public Consultations Fort St. George, 1741*, Madras: Government Printers, 1910, p. 86.

[110] According to Orme, the Europeans on the Coromandel coast distinguished 'all the different kinds of undisciplined militia by the general name of peons, and comprehend under this name, troops armed with swords and targets, with bows and arrows, with pikes and lances, with matchlocks and even with musquets'. Orme, *History*, vol. 1, p. 80. See also Bryant, 'The East India Company', p. 53.

[111] Madras Mil. Cons., 2 February 1755, *Diary and Consultation Book, 1755*, p. 28.

[112] Wilson, *History*, vol. 1, p. 148.

[113] In contemporary military parlance 'evolutions' meant such manoeuvers as forming into line from a column or vice versa and forming square. See for example Major-General Humphrey Bland, *A Treatise of Military Discipline in which is Laid Down and Explained the Duty of the Officers and Soldiers thro' the Several Branches of the Service*, London, 1753.

of sepoys to hold a low hill during the Battle of Tiruvannamalai in the Carnatic in 1767.[114]

Yet there is hardly any mention at this stage, of a standard system of training for the Company's troops. Individual officers probably used one or more of the numerous drill books available at the time. These manuals, though differing in details, were very similar as far as the broader aspects of eighteenth century drill and exercises are concerned. However the important point for our purpose is that by the early 1770s both sepoys and European troops were being drilled together, which obviously means that they were receiving the same training. For instance at Monghyr in 1773:

> The General reviewed the [European] Regiment, 5th and 7th battalions with eight guns. . . . He requested I would proceed in the usual manner. I then made the Line perform as follows: 1st, manual exercises and evolutions; 2nd subdivision firing, standing, advancing and retreating; 3rd Grand subdivision firing; 4th street firing, advancing and retreating; 5th, a General Volley; 6th marched by the General in open ranks, Officers saluting it as they passed. Concluded with forming the Escalier, or staircase, and from it the Battalion.[115]

The joint exercises and manoeuvers described above closely follow the guidelines issued to contemporary European armies, and in July 1779, the Commander-in-Chief, General Sir Eyre Coote made this mandatory when he ordered that the exercises practised in the King's army be adopted for the Company's army as well.[116] Within a decade—by June 1788—one finds sepoys and the Europeans—both King's and Company's troops—being reviewed together at Bombay—all performing the same routines.[117] In the same year, the Company adopted the drill manual devised by David Dundas as the standard for its army.[118]

But there was more to discipline in a European-style army than learning to shoot the firelock on command and forming line and column. Soldiers also had to conform to a rigorous pattern of life in camp and on the march. How did the British set about imposing this discipline on their sepoys?

[114] See the descriptions of these battles in Chapter 4 of this work.

[115] W.C. McPherson (ed.), *Soldiering in India 1764-1787: Extracts from Journals and Letters Left by Colonel Allan Mcpherson and Lieutenant Colonel John Mcpherson of the East India Company's Service*, London: William Blackwood & Sons, 1928, p. 50.

[116] Eyre Coote's minute, 15 July 1779, Bengal Mil. Cons., OIOC P/18/49, p. 49.

[117] Bombay Army General Orders, 1788-9, OIOC Mss. Eur. E. 419, pp. 104-5.

[118] Colonel David Dundas, *Principles of Military Movements, Chiefly Applied to the Infantry*, London: T. Cadell, 1788.

## CARROT AND STICK: COMPANY'S APPROACH TO CONTROLLING SEPOYS

One of the first steps taken towards building a regular sepoy army was to introduce uniforms. Until the middle of the eighteenth century the Company's native troops were attired exclusively in native dress.[119] But as drill became a feature of the native soldier's life, the Company began to toy with the idea of clothing him in some form of uniform in the manner of European soldiers. Clive showed the way by outfitting the Bengal sepoys with uniforms from the very beginning; the sepoys who traveled south with Colonel Francis Forde to take Masulipattanam in 1758 were all said to have been wearing red coats.[120] As for Madras, there are references to 'uniforms' there as early as 1754 and in 1756 we hear of the Madras Council sending Major Kilpatrick 600 sepoy coats in January 1756.[121] However, these early tentative moves seem to have had more to do with getting rid of some excess broadcloth than with regularizing the appearance of the native troops.[122] As late as 1758 the French troops who confronted Colonel Forde's force at Condore in 1758 mistook the Bengal sepoys (dressed in red) for the Company's European troops, probably because the Madras sepoys they were accustomed to seeing were still wearing native dress.[123]

But with the establishment of regular sepoy battalions uniform dress became mandatory. In Madras, regulation attire now consisted mainly of a basic red coat with facings of different colours to identify battalions (blue for the first battalion, yellow for the second).[124] In Bombay too, red coats were the order of the day after 1760.[125] By the early 1780s this basic uniform had been embellished by the addition of tight white breeches reaching halfway down his thigh, a turban carrying a plume of feathers or cloth and a sash of the same colour around the waist. Native officers wore the same uniform with slight variations. Their jackets were laced and their plumes were decorated with gold.[126]

[119] Orme, *History*, vol. 1, p. 81.

[120] Cambridge, *Account*, p. 274.

[121] Council to Kilpatrick, 24 January 1756, *Diary and Consultation Book, 1756*, p. 38.

[122] Wilson, *History*, vol. 1, p. 21.

[123] Cambridge, *Account*, p. 274.

[124] Wilson, *History*, vol. 1, pp. 143-4.

[125] Cadell, *History*, p. 67.

[126] Barat, *Bengal Native Infantry*, pp. 51-2. See also Major R. Money Barnes, *Military Uniforms of Britain and the Empire: 1742 to the Present Time*, London: Seeley Service and Co. Ltd., 1960, p. 42.

With regular organization came rigorous discipline. During the early stage, attention was more on general obedience. For instance, in December 1748 we hear of three sepoys being charged with threatening a European ensign[127] and during the campaign against Yusuf Khan in August 1763, a native commandant named Abdul Cader was brought against a court martial for 'not having acquitted himself properly of his duty when commanded', and sentenced to be reduced to the rank and pay of a *subedar*.[128] Soon after, the Company introduced a formal code of discipline in the form of the 'military regulations', first published in Madras in 1766, and in Bengal two years later. Bengal was advised by London to forward a copy of the regulations annually to the other presidencies, the object being to produce a uniform system of discipline throughout the Company's possessions. Furthermore, London ordered the Articles of War to be translated into the country languages and read to the sepoy companies assembled for parade at stated times. By 1776 they had been translated into both Tamil and Hindustani.[129]

Such regulations were aimed at maintaining a high standard of discipline down to the smallest behavioural details. Their effects were already apparent in the late 1760s. A muster book of the Bengal Army dating to 1768 mentions sepoys being punished with more than a hundred lashes for offences like losing a jacket, for quitting the guard and wearing the cummerbund under the coat.[130] More serious offences like desertion and disobedience could result in several months' suspension from service, severe floggings (up to 1,000 lashes) or dismissal from the service.[131]

The Company took a more serious view of collective insubordination. When a large number of Bengal sepoys refused to obey orders due to a dispute over allowances, the Commanding Officer, Major Hector Munro, stamped his authority by rounding up the ringleaders and blowing them from guns. A general order published after the event impressed on the minds of the sepoys that while all reasonable requests

[127] The three were eventually acquitted due to lack of evidence. FSD Cons., 27 December 1748, OIOC FR G/18/10, pp. 101-6.

[128] OIOC, O.V. 47, p. 73.

[129] Dodwell, *Sepoy Recruitment*, pp. 39-40.

[130] C. Ritchie, 'A Sepoy Muster Book of 1768', *Journal of the Society for Army Historical Research*, vol. 32, 1954, pp. 18-23.

[131] For example, see the accounts of various sepoy courts martial appearing in the general orders of the Bombay Army 1788-9, OIOC Mss. Eur. E. 419 and also Colonel Cosby's journal in Pasley Papers, B.L. Add. 29,000.

made by them would be complied with, insubordination would be 'punished with the utmost severity and no mercy shall be shown him or them who are guilty'.[132] This attitude was maintained in the decades that followed. When the 35th battalion of Bengal native infantry refused to march to an undisclosed destination and requested their discharge, their wish was granted, but not before two *subedars* and two sepoys were blown from cannon for leading the mutiny and the regimental colours burnt before all the troops present. Similarly when the 35th battalion of Madras native infantry mutinied in Colombo in March 1796 two of the ringleaders were shot while five others were sentenced to receive 700 to 1,000 lashes.[133]

But discipline was not without its limits. The Company showed a marked reluctance to demand obedience from their sepoys where their religious prejudices were involved. This was best demonstrated with regard to overseas travel, highly offensive to upper caste Hindus. In the Bengal Army with its predominantly upper caste Hindu background, embarkation aboard ships was made voluntary and volunteers were allowed to make their own living arrangements aboard ship to ensure ritual purity. For example, when the 15th battalion of native infantry was required to embark for Malacca in 1795, their Commanding Officer, Captain Grant was instructed to 'sound the inclinations of his men on the intended expedition and if he were pretty confident of a general aquiesance, to propose it to them under assurance of every possible attention being paid to their comfort and convenience on board of ship; of every indulgence being shown to their prejudices of caste in laying in water and provisions'.[134] This was not all. As Seema Alavi explains, the Bengal government took every precaution it could to help their sepoys maintain their high caste identity; they were allowed to maintain the rigid customs relating to their diet and the celebration of Hindu religious festivals were sanctioned within the cantonments.[135]

Somewhat similar care was taken at the other presidencies. For example, when the 9th battalion of Madras native infantry was required

[132] Bengal Sec. and Mil. Cons., 16 September 1764, OIOC P/A/5, p. 502.

[133] Colonel Stuart to Major-General Clarke, Commander-in-Chief, 28 March 1796, Madras Mil. and Sec. Cons., 4 April 1796, OIOC P/253/60, p. 1531.

[134] Bengal Mil. Cons., 9 October 1795, OIOC P/19/6, p. 602. Lord Cornwallis assured the Bengal native army in 1789 that he would 'never exact compliance from them which might be inconsistent with the tenets of their different religions'. Williams, *Historical Account*, p. 90.

[135] Alavi, *Sepoys*, pp. 76-80.

Plate 5: Madras sepoy with wife. Inscribed: 'A sepoy of the 36th Battalion Madras Native Infantry.' By a Tanjore artist dated 1797. OIOC Add. Or. 195.

to travel by sea from Anjengo to Bombay in 1775, the Commanding Officer Captain Kelly requested the authorities at Anjengo to provide the sepoys with all the necessities to make their journey comfortable. For example they were ordered to ensure that there was enough water provided for their ablutions and 'whether there are several large pots or kettles besides earthen vessels provided in every vessel for the various casts'.[136] Such indulgence was not limited to Hindus; when the Muslim sepoy officers of the Bombay Army complained in 1769 about having to wear leather boots, the Bombay government consulted their religious leaders about the propriety of requiring Muslims to wear leather.[137]

Apart from catering to the religious sensitivities of the sepoys the Company also strove to provide for their economic security. There is very little information as to the pay of the sepoys in the early period but it appears that there was no fixed rate. As has been seen the list of peons and sepoys of 1749 gives different rates for different companies. But in 1755 the Madras presidency established a pay scale whereby a sepoy was paid Rs. 6 per month, a *subedar* Rs. 60, a *jamadar* Rs. 16, a *havildar* Rs. 10 and a *naik* Rs. 8.[138] This pay scale seems to have been common throughout British India by the 1770s[139] and in 1779 it was officially adopted for all three presidencies.[140]

As Seema Alavi points out, this rate of pay was not superior to that offered by other country powers. But it was provided with regularity that the others could not match. The armies of most Indian rulers suffered from a case of chronic arrears in pay which was rarely the case with the Company's army.[141]

[136] Madras Pol. and Mil. Cons., 24 February 1775, OIOC P/251/77, p. 198.

[137] Bombay Pub. Cons., 29 August 1769, OIOC P/341/32, pp. 660-1.

[138] OIOC O.V. 288, pp. 213-15.

[139] Bengal Sec. Cons., 5 May 1773, G.W. Forrest (ed.), *Selections from the Letters, Despatches and other State Papers Preserved in the Foreign Department of the Government of India 1772-1785*, 3 vols., Calcutta: Superintendant of Govt. Printing, 1890, vol. 1, pp. 42-3.

[140] The sepoys were paid at the end of each month. Barat, *The Bengal Native Infantry*, p. 50.

[141] Alavi, *Sepoys*, p. 43. Ironically, according to some British observers, keeping their armies in arrears was one of the strategies adopted by Indian rulers to prevent desertion. See William Tooke's narrative of the capture of Fort William in 1756 in S.C. Hill, *Bengal 1757-58*, vol. 1, p. 265 and Dubois, *Hindu Manners*, pp. 674-5. The Company was also not always punctual in its payment of its troops. There were frequent instances when the sepoys went without pay for several months, sometimes suffering great hardships. For example, five battalions of sepoys engaged against Mahadji Scindia in 1780-1 went without pay and scanty provisions for several months. Williams, *Historical Account*, pp. 192-3.

Moreover, the Company was also quite generous with gifts and tokens of appreciation to those who behaved well in the field. I have already mentioned the rewarding of Yusuf Khan. This practice continued throughout the latter part of the century. For example, during the siege of Onore in 1783, a sepoy was presented with a pair of silver bangles for his exertions during an attack on Mysorean outposts.[142] Similarly, in August 1800, the Bombay Army ordered 'a badge of gold with an appropriate inscription' to be presented to Subedar Ibrahim Khan for his bravery in attacking a pagoda near Karwar. The *havildars* who were present were rewarded with badges of silver.[143]

There were other inducements as well. After twenty years' service every Madras sepoy received a cash pension of Rs. 3 per month.[144] In Bengal, the Company introduced in 1778 a system of providing invalid sepoys with plots of land. In 1796, the family and heirs of the invalid sepoys also became eligible for these land grants.[145]

To recapitulate, the salient features of the organization of the English East India Company's sepoy army in the eighteenth century were the establishment of a regular command structure, the introduction of European-style training and discipline. The main feature of the command structure was the gradual concentration of power in the hands of its European officers and the reduction of native officers to the status of mere figureheads while in the sphere of discipline, the Company strove to respect the religious prejudices of the sepoys. Care was also taken to provide regular pay and other inducements like pensions. In the area of training, the sepoys were exposed to the same training regimes as their European counterparts in the Company's service.

But all this still leaves a good deal undiscussed about the British attitudes to their Indian soldiers during the formative period of the sepoy army. What must be remembered is that military organization was ultimately measured by one yardstick—performance of the soldiers in battle. What did the British expect from their sepoys in this ultimate test of all their efforts at creating efficient and effective soldiers?

[142] Journal of General Mathew's campaigns against Mysore, 1782-3, OIOC Mss. Eur. C. 154, notebook no. 6, p. 466.

[143] Moor, *A Compilation*, Chapter XXXII.

[144] Alavi, *Sepoys*, p. 44. Colonel Braithwaite to Madras Council 9 March 1795. Madras Mil. and Pol. Cons., 10 March 1795, OIOC P/253/43, p. 675.

[145] See Seema Alavi, 'The Company Army and Rural Society: the Invalid Thana 1780-1830', *Modern Asian Studies*, vol. 27, no. 1, 1993, pp. 147-78. See also Barat, *Bengal Native Infantry*, p. 50.

*Four*

# The Sepoy at War, 1746-1805

In this chapter, I shall leave the barrack room and the parade ground and enter the smoke-filled and blood-splattered world of the battlefield. My search here is for the sepoy who fought in the numerous campaigns that helped establish the dominance of the East India Company over the subcontinent. The objective is to explore what the sepoy actually did—or was made to do by his English masters—in combat in order to understand the perceptions behind the organization of the Company's native army.

## THE YEARS OF APPRENTICESHIP 1746-1760

I shall start by looking at the period when the sepoy was still organized as an irregular soldier. Until the outbreak of the Carnatic War, the duties of the Company's garrisons in India were largely limited to mounting guard,[1] a circumstance that provided little scope for a significant differentiation in the roles of European and native soldiery. The situation however, changed with the commencement of active military campaigning in the late 1740s. Now the Company's army was called upon to do some real fighting, and against armies that included a nucleus of French infantry and artillery supported by very large numbers of native cavalry. True, these engagements were very trifling in comparison to the later wars with major powers like Mysore and the Marathas. In the south, the only real 'battles' in this period were the engagements between the Company and the French before Tiruchirapalli in 1753-4 and at Wandiwash in January 1760, while the only major engagement in Bengal during this phase was the show-down between the British and the Nawab Siraj-ud-Daulah at Plassey—hardly a 'battle' in a military sense. Yet, compared to the long period of

[1] Spear, *The Nabobs*, p. 15. See also Bryant, 'The East India Company', p. 37.

'peaceful trading' which preceded the hostilities in the Carnatic, this was genuine warfare.

Predictably, the semi-trained and ill-armed sepoys of the time were deployed very sparingly in these actions, and usually in an ancillary role—as when, in June and August 1753, EIC sepoys assisted the British grenadiers in their attack on French outposts on the rocky eminence called the 'Golden Rock'.[2] Thus, sepoys hardly ever fought against European troops except by accident—as when Clive's sepoys in May 1751 charged the French troops guarding the fort of Pithchundah, mistaking their demonstrations of submission for defiance,[3] or when a few days later, the English sepoys made a rush for the French troops at Valikondapuram.[4] Such unplanned, unpremeditated actions were the exceptions rather than the rule; usually, the approved place of the sepoys in combat was out of the way of European opponents.

It was a similar story during the Second Carnatic War (1757-61). The only real 'battle' between the English and the French, fought at Wandiwash in January 1760 was contested almost exclusively between the European troops on either side. The British deployed in two lines with the sepoys placed in the flanks of the European units. When the time for advancing came, the English Commander Eyre Coote moved on with only the European element of the army, leaving the sepoys behind to be spectators to the toughest battle the British had fought in India until then. Indeed, Orme even has it that the native commandants went up to Coote after the battle and thanked him for the spectacle![5]

There is also little mention in contemporary accounts of sepoys actively engaging with Indian cavalry that supported the French. In the following example, the writer is describing a skirmish before Tiruchirapalli in 1752, occasioned when a woodcutting party of European soldiers and sepoys was attacked by a number of French dragoons.

[2] On the engagement in June, see Stringer Lawrence's account of the action, OIOC O.V. 13, p. 56, Captain John Dalton's narrative, OIOC Orme India III, pp. 576-8 and Orme, *History*, vol. 1, pp. 294-6 and an anonymous account found in NAM Mss. no. 6309-619. On the engagement in August see Lawrence's journal, OIOC O.V. 13, pp. 57-9, Dalton's narrative, pp. 585-6 and Orme, *History*, vol. 1, pp. 304-6.

[3] OIOC Orme India III, pp. 543-4.

[4] Ibid., p. 547.

[5] Orme, *History*, vol. 3, p. 589. Battle description on pp. 587-9. For a description of this battle see also Eyre Coote's despatches of 21 and 22 January 1760 in OIOC Mss. Eur. F. 190, vol. 1, pp. 179-83.

we first met the dragoons, who halted on a little eminence to reconnoiter us, but a single platoon made them decamp, not willing we supposed to lose any men ineffectually, but they retreated only to bring up their black cavalry. . . . They then came up at full speed flourishing their swords and endeavoured to push in a strong party between us and the garrison, our soldiers on this occasion behaved with great calmness, they readily halted to wait their charge with fixed bayonets in very close order, the enemy made a halt within point blank range to draw our fire, we imagined they had not observed our field piece the first shot from which dismounted 3 of the moors, and Lieutenant Godwin (having had time to prepare his ammunition for quick fire) plied them so very warmly that they very soon began to move off. . . . [6]

Note that the sepoys are not mentioned in this action although a considerable number of them were present. The 'soldiers' mentioned are almost certainly Europeans as it was customary during this period to distinguish between native and European troops as sepoys and 'soldiers'. The question is, why the omission?

It is tempting to dismiss such accounts as the biased works of English officers keen to magnify the contribution of the European troops in battle. But the implied low profile of the sepoys is really not surprising if we recall the limited training provided for them. The clashes between the French and the English may have been little more than short, sharp skirmishes, but the scale of these encounters did not diminish the demands they placed on discipline. For example, during an action fought before Tiruchirapalli in June 1753, the English troops drew up within 20 yards of the French and received their fire before opening fire themselves[7]—a typical tactic, as we have seen, of contemporary European warfare. However, steadfastness of this sort did not come naturally; it had to be learned, instilled on the parade ground. It was a product of training. Since the sepoys of the 1740s and 1750s were still largely untrained, risking them against French infantry would have been foolhardy. When Colonel Francis Forde described sepoys as being 'very good behind walls' he was making a strictly professional observation.[8] It was no good expecting sepoys to perform tasks for which they had not been adequately prepared.

But fighting the French or native cavalry were not the only type of actions that took place at the time; there were also forts to man and convoys to escort and delegating such duties to sepoys was seen as a

[6] OIOC Orme India III, p. 525.
[7] Orme, *History*, vol. 1, p. 296.
[8] OIOC O.V. 292, p. 35.

good way of sparing the Europeans for duty in the field. Advising the withdrawal of European troops from minor forts to strengthen Tiruchirapalli in 1754, Stringer Lawrence recommended a 'force barely to maintain those [forts] that have prisoners is sufficient which can be done by sepoys'.[9] Similarly, when war broke out in the Carnatic again a few years later, a large number of sepoys were raised in order to replace the European troops withdrawn from outlying garrisons to fight with the main army pursuing the French. Interestingly, during this campaign in the Carnatic in 1760, the Fort St. George Council advised Colonel Eyre Coote, the Commander of the Company's forces to 'find the best situations possible for the European troops with a view as well to their security against the heat of the weather as against the attack of the enemy, so posted they take some repose while the horse and sepoys are employed in preventing any supplies from the country being thrown into Pondicherry'.[10]

Moreover, it seems that the English had enough confidence in their sepoys to use them now and then in expeditions against lesser opposition, such as the armies of local lineages. That the English did not think much of the military power of these lineages can be gleaned from a letter written by Colonel Charles Campbell in 1764. 'The Hamuldars and Renters,' wrote Colonel Charles Campbell in 1764, 'have a few sepoys and colleries and a little artillery [and] small forts for the security of their villages against Robbers. They will probably now and then have little skirmishes with the neighbouring poligars . . . those little forays always ends with perhaps the loss of a few sheep on the side that gives way and has been their manner of acting for hundreds of years.'[11] Against such relatively weak opponents, the Company was sometimes prepared to send sepoys without any European officers, particularly when trusted sepoy officers were involved. For instance in February 1758, Jemal Sahib was sent with four companies of sepoys to subdue some poligars around Tripassore and Poonamaalee,[12] and in July the same year two sepoy companies each were sent to Chinglepet and Conjeewaram to assist the *amuldars* in collecting revenue.[13] As

[9] Stringer Lawrence to Madras Council, 2 February 1754, *Diary and Consultation Book, 1754*, pp. 39-40.

[10] Madras Mil. and Sec. Cons., 12 April 1760, OIOC P/D/43, pp. 350-1.

[11] Charles Campbell to Madras Council, 5 December 1764, Madras Mil. and Sec. Con., 11 December 1764, OIOC P/251/51, pp. 1042-3.

[12] Madras Sel. Com. Cons., 9 February 1758, OIOC P/C/53, p. 88.

[13] Madras Sel. Com. Cons., 7 July 1758, OIOC P/C/53, p. 268.

noted earlier, Jemal Sahib was one of the *subedars* enjoying a position of great trust in the sepoy establishment and that would have been an added incentive to send a detachment under his command.[14]

Again, Indian soldiers were valued for their specialist knowledge as apparent from Orme's praise for Yusuf Khan's efforts to keep Tiruchirapalli well-supplied during its investment by the French in 1753-4: 'he constantly procured intelligence of the enemy's motions, and, having a perfect knowledge of the country, planned the marches of the convoys so well that by constantly changing the roads and the times of bringing the provisions out of the woods, not one of them was intercepted for three months'.[15] Yusuf Khan's other major assignments were also of a partisan nature: the pacification of Madura in deep jungles in 1756 and creating disturbances behind French lines in 1758-9. But when Vellore was to be taken in 1755 the Company refused to entrust the task to Yusuf Khan's sepoys because the fortress was considered too strong to be taken by sepoys alone.[16] To the English, Yusuf Khan was little more than a sepoy with exceptional abilities in the type of activities sepoys were good for. It was Stringer Lawrence who best expressed the English perspective of his beloved 'Nellore Subedar'. 'He is a born soldier,' he said, 'and a better of his colour I never saw in the country.'[17]

Thus, during the first few years of active military campaigning by the Company's army, only a very modest combat role was allowed for the Company's native troops. Essentially the sepoy army at this period was a semi-trained, irregular force employed more in performing paramilitary rather than military tasks. But, as seen in the previous chapter, it was not long before the Company upgraded the organization and training of their sepoys under increasing European control. Significantly, these improvements in the Company's sepoy army coincided with the emergence of formidable country powers like the

[14] What was expected in such expeditions is revealed by Colonel John Caillaud's description of what he calls a 'country battle' fought between Yusuf Khan's force of sepoys and the followers of Maphus Khan, the Nawab's brother. Caillaud says that the engagement 'lasted from 7 in the morning till sun set. Usuf Khan had four men killed and six or seven wounded. Maphus Khan's party had lost about three hundred . . . these little engagements tho' not so decisive as could be wished may in time however produce good order and tranquility in the country.' Caillaud to Council, 12 March 1757, Madras Sel. Com. Cons., 28 March 1757, OIOC P/C/51, pp. 199-200.

[15] Orme, *History*, p. 347.

[16] Hill, *Yusuf Khan*, p. 47.

[17] OIOC O.V. 13, p. 78.

Marathas and Mysore. Under the influence of the 'Indian Military Revolution' described in the first chapter, these states began to deploy large numbers of disciplined infantry, and powerful trains of artillery. Consequently, the Company's battles in the late eighteenth century were much bigger affrays than those which had been fought against the French and their allies in the 1750s—both in scale and destructiveness.

How did the British employ their regular sepoys against these powerful enemies? I shall seek an answer to this question through a close scrutiny of a number of major engagements during the latter part of the eighteenth century, namely the battles of Buxar, Tiruvannamalai, Porto Novo, Assaye, Laswari and the storming of Srirangapattanam. These were not only politically decisive battles but also very formidable military challenges to the Company's army. The Mughal army at Buxar was one of the most powerful forces the Mughal empire could muster at the time. Apart from the usual quota of heavy cavalry, and a large train of artillery, the Mughal forces at Buxar also consisted of a number of infantry units drilled in the European fashion and commanded by European and Armenian adventurers. Likewise, Hyder's army at Porto Novo was reckoned to exceed 60,000 horse and 50,000 foot—again, a considerable number of the latter drilled and armed in the European fashion—besides 100 pieces of artillery.[18] As for the Maratha Wars, I have already described the quality of the Maratha artillery at Assaye and Delhi. These were real contests, fought against adversaries considerably superior in numbers, not always inferior in materiel and quality of training, and, like Tipu Sultan, possessed formidable strongholds.

## THE TEST OF BIG BATTLES

### *Buxar, 23 October 1764*[19]

The British army that fought against the Nawab of Awadh at Buxar was commanded by Major Hector Munro and consisted of about 1,000 European troops and nearly 7,000 sepoys supported by 28 guns.

[18] These figures are taken from Munro, *A Narrative*, p. 130. The narrative of the campaign attributed to one Major Sydenham gives Hyder's force as '47 guns well served, 600 Europeans, 400 Topasses, cavalry 40,000, 23 battalions of sepoys cloathed, in number 18,402, Irregular Foot armed with matchlocks pikes and rocket men, 1,20,000'. OIOC Home Misc. 248, p. 89.

[19] The description of this battle is pieced together from Hector Munro's despatch

Opposed to them was a Mughal army nearly 50,000 strong, including several thousand trained infantry and a strong artillery train. The battle began with a cannonade by the Mughlal line at about 9 o'clock in the morning of 22 October. The fire and the sight of swarms of Mughal cavalry forming in the distance force Munro to hastily withdraw an advance guard of sepoys. Soon, Shuja's army was seen advancing towards the English camp. In the centre of his line, the trained battalions of Sumroo, their artillery manned by renegade European gunners, were clearly discernible, while on their right hovered several thousand heavy cavalry under the Raja of Benares.

Munro decided to battle, and formed his army in two lines.[20] The centre of the first line was occupied by two companies each from the Bengal and Bombay European regiments and by Royal troops and marines. These European troops were flanked by two battalions of sepoys each, the intervals of the battalions occupied by two pieces of artillery. The second line was formed about 100 yards to the rear of the first. Its centre comprised the remaining companies of the Bengal European regiment together with four battalions of sepoys and artillery placed in the same disposition as the first line. Between these two lines was the reserve composed of the grenadiers of the Bengal European regiment. The baggage was left in a village in the rear, under the protection of native cavalry.

The British began their march towards the advancing enemy, the Mughal heavy artillery coming within range long before the light pieces of the British army. The Mughals gradually advanced close enough to occupy a *tope* or grove of trees in front of the British centre with their infantry. A strong Mughal battery was also posted in a village, to the right of the English line, at the edge of the grove. As the British line advanced, this battery began to gall the British right flank. In an attempt to silence this, Munro detached a battalion of sepoys from the right of the first line. The sepoys were beaten back twice and Munro ordered

dated 25 October 1764 in Bengal Sel. Com. Cons., OIOC P/A/5, pp. 567-8, a description of the battle left by an officer who took part in it appearing in OIOC Home Misc. 198, pp. 98-107 and the descriptions appearing in Charles Caraccioli, *The Life of Robert Lord Clive, Baron of Plassey*, 3 vols., London, 1775, vol. I, pp. 50-6; and Broome, *History*, pp. 474-9.

[20] The European troops in this battle were H.M. 84th, 89th, 90th regiments, Bengal European battalion and detachments of Royal Marines and Bombay Europeans. The sepoys comprised the 3rd, 6th, 8th, 10th, 11th, 14th and 15th Bengal battalions. James P. Lawford, *Britain's Army in India*, London: Allen and Unwin, 1976, Appendix III.

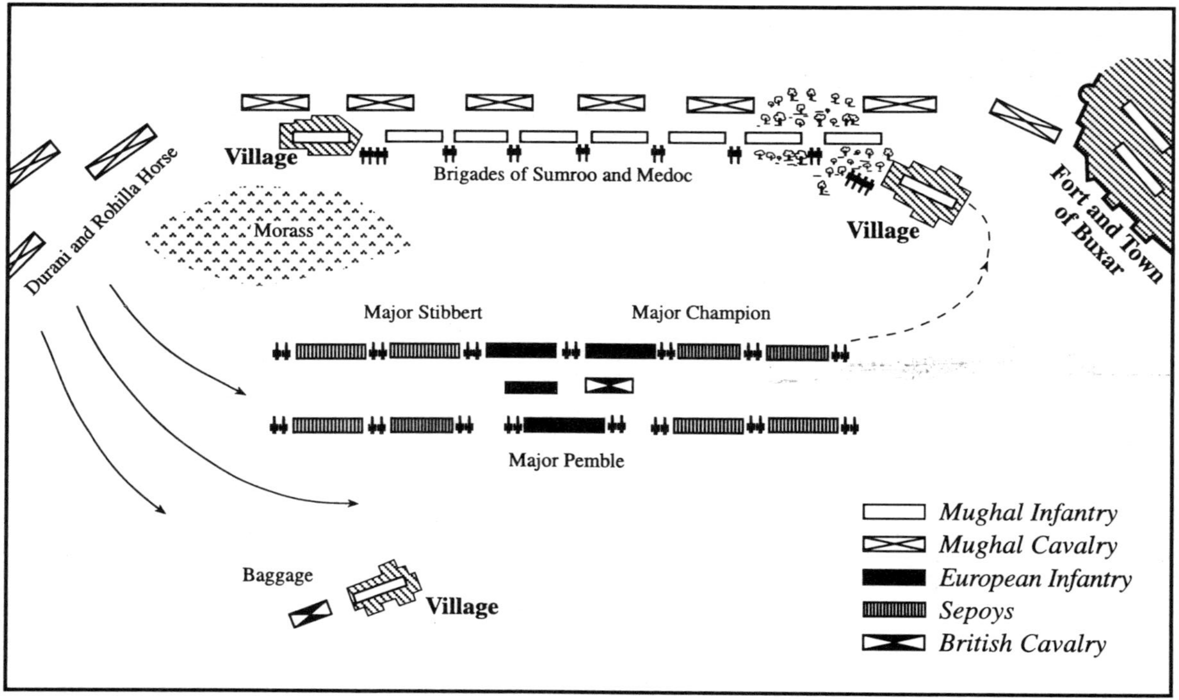


Plan 1: The Battle of Buxar, 23 October 1764.

another sepoy battalion from the extreme right of the second line to support them. Together, the two contingents of sepoys prevailed, but only after a firefight lasting nearly two hours.

While the struggle for the village was going on, the English advance had been interrupted by a large swamp to the left of their front. To avoid this, both lines had to turn and move slowly to the right. Once the morass had been by-passed the line continued its advance but it was now faced by a new, more serious menace. The Mughal cavalry that had bided its time now came thundering down on their left flank and rear. It looked as if the two British lines would be separated by the enemy cavalry pouring into the gap between them. But the reserve of grenadiers now formed a line facing left and Munro ordered half a battalion of sepoys from the left of the front line to pull back and another sepoy battalion from the left of the second line to wheel inwards to join the grenadiers and form a solid line on the left flank. At the same time, the remaining units of the second line turned around to face the rear. The fire from the British left and rear repulsed the cavalry charge but not before the entire baggage was overrun.

Now the sepoys who took the village were ordered against the left flank of the enemy position in the grove. But this attack too was beaten back, which exposed the retreating sepoys to attacks from the Mughal cavalry. Sensing the battle had reached a critical stage Munro ordered Major Champion with the Bengal Europeans and the Royal troops from the centre of the first line and the remaining two battalions of sepoys from the right flank of both lines to lend support. It had the desired effect. The enemy cavalry drew off and the surviving sepoys from the first party now joined Champion's troops to resume the advance on the grove, which was duly captured.

With the grove lost, the Mughal left was pressed back on their centre. Simultaneously, the British left resumed its advance. Soon its field pieces were within killing range of the massed Mughal line. As the British guns came to bear, the Mughal centre, already under pressure from their left, began to move off, soon breaking into full retreat (although some units like those of Sumroo and Medoc maintained a good order). Several sepoy battalions now broke formation without orders and rushed on the enemy but this indiscipline made no difference to the outcome. Very soon, the retreat had turned in to a rout. In a melancholy finale to the battle, many thousands of imperial troops and camp followers perished in a frantic scramble across the stream that flowed beyond Buxar village.

On the battlefield the English counted 2,000 dead Indian bodies but the total Mughal losses were certainly much higher considering the large numbers that perished in the mad rush across the stream. The Mughals also left behind them a total of 172 pieces of artillery and the greater part of camp equipage. On the British side the sepoys bore the brunt of the casualties, 205 killed and 414 wounded compared to 32 Europeans killed and 47 wounded. It was quite a heavy price, but it gave the EIC political supremacy in eastern India.

### *The Mysore Wars: Tiruvannamalai, 26 September 1767*[21]

The Battle of Tiruvannamalai was one of the few set-piece battles of the First Mysore War. The battle flared up when Hyder's army tried to intercept the march of a British force under Colonel Wood in late September 1767. British army, and when the British encamped closer to a stretch of swampy ground near Tiruvannamalai, with a force of 9,000 sepoys, 1,400 Europeans and 24 guns. Hyder became optimistic of his chances of surrounding the enemy in difficult ground. After reconnoitering the English position early on 26 September, Hyder began the action by opening his guns from a rising ground in the distance. However, his gunners wasted their advantage; the fire was largely ineffective and achieved little more than 'frightening the feathered inhabitants of the underwood that grew on the hill-side'.[22] Now alerted to their peril, the British swarmed out of their encampment to meet the Mysoreans who drew up in the distance, ready for battle.

To avoid the swamp, the British army had to move to their right and, in doing so, had to skirt a hill of considerable height. But they took care to post a battalion of sepoys commanded by Captain Cooke on the hill to prevent the enemy from occupying it. The Mysoreans however, mistook this for a retreat and sallied forth to intercept, deploying themselves face to face with the English army that had rounded the hill. Soon the two armies engaged each other.

Hyder moved first, despatching a body of his Topasses and sepoys to take the hill. Fearing of being outflanked, Colonel Wood now sent

[21] The main sources for this battle are: journal and orderly book of Brigadier-General Joseph Smith, OIOC O.V. 215, pp. 38-41; the journal kept by Lieutenant-Colonel Henry Cosby, BM Add. 29898, pp. 31-5; 'Memoranda of Colonel Robert Kelly', OIOC Mss. Eur. D. 1146/6, pp. 23-5 and M.M.D.L.T., *Hyder Ali*, pp. 312-17.

[22] M.M.D.L.T., *Hyder Ali*, p. 313.

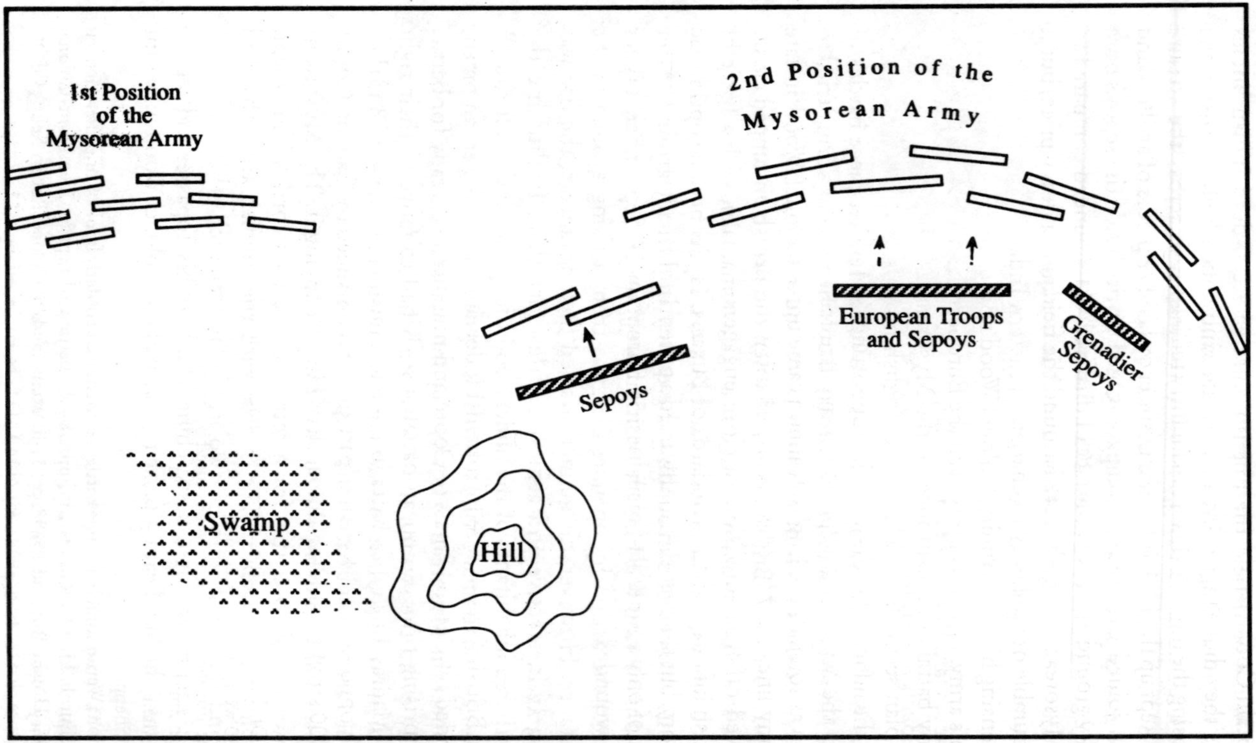


Plan 2: The Battle of Tiruvannamalai, 26 September 1767.

Captain Cooke back with his sepoys to dislodge the Mysorean force. This they did with help from a second sepoy battalion. Disconcerted at losing the hill, the Mysorean infantry fell back, but rallied at a distance and kept up their fire on the English sepoys. Two more sepoy battalions soon joined the sepoys already engaged in holding the hill and the rocky ground in front in the face of this fire. All this time, large numbers of Mysorean cavalry hovered around the field of action, waiting for a favourable opportunity to charge.

Sensing his opportunity, Colonel Wood now ordered the main body of his army, which comprised all the Europeans and the remaining five sepoy battalions to advance on the Mysorean army in front. At first the plan seemed to backfire, the English moving with a rapidity that put the infantry far ahead of the supporting field pieces while for their part, the Mysoreans kept up a heavy fire from their artillery. But as soon as some of the English cannon came up, and were trained on the enemy line, the Mysorean army, infantry and cavalry, broke up, and moved off without risking a close engagement with the advancing British infantry. By the standards of Buxar, this was hardly a dazzling victory, but the British had thwarted a potentially devastating attack at cost of only a handful of casualties: 50 Europeans and 100 sepoys killed and wounded.[23]

### *Porto Novo, 1 July 1781*[24]

The British force that confronted Hyder at Porto Novo was commanded by General Sir Eyre Coote and numbered about 7,600 men, comprising three European battalions—King's 73rd and the Bengal and Madras European battalions—and nine sepoy battalions. They were opposed by the greater part of the Mysorean main army nearly 70,000 strong including almost all of Hyder's trained infantry, a strong

[23] Of these, 25 Europeans were killed and 25 wounded. Of the sepoys 40 were killed and 60 wounded. Cosby's journal, BM Add. 29898, p. 35. According to Joseph Smith all the European casualties were caused by cannon shot. Journal and orderly book of Joseph Smith, OIOC O.V. 215, p. 41.

[24] Main sources for this battle are: General Eyre Coote's despatch reproduced in E.W. Sheppard, *Coote Bahadur: a Life of Lieutenant-General Sir Eyre Coote, K.B.*, London: Werner Laurie, 1956, pp. 208-14; narrative of Eyre Coote's campaign, OIOC Mss. Eur. F. 190, box 1; the description of the battle attributed to Major Sydenham, OIOC Home. Misc., 248, pp. 85-9; Munro, *A Narrative*, later descriptions of the battle are also found in Wilks, *Historical Sketches*, vol. 2, pp. 311-13; and H.C. Wylly, *Life*, pp. 200-2.

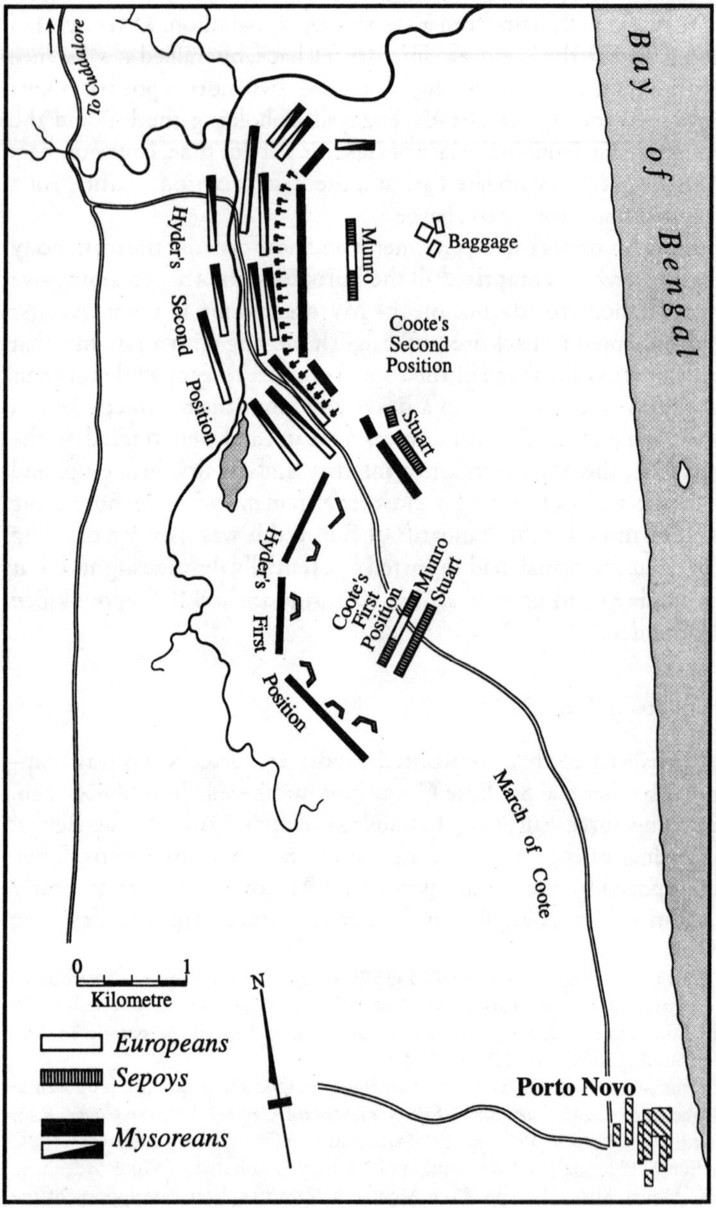


Plan 3: The Battle of Porto Novo, 1 July 1781.

train of artillery and the flower of Mysorean cavalry. Nevertheless, despite these odds, Coote accepted Hyder's challenge, and on 1 July marched northwards. He moved in two lines, the first under Hector Munro comprising two regiments of native cavalry, the three European and five sepoy battalions and 30 guns, the second under Colonel Stuart, with four sepoy battalions and 26 guns. The baggage was entrusted to the care of a sepoy battalion and two native cavalry regiments and was kept at a distance, somewhat closer to the sea.

The Mysore Army soon came into view, spaced out over a broad stretch of ground to the west. The position was well-defended by redoubts mounted with artillery. Of more immediate concern to the British however, was the appearance of large bodies of enemy cavalry. This forced Coote to pull back the two battalions in the extreme left of his first line at right angles to the line of march, to prevent his flank being turned. Then the Mysore artillery came into action which brought Coote's advance to a halt. Nevertheless, Coote thought he saw an opening—a small gap between the enemy's left and the ocean. Seizing on this, he ordered his two lines to file off to the right in two columns, behind a line of low sand hills. Under cover of the sand hills, the second line commanded by Stuart took position facing the enemy's centre while the main body under Munro continued north until it came in line of the Mysore left.[25] Simultaneously, an 18-pounder and two 12-pounders with the second line were now unlimbered on the heights where Stuart took position, and trained on the Mysore positions to cover the advance of the first line. A gifted general, Hyder did not take long to grasp the British plan. Quickly, he led his infantry out of their positions to attack Munro while flinging large bodies of cavalry and infantry against Stuart's line. However, the sepoys in Stuart's line beat off these assaults helped by the timely intervention of. a British Schooner, *Intelligence*, which had been cruising off the coast. The naval gunfire scattered the Mysore cavalry, and in so doing, saved the British baggage which was placed behind the English positions.

Meanwhile, Coote advanced on the enemy positions. 'The minute was critical', he wrote in his despatch. 'I had gained the flank of the enemy's batteries, waited with impatience under a heavy fire of cannon, till I had ascertained that the heights in my rear were possessed by the

[25] The sources are not clear as to the order in which the line was deployed, but Fortescue's plan of the battle shows the sepoys flanking the Europeans. John Fortescue, *History of the British Army*, 13 vols., London: Macmillan, 1902-30, vol. 3, Plate IX.

second line, then instantly moved on with the first, as far as order and an advancing fire of artillery on our side would permit.'[26] As they did at Tiruvannamalai, the Mysorians did not wait to receive the British infantry. Their infantry fired one volley—at too great a distance to harm the British—and fell back, the entire Mysore Army soon following suit.

Coote later estimated enemy casualties to be about 4,000 which was trifling considering the massive numbers involved, but the Mysorian dead included some of their best cavalry and Hyder's second-in command at the battle, Meer Sahib, who was the victim of the opportune intervention of the schooner. English casualties were remarkably light: 83 killed (19 Europeans and 64 sepoys), 235 wounded (37 Europeans and 198 sepoys) and 19 missing (1 European and 18 sepoys).[27]

### *The Storming of Srirangapattanam, 4 May 1799*[28]

The Second Mysore War left the Carnatic devastated but within seven years of its completion war clouds gathered again. In December 1789, Hyder's son and successor, Tipu Sultan, attacked the Raja of Travancore, an ally of the EIC. This gave the British a golden opportunity to reduce the power of their erstwhile enemy. The war which followed Third Mysore War 1790-2 saw Mysore invaded from both east and west, Bangalore captured and Tipu's fortified camp before Srirangapattanam successfully stormed. The war ended in a humiliating treaty for Tipu, resulting in the cession of one half of his kingdom to the British. But it was not the end of Mysore as a potential threat to British interests—the tiger's claws were clipped but he was still not caged. In 1798 Tipu entered into an alliance with Napoleonic France and a joint French-Mysore enterprise to eject the British from India was greatly feared.

[26] Sheppard, *Coote Bahadur*, pp. 210-11.

[27] Casualty figures in Wylly, *Life*, p. 205.

[28] The description of this action is based on: Alexander Beatson, *A View of the Origin and Conduct of the War with Tippoo Sultan Comprising a Narrative of the Operations of the Army Under the Command of Lieutenant-General George Harris and of the Siege of Seringapattam*, London, 1800, pp. 125-38; the narrative of Major L. Macquarie of the Bombay Army in OIOC Home Misc., 814, pp. 140-54; General orders of the army before Seringapattanam 1 January-27 June 1799. OIOC Mss. Eur. E. 386; and a letter from an officer serving with the army before Srirangapattanam, OIOC Mss. Eur. B. 276. See also Wilks, *Historical Sketches*, vol. 3, pp. 434-45.

Plate 6: 'And a most noble sight it was—columns of grenadiers dashing at noonday across a broad river.' The storming of Srirangapattanam, 4 May 1799. Coloured lithograph after Captain Allan, published for 'Cannons Military Records'. OIOC P. 471. Quote from OIOC Mss. Eur. B. 276.

To pre-empt such a move, the British again declared war on Tipu in early 1799.

In February 1799, the British launched their invasion of Mysore with a force comprising nearly 20,000 troops. An attempt by Tipu to check its advance was easily overcome at Malvelly on 27 March and the army encamped before Srirangapattanam on 5 April. A detachment form Bombay—6,400 strong—reached the camp on 14 April and soon after, the siege of the stronghold began in earnest. On 2 May, the English battering cannon zeroed in on the point on the walls of the fort chosen to be breached. This point, a section in the west wall just south of the north-west bastion, had already been under systematic bombardment since the beginning of the siege. Within a day, the battering cannon had succeeded in forming a practicable breach and by daybreak on 4 May, everything was ready for the final assault.

The assault was made in two columns. The left column was led by flank companies of the King's regiments followed by the King's 12th and 33rd royal regiments and flank companies of ten Bengal sepoy battalions. At the head of the right column were flank companies of the Scots brigade, followed by the Swiss regiment de Meuron, the entire King's 74th and 73rd regiments and eight flank companies of Madras sepoys. The plan was for these two columns to mount the breach and then turn right and left in order to take control of the rampart encircling the city.[29]

At half-past one in the afternoon on 4 May, the storming parties moved out of the trenches supported by a heavy covering fire from the advanced artillery emplacements and 'in the face of a heavy and unremitting fire of musketry and cannon'.[30] The breach was mounted against heavy opposition but once the two columns had performed their manoeuver to the right and left, Tipu's troops on the rampart were caught between two fires. In a frenzied attempt escape into the body of the fort, the defenders headed for the two nearest exit points—a gateway in the inner rampart and a water gate that led into the Kaveri river—where they were picked off almost at will by the flintlocks of King's 12th. Shortly after, organized resistance ceased. After a lengthy search, the Sultan's body was found among the corpses that choked the water gate.

[29] See the orders for the assault on the fortress in OIOC Mss. Eur. E. 386.

[30] OIOC Mss. Eur. B. 276.

The 'Tiger of Mysore' was finally vanquished, but at a heavy cost. The assault had cost 349 casualties and the entire siege almost 1500—a very large number for those days.[31]

### *The Second Maratha War: Assaye, 23 September 1803*[32]

The Second Maratha War was fought in two major theatres: the Deccan, where Scindia and Berar operated, and northern India where the Maratha forces were deployed under the command of the French mercenary, Cullier Perron. The forces in the Deccan included about 10,500 regular infantry and nearly 50,000 cavalry along with about 100 pieces of artillery. In Hindustan Perron had close to 10,000 regular infantry plus 15,000 cavalry. On the way to Hindustan from the Deccan were another 25,000 men, including 8,000 regular infantry, sent by Scindia under a trusted general Ambaji Inglia to reinforce the troops in Hindustan. To meet this formidable army the British had two main field forces in the Deccan, under Major-General Arthur Wellesley and Colonel Stevenson, amounting to about 17,000 men in all. The force operating in Hindustan, about 10,500 in number were placed under the personal command of General Gerard Lake, the British Commander-in-Chief.

In the Deccan, Wellesley opened the British campaign in August 1803 by capturing the Fort of Ahmadnagar south of the Godavery river after a brief siege. With Ahmadnagar secured as a strategic base for future operations, Wellesley and Stevenson were free to move

[31] Details of British casualties were as follows: Europeans: 181 killed, 622 wounded and 22 missing; sepoys: 119 killed, 420 wounded and 100 missing. Figures from Lieutenant-Colonel William Gurwood (ed.), *Despatches of the Field Marshall the Duke of Wellington During his Various Campaigns in India, Denmark, Portugal, Spain and the Low Countries and France from 1799 to 1818*, 8 vols., London: John Murray, 1834, vol. 1, p. 28.

[32] This battle is well documented by several participants. We have Arthur Wellesley's own despatches appearing in Sydney J. Owen (ed.), *A Selection From the Despatches, Treaties and Other Papers of the Marquess Wellesley, K.G. During his Government of India*, Oxford: Clarendon, 1877, pp. 299-309 and the two excellent descriptions left by Captain John Blakiston, *Twelve Years*, vol. 1, pp. 165-85 and Arthur Wellesley's aide-de-camp Mountstuart Elphinstone, Colebrooke (ed.), *The Life*, vol. 1, pp. 47-85. Two other eye-witness accounts are provided by Sergeant Thomas Swarbrook, 19th Dragoons, NAM Mss. 8207-64, and Captain Frazer of the King's 78th, BM Add. 13857.

against the main force of the Marathas in two separate columns. Wellesley was the first to make contact, running unexpectedly into the enemy force at Assaye on 23 September. Stevenson was still a fair distance away, but fearing a possible attack on his camp before Stevenson's arrival, Wellesley decided to take the initiative and attack the enemy on his own.[33]

The Maratha position at Assaye lay between the rivers Kaitna and Juah. When Wellesley first sighted them they had formed their line along the northern bank of the Kaitna. Wellesley decided to try to turn the Maratha left and with this intention he crossed the Kaitna a few miles to the east. Seeing what was afoot, the Marathas opened a heavy cannonade—which however, proved largely ineffective, achieving little more than decapitating Wellesley's orderly, whose headless torso remained in the saddle offering a gruesome spectacle to the army.[34] Accordingly, the Maratha commander changed tactics shifting their front to face the British, 'in the most steady manner possible, though not exactly according to Dundas'.[35] Their new position extended north-south from the village Assaye on the bank of the Juah to the Kaitna. Their infantry was lined up behind the cannon.

The British crossed the stream without much loss and deploying their infantry in two lines one behind the other in echelon, prepared to attack the new Maratha position. The extreme left of the first line was occupied by the King's 78th which was expected to attack and turn the enemy's right flank. The extreme right of the second line was held by the other European regiment, the King's 74th. As the advance began, the Marathas intensified their fire and 'shots which were so ineffective before now fell like hail and knocked down men, horses and bullocks every shot'.[36] Indeed so devastating was the Maratha artillery that the sepoys in the centre began to panic, many crowding behind the 78th in order to avoid the deadly fire.[37] But it stopped

[33] Wellesley's army at the time comprised two regiments of European infantry (the King's 78th and 74th), four regiments of sepoys, one regiment of European and three regiments of Indian cavalry and 12 guns.

[34] Colebrooke, *The Life*, p. 66.

[35] Blakiston, *Twelve Years*, vol. 1, pp. 161-2. The 'Dundas' referred to here is Colonel David Dundas whose system of military training was in use in the Company's army at the time.

[36] Colebrooke, *The Life*, p. 66.

[37] Blakiston, *Twelve Years'*, p. 163. Blakiston also voiced many sepoys taking advantage of 'any irregularities in the ground to shelter themselves from the deadly shower, or

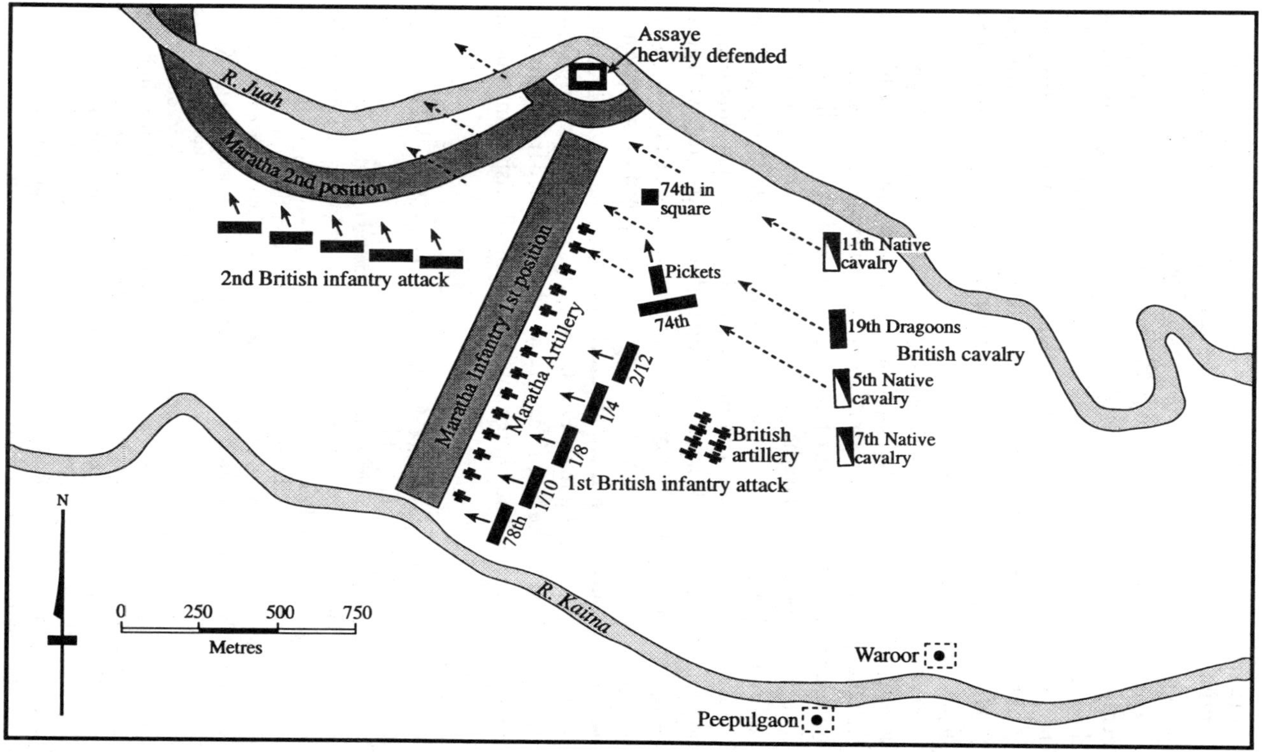


Plan 4: The Battle of Assaye, 23 September 1803.

short of wholesale disintegration. Despite heavy losses the British continued to move forward and eventually they got close enough to launch a bayonet charge on the enemy artillery.

The struggle for the guns was bloody but brief. In a remarkable demonstration of courage, Scindia's artillerymen continued to load their guns until struck by British bayonets.[38] However, the Maratha infantry proved to be of lesser mettle, 'standing no longer than the guns fired'.[39] Their right and centre now abandoned their first position and fell back on a second line along the river Juah, leaving a large number of cannon in British hands.

In the meantime, disaster had struck the British. The King's 74th which formed the extreme right of the second line, had made the mistake of straying close to the heavily fortified village of Assaye. It suffered heavily from the fire from the village and from a full-blooded charge by a body of Maratha cavalry which cut in among its shaken ranks. The situation was rescued however, by a counter-charge from the British cavalry, which had been guarding the British line from a possible outflanking movement and pursued across the Juah with great slaughter.[40] Meanwhile the British infantry had renewed its attack on the Maratha second line. The first assault by the sepoy units were beaten back but before the 78th could reform the Marathas turned around and hastened across the Juah. One body of this retreating infantry was at once charged by the British cavalry who had returned from pursuing the Maratha horse. The charge miscarried, the British commanding

---

that even, in some few instances, not all the endeavours of the officers could pursuade them to move forward'. Ibid., pp. 164-5.

[38] It is not quite clear whether the British infantry opened fire before going in with the bayonet. The description of the battle given by sergeant Swarbrook does mention the use of musketry by the British side: 'When our Infantry was all formed they opened a severe fire of musketry but the Enemy keeping such a heavy fire of round and grape shot our infantry suffered severe. The Right Brigade charged but was forced to retreat.' NAM Mss. 8207-64. However, it is quite possible that this was limited to the King's 74th. This regiment which was on the extreme right of the British line, was also the infantry unit that was closest to the British cavalry, and Swarbrook's account of the battle deals almost exclusively with the action which occurred on the right of the British line. Captain Blakiston, who was with the King's 78th on the extreme left does not mention firing. Therefore, the likelihood is that the use of musketry was limited to the British infantry on the right of their line and the King's 78th, which was pivotal in turning the Maratha right flank charged home without waiting to open fire.

[39] Blakiston, *Twelve Years'*, p. 165.

[40] Ibid., p. 169.

officer being killed, but by now the Maratha army was in full retreat. Assaye had been a fearsome encounter. The Marathas were left with nearly 1,200 dead and almost all their artillery and British casualties were also heavy.[41] Nevertheless it was a clear British victory and a decisive stroke in the destruction of Maratha military power.

### *Laswari, 1 November 1803*[42]

While Wellesley was settling scores with Scindia and Bhonsle in the Deccan, Lake was crossing swords with what was left of Scindia's foreign mercenaries in the Deccan. On 11 September he defeated twelve battalions of regular Maratha infantry under their French commander Louis Bourquin within sight of the minarets of Delhi, and shortly after, entered the city bringing the aging Mughal emperor under British protection. Bourquin and almost all the other remaining European mercenaries deserted with the defeat at Delhi but the Maratha survivors from the battle were now joined by the force sent from the Deccan under the command of Ambaji Inglia, confronting Lake with a rather more formidable challenge when he caught up with them on 1 November near the village of Laswari.

When he met the Marathas, Lake had only eight regiments of cavalry. With these slender resources he decided to attack Inglia who had under his command nearly 10,000 infantry, 5,000 cavalry and 75 guns. Again, the guns were posted in the front of the Maratha line whose right flank lay on a deep stream and the left flank near the village of Mohalpur. Despite breaking through the Maratha line, the British cavalry could not capture the guns in the absence of infantry support and draught animals. When the infantry arrived later in the day, Lake decided to attack the Maratha right flank with his infantry. The British infantry was formed in two columns. The first column was led by the King's 76th and also included five battalions of native infantry. Their task was

[41] The British casualties were: killed: 198 Europeans and 230 sepoys; wounded: 442 Europeans and 650 sepoys. Figures from Thorn, *A Memoir*, p. 280.

[42] The following battle description I have depended on Lake's two despatches appearing in Owen, *Wellesley Despatches*, pp. 404-7; and Robert Montgomery Martin (ed.), *The Despatches, Minutes and Correspondence of the Marquess Wellesley During his Administration in India*, 5 vols., New Delhi: Inter India Publishers, 1984; 1st pub. 1836, vol. 3, pp. 444-5; Thorn, *A Memoir*, pp. 213-29; and two other eye-witness accounts left by one C. Russell, BM Add. 13857, pp. 48-51 and the description left by an anonymous participant, OIOC Mss. Eur. B. 401.

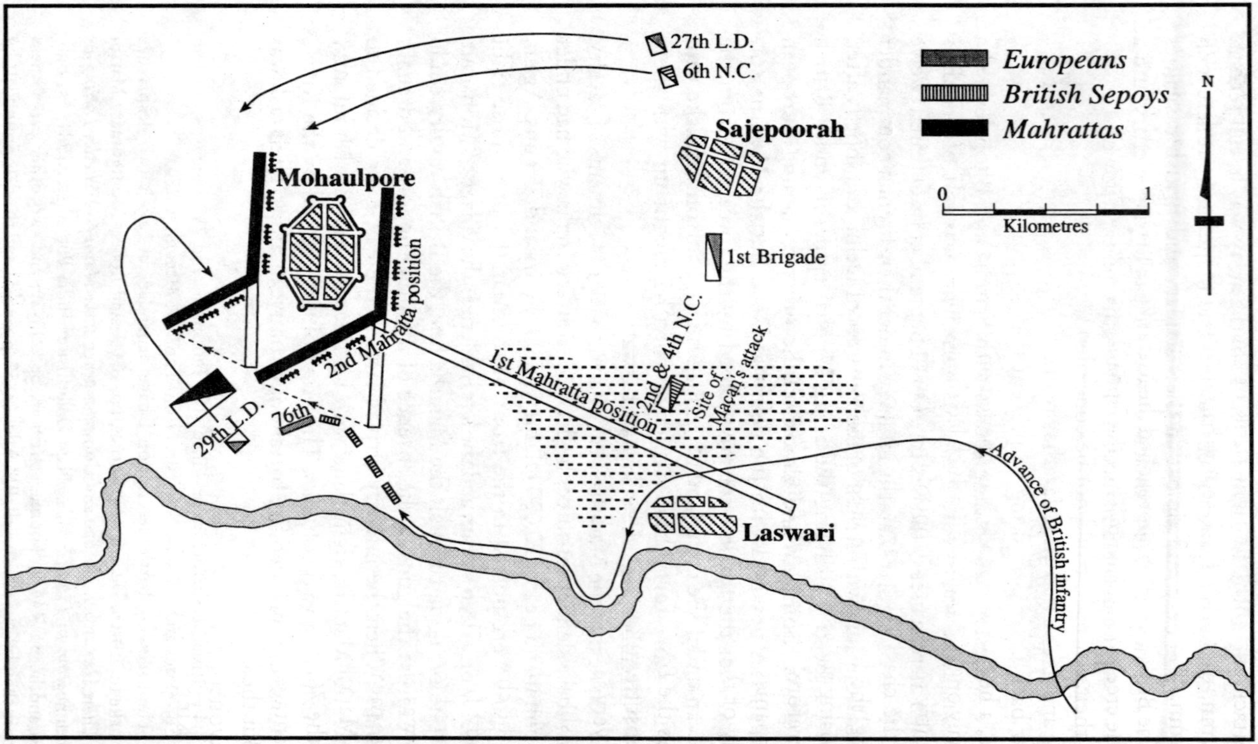


Plan 5: The Battle of Laswari, 1 November 1803.

to attack and turn the right flank of the Maratha line. The second column, comprising six sepoy battalions, was to support the first column.

The British infantry approached the Maratha position along the banks of the creek, concealed by the tall elephant grass that covered the plain. But their objective could not be concealed from the Marathas for too long and as soon as the Marathas realized what was happening, they drew back their right wing to prevent it being turned. At the same time, a heavy cannonade was opened on the British infantry who fell heavily on the King's 76th, which led the column. Eventually, the British infantry reached the front of the Maratha left flank, ready to draw up for the charge. However, the rest of the column was still struggling along the bank of the creek and waiting for them to arrive risked exposing those who had already formed up to a very destructive fire. Therefore, Lake ordered the 76th, one sepoy battalion and a few companies from another sepoy battalion that had got ahead of the body of the column to commence the attack without waiting for the rest.

As the British infantry came within range of Maratha canister shot 'a most tremendous fire was opened upon them. The loss they suffered was very severe, and sufficient prevent a regular advance.'[43] As desperate British officers struggled to prevent the sepoys from breaking up,[44] the Maratha cavalry appeared in the distance, on the British left, ready for the charge. The British infantry though received the charge with a steady fire, breaking up the closely bunched horsemen. Now Lake ordered the 29th dragoons to disperse the broken Maratha horse and this was effected without much difficulty. Not only did the dragoons chase the Maratha cavalry from the field, they also charged the right of the Maratha line and broke through the line of cannon and infantry. As the 76th and the sepoy units accompanying it pushed home their advantage, the Maratha first line abandoned their guns.

But the battle was far from over. The second Maratha line delivered a bayonet charge on the advancing British. The attack was repulsed by the King's 76th, forcing the Marathas to give way. A portion of the

[43] Lake to Lord Wellesley, 2 November 1803. Owen, *Wellesley Despatches*, p. 406.

[44] There is some evidence of confusion in the sepoy ranks at this stage. For instance, we hear how Major-General Ware was cut down by a cannon ball soon after he frantically urged another officer to 'put the sepoys in some kind of order' so that they could support the King's 76th in their charge on the Maratha cannon. OIOC Mss. Eur. B. 401.

fleeing Marathas tried to make a stand near a mosque behind the village of Mohalpur but the 29th dragoons now returned to the charge, this time from the rear. The Marathas, already in disarray, were caught between two fires and many were cut down. Although the left wing attempted to make an orderly retreat, they were charged by the remaining British cavalry and decimated.

By this stage the battle was effectively over, the Maratha casualties testifying to the completeness of their destruction: 7,000 killed and 2,000 captured. As well, the Marathas lost 72 guns and the entire baggage train. British casualties on the other hand were comparatively light: in all 823 killed and wounded.[45]

The actions just described were not the only major encounters between the British and their Indian opponents during our period, but they were certainly among the fiercest. As such, they are also good examples of what the British expected from their regular sepoys in high-pressure battlefield conditions. What do these great battles of British conquest say about the sepoys' place in the Company's army?

## THE DIVISION OF LABOUR IN THE COMPANY'S WARS

The deployment of troops in the above actions show a confidence in the sepoys on the part of the British military that is in sharp contrast to the skepticism of the 1750s. In contrast to the pre-1760 period, the sepoys were now routinely exposed to the fury of the enemy's attack. At Buxar, Tiruvannamalai and Porto Novo, the sepoys had to withstand attacks by the enemy infantry and cavalry while at the first two battles they were also thrown against strong enemy defences. At Assaye and Laswari the sepoys faced deadly artillery fire. There was certainly no attempt to 'hide' the sepoys as there had been, to some extent, during the 1750s. The performance of the sepoys by and large, vindicated that confidence. There were occasional signs of wavering and confusion, as at Buxar and Assaye, but generally, the sepoys' behaviour was above reproach.

Thus, one could say that the lengthy process of reorganizing the sepoys since the late 1750s had translated into greater confidence in

[45] The British deaths in action amounted to 95 European and 77 sepoys while 310 Europeans and 339 sepoys were wounded. They also lost 277 horses killed and 154 missing. Figures from Thorn, *A Memoir*, p. 230.

the native soldier's ability to handle formidable opposition. But Srirangapattanam defies this pattern of confident deployment. The assault on Srirangapattanam clearly showed a marked preference for European troops to lead the assault. A very considerable number of Europeans—a little over five regiments—led both attacking columns while only sixteen companies—about a regiment and a half—of sepoys followed them.

Moreover, Srirangapattanam was not an isolated case. As shown in the Appendix, the choice of Europeans to lead attacks on fortifications seems to have been the rule rather than the exception. The list is of course, not exhaustive; it includes only the major assaults carried out by the EIC forces during our period. As in the early period, sepoys were often used without European troops in countless minor operations designed to 'pacify' the countryside[46] and the storming duties during these operations were naturally carried out by sepoy assault parties. But these actions were trivial when compared to the assaults on major fortifications like Bangalore or Srirangapattanam which belonged to powerful enemies. As shown in the Appendix, European troops always led these major assaults. Interestingly, this division of labour prevailed even during minor operations when small European detachments happened to accompany sepoys on pacification operations as it was the case during the pacification of the poligars in the 1760s and 1780s.

[46] For example, when Raja Cheyt Singh of Benares rebelled in 1781 in protest at Hasting's extreme demands for tribute, several sepoy battalions were despatched to bring the disaffected rajah to heel. In the main battle of the campaign fought at Patteeta (September 1781) only one sepoy battalion supported by two grenadier companies drawn from another sepoy battalion took part. See Captain Thomas Blair's description of the battle in Warren Hastings, *A Narrative of the Insurrection in the Zameendary of Benaris in 1781 and the Transactions of the Governor-General in the District*, Calcutta, 1782, p. 100. Often such pacification duties were entrusted to detachments composed only of a few companies of sepoys. See the description of the campaigns against the *fakirs* in western Bengal in the early 1780s in Atis K. Dasgupta, *The Fakir and Sanyasi Uprisings*, Calcutta: K.P. Bagchi, 1992, pp. 84-97. On the use of sepoys in Pacification operations see also Bryant, 'Pacification', p. 3. At times, sepoys were used in very small numbers to deter incursions by forest and mountain tribes into more settled areas. For instance, in March 1770, a British official stationed at Rajamahal suggested to Richard Beecher, the British Resident at Murshidabad that 4 or 5 sepoys be stationed at every village between Rajamahal and Faruckabad, 'so that the sepoys from two or three villages will be able to assemble on any alarm and when joined will be a sufficient force against ten times the number of mountaineers'. William Harwood to Richard Beecher, 3 March 1770. *Records of the Government of Bengal: Letter and Copy Book of the Resident at Durbar at Murshidabad 1769-70*, Calcutta: Bengal Secretariat Press, 1919, p. 46.

On these expeditions, the Europeans were invariably given the task of leading assaults on forts. For example, when the fort of Wissnellore had to be stormed in May 1768, twenty European volunteers and the grenadiers from the Madras European regiment were ordered to lead the assault ahead of the grenadiers of the three sepoy battalions present.[47] As James Welsh observed in 1801, it was 'next to madness' to take a poligar fort 'without even a few Europeans to lead the storming party'.[48]

In other words, where Europeans were present, sepoys never headed assaults and Europeans were present in all major and some minor operations. Interestingly, this preference for Europeans in attack was not altogether absent in the other actions either. Note at Assaye how Wellesley placed a European regiment on the extreme left of the line where he intended to break through the Maratha defences.[49] It was a similar story at Laswari too. Lake's object was to turn the Maratha right and, by placing the European regiment at the head of the attacking column, he signaled that he intended to use the Europeans for the task. Given the approach in column, the leading unit of the column—the 76th—would have formed the extreme left of the attacking line when it was formed—just as at Assaye. This would have given the King's 76th the same duty as the King's 78th at Assaye, which was to break through and roll the Maratha right flank.

Thus, at both Assaye and Laswari, European units occupied the points in the British battle formation that was crucial to forcing the decision. Where does this leave the other encounters we have looked at?

[47] OIOC O.V. 77, p. 52. A good example of the priority reserved for European troops in leading assaults even against minor forts was provided during Lake's campaign against the Marathas in 1803. In the Fort of Sasni was unsuccessfully attacked using an advanced party of sepoys before the King's 76th had come up. When the fort was attacked again after the arrival of the 76th, the British grenadiers were promptly chosen to lead the attack. John Pester, *War and Sport in India: an Officer's Diary*, London: Heath, Cranton and Ousley Ltd., 1914, p. 51.

[48] Welsh, *Military Reminiscences*, vol. 1, p. 54.

[49] Wellesley wrote that, as he 'had foreseen, the corps at Assaye was not defeated till worked upon by the centre and left of our lines, not withstanding the movement of the piquets, the 74th and the cavalry'. Gurwood, *Despatches*, vol. 1, pp. 729-30. This clearly shows that Wellesley's objective was to turn the Maratha right which was facing the left and centre of the British line, and in such a manoeuver the unit on the extreme left, the King's 78th, would have provided the first breakthrough. The rest of the British line would follow suit along the line, thus 'rolling up' the Maratha flank.

At Assaye and Laswari the thrust of the attacking formation was generally spread along the line rather than being concentrated on a particular point. Still, even at Tiruvannamalai and Porto Novo, all available European units were placed, along with some sepoy units, in the body which attacked the main force of the opposition while detachments composed exclusively of sepoy units held some of the strategically important features. At Buxar, where the attack was delivered in two lines, European units were included in the centre of both. One cannot be too certain, but it was possibly a measure taken to 'strengthen' both lines in anticipation of an attack from the swarms of cavalry that surrounded the Company's troops while they advanced to the attack.

These examples demonstrate that, despite an increased confidence in their sepoys, the European troops were still treated as the main strength of an attacking party and when, as at Laswari and Assaye there was a clear point of focus in the attacking formation, European troops were clearly preferred over the native troops. It is true that at Tiruvannamalai and Porto Novo, sepoys also accompanied European soldiers in delivering the main attack. Yet, in acknowledging that, it need be asked why did the British not make these bodies *exclusively* native? Why didn't they get the Europeans to hold the hills and rocks while the sepoys alone delivered the main attack? I shall endeavour to find the answer to this in the next chapter.

*Five*

# The Sepoy and British Perceptions

THE FOREGOING DISCUSSION has revealed some interesting features in the English East India Company's approach to creating an army of native soldiers. I have already shown how the British superseded the segmented command structure in the early sepoy army with a regular chain of command dominated by European officers. At the same time, rigorous discipline was introduced but still the Company showed a reluctance to press for obedience where the religious prejudices of the sepoys were concerned. But the most interesting aspect of the sepoy army was in its deployment in the field. The British showed a marked reluctance to depend on sepoys when it came to hard fighting, particularly when storming fortified places. My aim in this chapter is to explore the rationale behind these decisions. I shall begin by examining the perceptions behind the Company's recruitment policy.

## BRITISH PERCEPTIONS AND THE RECRUITMENT AND MANAGEMENT OF SEPOYS

It was seen in the third chapter that when recruiting sepoys, the Company gravitated mainly towards men of Turkish and Arabian descent during the Anglo-French hostilities in the Carnatic. This preference was probably due to their reputation as loyal and brave soldiers. As pointed out in the 'Introduction', in the early nineteenth century, Arabs had a reputation for being brave soldiers. Similar situation most probably existed in the mid-eighteenth century when the French and the British began recruiting sepoys. The value placed on Arabian troops is clearly shown by the fact that when 1,000 Arabians in the French service offered their services to the British in 1760 the British decided to pay them Rs. 16 each while only Rs. 11 were offered to non-Arabs.[1] The Arabs certainly had a reputation for loyalty; when

[1] Madras Mil. and Sec. Cons., 10 January 1760, OIOC P/D/43.

Fort St. David asked for Arabs in 1747 the reason given was that they were 'less liable to desertion' than the Company's peons.[2] The Turks also shared a reputation for valour, among Europeans, thanks to their ferocious encounters with European forces in Europe and the Middle East. The Turks were thought, for the same reason, to be more familiar with European methods of fighting.[3] Turks and Arabs probably had an advantage in terms of physical stature too, being generally taller and strongly built than most natives of the subcontinent.

Considerations for physical fitness also operated in favour of the north Indian peasantry. But here, physical attributes were linked to the pastoralist background of the soldiers rather than their ethnicity. Contemporary European armies preferred men from a peasant stock due to their being inured to physical hardships and the current belief in the connection between climate and physical toughness favoured men from colder, harsher climates. In the British Army, the Scottish highlanders in particular, were considered ideal soldiers due to their rustic environment and lifestyle.[4] As I have already shown, Orme classed the men from the wheat-growing regions of northern India to be physically more robust and stronger than the more 'effeminate' men from the south and Forbes associated the athletic form of Rajputs to the bracing climate of Rajasthan.

Given these considerations it is not difficult to understand the preference—particularly in the Bengal Army—for the peasantry from northern India. The poorer 'ashrafi' gentry from Bihar were described as 'excellently adapted for soldiers, being hardy men of high spirits'.[5] So were the Rajput peasantry. Indeed, one early nineteenth century English officer even spoke of the 'Brahmin and Rajpoot yeomanry of the Upper Provinces' when talking of the Bengal sepoys.[6] Tall, sturdily

[2] FSD Cons., 16 March 1747, OIOC FR G/18/6, pp. 46-7. Significantly, the Marathas also valued Arabs highly as brave soldiers. Arthur Wellesley to the Governor of Ceylon, 14 October 1803. Gurwood (ed.), *Despatches*, vol. 1, p. 785.

[3] Horn, *Kriegwesens*, p. 24.

[4] Alavi, *Sepoys*, pp. 35-7. Peers, 'The Habitual Nobility', p. 50. As General David Stewart of Garth put it in 1822, 'the simplicity of his [the highlander's] life gave rigour to his body, so it fortified his mind. Possessing a frame and constitution thus hardened, he was taught to honour courage as the most honourable virtue, cowardice the most disgraceful thing'. Peter Simpson, *The Independent Highland Companies 1603-1760*, Edinburgh: J. Donald, 1996, p. 18.

[5] Francis Buchanan, *An Account of the Districts of Bihar and Patna in 1811-1812*, New Delhi: Usha Publications, 1986, 1st edn. 1934.

[6] Cited in Peers, *Between Mars and Mammon*, p. 89. Interestingly, Sita Ram describes himself as of 'yeoman' stock. Here, we are probably hearing the voice of his commanding

built men, they fitted the bill perfectly. According to a British officer who campaigned in Ceylon in 1803, the Bengal sepoys who served on the island were all 'tall and well-proportioned men, well-featured, of a light bronze colour'.[7] Many of the sepoys from the north even towered above the Company's European troops who appeared like 'a regiment of dwarfs'[8] in their presence.

Peasant background was not the only factor that favoured Rajput recruitment. As noted earlier, caste also played a role. This was on the one hand, largely circumstantial. Since the Company was utilizing indigenous recruiting networks it had to necessarily gravitate towards the Rajputs and other military castes who dominated the military labour market on the subcontinent. Related to this was the reputation the Rajputs had as a martial caste. As James Welsh explained, 'Rajahpoots' were 'the bravest and most devoted soldiers, far surpassing all other natives in a romantic [though] sometimes mistaken notion of honour'.[9]

But at another level, recruitment of Rajputs—and indeed all higher castes—also made political sense because of the social and political dominance of these groups. In the north, the Raja of Benares and the Nawab of Awadh had set the example by raising large armies of Rajput warriors which cemented their alliance with the local lineages, and the British were only too eager to follow that lead.[10] But there was more to this appreciation of the political importance of winning over the political and social elites. The policy was also heavily influenced by the growing awareness in the Company's official circles of the importance of the institution of caste, thanks mainly to the efforts of Orientalist scholars, who were unravelling the complexities of the Indian caste

---

officer who wrote the old subedar's 'autobiography' for him. Pandey, *Sepoy to Subedar*, p. 3.

[7] Alexander Alexander, *The Life of Alexander Alexander Written by Himself*, 2 vols., London, 1830, vol. 1, p. 166.

[8] General Joseph Smith to Bengal government, 2 November 1768. Cited in Michael H. Fisher (ed.), *The Travels of Dean Mahomet: an Eighteenth Century Journey Through India*, Berkeley: University of California Press, 1997, p. 15. Lord Cornwallis expressed similar views about the Bengal sepoys in 1786 when he wrote to the Duke of Yorke that the sepoys were 'fine men and would not in size disgrace the Prussian ranks'. Cited in Raymond Callahan, *East India*, p. 71.

[9] Welsh, *Military Reminiscences*, vol. 1, p. 14. One Colonel Cathcart, a King's officer described the Bengal sepoys in the 1780s as having a 'nice sense of honour' and 'soldiers by birth'. Crisp, *British India Analysed*, 3, p. 807.

[10] Alavi, *Sepoys*, p. 39.

system. It is certainly no coincidence that Warren Hastings, who was one of the earliest patrons of Orientalism was also responsible for laying the foundations for a high-caste dominated army in Bengal.

Likewise, the Company's efforts to respect the sepoys' religious sensitivities were only a natural consequence of the rising general awareness of the prejudices peculiar to the caste system. But where the attempts to satisfy the material needs of the sepoys were concerned, the British were influenced by the perception of a strong mercenary streak at work in the Indian military culture. As Colonel John Carnac explained to Henry Vansittrat in 1761, it was 'from the superiority of pay alone' that the British could 'expect to have the best of the country forces'.[11] Carnac was writing in the early 1760s when the sepoy army was just emerging as a regular force, but the British conviction that the sepoy was essentially a mercenary soldier did not wane with the growth of the sepoy army. Thus we hear Captain Henry White of the Madras Army explaining in 1795 that all sepoys were mercenaries 'unsusceptible to the sentiment of public spirit' who entered the Company's service 'on a principle of self-interest, the superior certainty of regular pay and allowances'.[12] Such men could not be satisfied by attention to spiritual needs alone.

Thus, the appreciation of cultural distinctiveness and the recognition of the mercenary character of military service on the subcontinent were influential in shaping the Company's policy towards the discipline and the general management of their sepoy army. The interesting thing however, is that the sepoys themselves played a major role in encouraging these perceptions. The numerous small-scale sepoy mutinies that took place during this period clearly revealed the major concerns of the Company's native soldiers. The already noted mutiny of the Bengal sepoys in 1764 occurred over the distribution of prize money. The later mutinies in the Bengal Army, however, had religious undertones to them. The most serious of these mutinies occurred in 1795 when the 15th battalion of Bengal native infantry refused to sail for Malacca to fight the French for fear of losing caste.[13] Attempts to

[11] Carnac to Vansittrat, 3 March 1761, OIOC Mss. Eur. F. 128/4.

[12] Captain Henry White to Madras government, 24 March 1795. Madras Mil. and Pol. Cons., 26 March 1795, OIOC P/253/43, p. 949.

[13] For example, the 15th battalion of Bengal native infantry broke into mutiny in August 1795 when ordered to Malacca. See Bengal Mil. Cons., 9 October 1795, OIOC P/19/6.

Plate 7: Sepoy and family with wife and children, riding a bullock, sepoy in undress carrying a sword, by a Tanjore artist *c.* 1800. OIOC Add. Or. 2528.

persuade the mutinous sepoys to lay down their arms led to violence, resulting in the death of many mutineers.[14]

The grievances of the sepoys in the more heterogeneous Madras and Bombay presidencies were more complex. For instance, when the 35th battalion of Madras native infantry mutinied in Colombo in March 1796 it was in reaction to the hardships they suffered due to separation from their families.[15] In 1785, long standing arrears in pay had driven two other Madras battalions—the 31st and 32nd—into open mutiny,[16] while hardships associated with separation from their families drove the 35th battalion of Madras native infantry to down their arms in Colombo in March 1796.[17] But even in Madras, religion was not a non-issue. The most serious act of insubordination—the Vellore mutiny and related incidents of 1806—had religious undertones, the unrest being sparked by the introduction of a headdress which closely resembled a Europeans' hat and the prohibition of the display of caste marks. The disturbances at the out-stations also revealed deep-seated grievances relating to intolerable service conditions like low pay and excessive drill.[18] These grievances were exploited by the disgruntled local elite incarcerated in the Vellore Fort, resulting in a bloodbath of unprecedented scale.

Thus, as far as these mutinies are concerned the Company's native soldiers rebelled for want of pay, prize money and *batta*, as a result of fears about separation from their families and perceived threats to religious identity. In almost all mutinies it was a combination of several

[14] Lieutenant-Colonel Erskine to Colonel Peter Murray, 6 October 1795. Bengal Mil. Cons., 9 October 1795, OIOC P/19/6, pp. 592-6.

[15] Colonel Stuart to Madras Council, 21 March 1796. Madras Mil. and Sec. Cons., 5 April 1796, OIOC P/253/59, pp. 2560-2.

[16] Brigadier-General Matthew Horne to J. Huddlestone, Resident of Tanjore, 25 September 1785. Madras Mil. and Pol. Cons., 29 September 1785, OIOC P/252/3, pp. 1418-23.

[17] Colonel Stuart to Madras Council, 21 March 1796. Madras Mil. and Sec. Cons., 5 April 1796, OIOC P/253/59.

[18] Evidence to this effect comes mainly from Wallajabad where unrest materialized soon after the mutiny in Vellore. A British officer reported hearing the sepoys complain about having to clean their weapons after parade, declaring that they would rather kill their officers than submit to such rigours. The report of the Adjutant-General, 27 July 1806, OIOC Home Misc. 507, pp. 483-5. Later the wife of an English officer stationed at Wallajabad claimed she overheard sepoys speaking of their officers 'in the vilest language unfit to be repeated' and talking about throwing their miserable pay in their officers' face. Evidence of Mrs. Revier, 28 July 1806, OIOC Home Misc., 507, pp. 494-5.

of these factors that provoked insubordination. The violence they were sometimes willing to resort to in order to defy their masters shows the strength of their feeling regarding these issues.

Therefore, it is fair to say that the Company's recognition of the need for tolerance towards religious practices and adequate pecuniary rewards was also based on feedback from the sepoys themselves. In other words, it was not purely out of respect for the indigenous alien culture that overseas travel was made voluntary in the Bengal Army; there were pressing military concerns as well. Just as European leadership was thought to be essential to make the sepoy efficient as a soldier, pandering to the sepoy's religious prejudices was generally considered the surest way to keep him loyal and under control. As one British officer, Major James Rennel explained, 'the indulgence of those very habits and prejudices constitute the chief hold the European employers have on their [sepoys'] minds and affections'.[19] The British response to the mutiny at Vellore clearly demonstrated the Company's reliance on conciliation rather than force where the sepoys' loyalty to the Company was threatened by his religious sensitivities. As always, British retribution was swift and ruthless. The mutiny was crushed with the aid of reinforcements from Arcot and nearly 350 mutineers were killed on the spot. The ringleaders among the survivors were severely punished—six blown from guns, eight shot by firing squad and six transported for life.[20] The two guilty regiments were also erased from the Madras Army. However, in spite of the severity of the punishments the British also reiterated their 'tenderness to religious scruples' by recalling the Commander-in-Chief Craddock and rescinding the offending regulations. Commenting on the lack of attention paid to sepoy grievances about the new regulations, the Directors pointed out that had it been revealed that widespread objection to the new turban existed, no compliance should have been expected from the sepoys, 'whatever might be the sacrifice'.[21]

[19] Major James Rennel, *The Marches of the British Armies in the Peninsula of India during the Campaign of 1790 and 1791*, London, 1792, p. 9. According to James Welsh, 'when their prejudices were humoured', the Rajputs were 'the bravest and most devoted soldiers'. Welsh, *Military Reminiscences*, vol. 1, p. 14.

[20] Wilson, *History*, vol. 3, p. 188.

[21] Wilson, *History*, vol. 3, pp. 198-200. The mutiny at Vellore was followed by minor disturbances at the garrisons at Wallajabad and Hyderabad. At Hyderabad the discontent was directly in opposition to the new dress code and subsided only after the new turban was withdrawn. At Wallajabad, sepoy discontent also took the form of dissatisfaction

The Company's commitment to conciliation as a major means of controlling sepoys is further underlined by their approach to the enforcement of physical punishment in the sepoy army. Some scholars have argued that the British consciousness of the upper caste Indians' abhorrence of physical punishment made them reluctant to employ corporal punishment as a means of enforcing discipline among sepoys—particularly in the Bengal Army.[22] While this may have been the view of some officers, the seriousness of this concern is doubtful, at least during our period. The directors did stress the need to use the sepoys 'with humanity'[23] but such directives do not seem to have been vigorously pursued. Corporal punishment was not inflicted in the Bengal Army as often as in the other presidencies but casual violence towards sepoys was widespread. According to a Bengal sepoy giving evidence before a court martial in 1795 it was usual for British officers to beat them with rattans as punishment.[24] Such treatment was not limited to ordinary sepoys either. Even sepoy officers were routinely abused and beaten with canes in the presence of their sepoys.[25] The reason for such apparently frequent mistreatment was probably the lack of concern among the sepoys themselves. Many Indian armies probably treated their soldiers worse than the EIC and when on the odd occasion the sepoys did complain about physical abuse, the Company took a stern view of it. For example, when, in 1768, some Indian officers in the Bombay Army complained of being 'often beaten and abused' by their European non-commissioned officers the Bombay Army issued a general order cautioning their European officers against using violence towards native troops.[26] But evidently, such complaints were not frequent or vehement enough for it to be of too great a concern for the Company.

---

over measly pay and rigorous discipline, the sepoys openly praising the Vellore mutineers and threatening their officers with a similar fate. However, little came out of such threats and the disaffected sepoys at Wallajabad were disarmed with the aid of reinforcements and their officers confined. See Maya Gupta, *Lord William Bentinck in Madras and the Vellore Mutiny 1803-07*, Delhi: Capital Publishers, 1986, pp. 219-34.

[22] See for example, Peers, 'Sepoys, Soldiers and the Lash: Race, Caste and Army Discipline in India 1820-1850', in *Journal of Imperial and Commonwealth History*, vol. 23, no. 3, 1995, pp. 211-47.

[23] Barat, *Bengal Native Infantry*, p. 34.

[24] Bengal Mil. Cons., 9 October 1795, OIOC P/19/6 p. 737.

[25] *Observations and Remarks*, 1798, pp. 37-8.

[26] OIOC Mss. Eur. C. 155, p. 55.

Thus, the Company's attitudes to the discipline and general management of the sepoy army were influenced by their perception of the peculiar needs and sensitivities of the sepoys. But how can we explain the command structure of the sepoy army and the deployment of the sepoys in battle?

## BRITISH PERCEPTIONS AND THE COMMAND AND DEPLOYMENT OF SEPOYS

The relegation of sepoys to a secondary status—both as officers and soldiers—presents an interesting situation. In terms of discipline, training and leadership, there was no difference between the sepoys and their European counterparts. The only difference was in the human material and this was evidently the basis of the distinction made between Sepoys and European troops. What does this tell us about the British perceptions behind this discrimination?

The rationale behind this was not clearly explained but it seems that there were strong concerns for security when it came to entrusting sepoy officers with command. As the Madras government explained when abolishing the native commandant's post, 'when they [commandants] are clever men their influence over the native officers and sepoys become dangerous, and when they are not so they can be of no use'.[27] But the need for European command was more frequently expressed in terms of the incompetence of sepoy officers. The Madras government had decided to form sepoy battalions in December 1758 but it was the behaviour of the sepoys during the French siege that seems to have convinced the Fort St. George Council of the urgency for European control. Soon after the siege was raised, the Madras Council minuted: that having found it 'impracticable to maintain that order and regularity among the sepoys under their own commandants as the nature of their services requires. . . . There is reason to believe that they may be made more useful by being put under the command of a careful European officer.'[28] When he formed the first sepoy battalions in Bengal, Clive was no doubt going by his experiences with the sepoys in the Carnatic. The Bombay government evinced a similar conviction when they formed their first regular sepoy battalions with permanent European leadership. The turning point came in 1767 when

[27] Quoted in Wilson, *History*, vol. 2, p. 174.
[28] Quoted in Love, *Vestiges*, vol. 3, p. 547.

their sepoys fared poorly in a campaign against the Sidis in 1767. The Bombay government was quick to attribute it 'solely to the want of European officers as on the other coast', and resolved to form their sepoys into battalions under European officers.[29]

The gradual increase in European control was but the logical extension of this rationale behind the formation of the first sepoy battalions. In 1769, the Court of Directors in London advised the Bengal Council to appoint as many European officers as possible to the sepoy units as European officers were considered essential to the establishment of discipline and subordination among the native troops.[30] As shown by the following resolution by the Bengal government, the European officers were expected to discipline the sepoys by keeping the Indian officers themselves in line:

> The good discipline of all troops is owing to the care the officers take to enforce it; the black sepoy officers are but too often remiss—it is therefore recommended to the European officers, to enforce command and obedience amongst them, and endeavour, by encouragement and good treatment to the active and by punishing the remiss, to make them keep good order and discipline among their sepoys.[31]

But there was more to European leadership than instilling discipline. European officers were also expected to provide a moral example to the sepoys; Colonel Robert Kelly of the Madras Army claimed in 1782 that the biggest strength of the sepoy army was its English officers who infused a 'martial spirit' to the sepoys.[32] Likewise, the contemporary historian of the Second Mysore War, Innes Munro, assured his readers that, according to veterans in the army, when led by European officers, the sepoys behaved 'with astonishing conduct and intrepidity'.[33]

[29] Bombay Pub. Cons., P/341/30, pp. 703-4.

[30] Secret Committee of the Directors to Fort William, 11 November 1768. N.K. Sinha (ed.), *Fort William India House Correspondence and Other Contemporary Papers Relating Thereto*, Public Series, 21 vols., New Delhi: National Archives, 1949, vol. 5, p. 153.

[31] OIOC MR L/MIL/17/2/438, p. 299. The same instructions appear in most orders and regulations relating to the organization and discipline of the sepoys. See for example the regulations governing the formation of the first sepoy battalions at Madras in September 1759 and the Madras military regulations of 1 January 1766. Wilson, *History*, vol. 1, pp. 149 and 233.

[32] OIOC Mss. Eur. D. 1146/6, p. 80.

[33] Munro, *Narrative*, pp. 23-4.

When sepoys suffered reverses, they were often attributed to the lack of European officers. Following the ill behaviour of some sepoy units during the campaign against the Marathas in 1774 Brigadier-General Robert Gordon of the Bombay Army promptly called for more European subalterns for each sepoy battalion. Without at least one to each company, he felt, 'posts of importance' could not be entrusted to the sepoys, 'nor their services depended upon'.[34] His views were echoed by Lieutenant Edward Moor during the Second Mysore War (1790-2) who explained a defeat suffered by a company of grenadier sepoys as the result of both their European officers being killed at the beginning of the action. He recommended more European officers, emphasizing: 'So long as their officers are with them, sepoys will behave like soldiers and no longer.'[35]

If competence and security were the main concerns that governed British attitudes to sepoy officers what was the rationale behind relegating the sepoys to a secondary role in combat, particularly when acting in an offensive capacity? To understand the reasoning behind the preference for Europeans to play a major role in attack, especially in leading assaults, one needs to look closely at the various military implications of attacking a fortress. An assault was always made in the formation of a column of about one or two companies (anything between 80 to 100 men) across and much deeper than that depending on the number of people involved.[36] Assaulting a breach in this formation was always a very daunting task, especially for those who led the attack. They had to proceed in the face of a heavy fire, and, usually, the fire of the majority of the defendants would be concentrated on the head of the assault column. To some extent, it is true, this could be countered by maintaining a 'covering fire' on the walls—as happened at Srirangapattanam—but once the assailants were in the breach they

[34] Quoted in Cadell, *Bombay Army*, p. 111.

[35] Moor even claimed that the enemy deliberately targeted the European officers in order to create panic among the sepoys. Moor, *A Narrative*, pp. 385-7. Arthur Wellesley's views in this regard, expressed in a memorandum in 1805, is also interesting. 'Those acquainted with the sepoys,' he wrote, 'know well that they will do nothing against their enemy excepting led by, and in the sight of their officers.' Memorandum on a proposed plan of an interchange of native troops of India and the Negro troops of the West Indies, Sydney J. Owen (ed.), *A Selection From the Indian Despatches, Memoranda & ca. of the Duke of Wellington*, Oxford: Clarendon, 1880, p. 459.

[36] See John A. Lynn, *The Bayonets of the Republic: Motivation and Tactics in the Army of Revolutionary France 1791-94*, Chicago: University of Illinois Press, 1984, p. 245.

were on their own, left to clear the breach in a confused hand-to-hand struggle with the enemy who often outnumbered them.[37] It was a daunting task: there was a very good reason for calling the leading men in an assault party the 'forlorn hope'.

Therefore, the leading units in an assault column were expected to meet with and overcome the initial and toughest opposition from the defenders. By contrast, the tail of the column was required merely to mop up the broken resistance—a comparatively less daunting task. At Srirangapattanam, this was clearly shown by the overwhelmingly large number of casualties suffered by the leading European units in contrast to the comparatively light losses suffered by the sepoys.[38]

To use a metaphor, throwing an assault column at a breach was like driving a nail into a wall; the harder and sharper the point, the greater the penetrative power. The persistence with Europeans to lead assaults shows simply that, as far as the Company was concerned, Europeans were more reliable than the sepoys in providing this hard, penetrative edge. In major actions like the assaults on Srirangapattanam in 1792 and 1799, this sharp European 'point' was very long. The sepoys, it seems, were to provide the weight of numbers, or to 'pack the punch', to use a colloquialism.

Why was it so? Arthur Wellesley provides the answer. According to him, the operations in India were often of an offensive nature and,

> it is possible in an offensive operation to have some of the troops who are to perform it, however desperate it may be, of an inferior nature. Accordingly, in proportion to the service to be performed, we have seen 1/2, 1/4, 1/6, 1/10 of the number of the army English soldiers . . . and it has always been customary

[37] Geoffrey Best, *War and Society in Revolutionary Europe 1770-1870*, Leicester: Leicester University Press, 1982, pp. 101-2; According to one English officer, Lieutenant-Colonel Fitzclarence, storming Indian fortresses was particularly daunting due to the unusually stiff opposition from the defenders: 'The Indians, in their defence of their forts, behave with the greatest gallantry and courage, and in this differ from the Europeans, who often fancy that, when a practicable breach is made in their walls, surrender becomes justifiable. But here [in India] all feel desirous of fighting man to man, and look upon the contest in the breach as the fittest occasion for meeting their enemies with sword and dagger.' Quoted in Irvine, *Army*, p. 273.

[38] Colonel John Caillaud's dispatch to the Madras Council regarding the abortive attempt on Madura in 1757 is illuminating in this regard. Lamenting the heavy losses suffered by the assault party he explained that 'the best, who were in the forefront as usual were all killed and wounded'. Caillaud to Council, 9 July 1757. Cited in Hill, *Yusuf Khan*, p. 68.

in wars in India to increase the proportion of the European troops to the natives, as the service should appear more arduous.[39]

Here, Wellesley is clearly treating the European troops as an essential stabilising or strengthening factor in the army. Eyre Coote's observation that 'no European could have been steadier'[40] than the sepoys at Porto Novo also underlines the perception that the European soldier set the standard in combat. As Lake declared after the Battle of Agra in September 1803 it was 'impossible to do great things in a gallant and quick style without Europeans'.[41]

Thus, European troops were expected to add to the army a steadiness and an aggressive spirit which the sepoys were not capable of providing on their own. But there was more to this 'European contribution' than strengthening the line and providing the 'sting' in attack. The European troops were also expected to produce a moral effect by inspiring the sepoys with confidence. This role had been recognized from an early time. The daring attack on the French detachment at Valikondapuram in 1752 was promptly explained as inspired by European troops: 'the continued series of successes which had attended our arms made 'em [sepoys] look upon themselves as sure of victory when supported by an English battalion' as one British officer explained.[42] Likewise, during

[39] Owen, *Wellington Despatches*, p. 458. A Company official giving evidence before the House of Commons Committee on the East India Company in 1767 declared that the sepoys were 'not to be depended without Europeans'. This was probably a reference to major campaigns. 'Minutes of the House of Commons Committee on the EIC', OIOC, Mss. Eur. D. 1018., pp. 5-6. It is also interesting what Wilks has to say about Eyre Coote's use of an exclusively sepoy force to attack Chidambaram in 1780. According to Wilks, it was the small number of European troops and 'a desire for reserving them for greater emergencies' that prevented the deployment of Europeans against the fort. Wilks, *Historical Sketches*, vol. 2, p. 307. This attitude was underlined by Eyre Coote when he requested more Europeans from Bengal during the Second Mysore War. Coote informed Hastings that without 'a great augmentation of European infantry' he dared not 'risk an engagement with Hyder Ali'. Quoted in G.R. Gleig, *The Life of Sir Thomas Munro*, 2 vols., London: Murray, 1849, vol. 2, pp. 336-7.

[40] Sheppard, *Coote Bahadur*, pp. 212-13.

[41] Martin, *Wellesley Despatches*, vol. 3, p. 396; Mountstuart Elphinstone, who was present at Assaye was equally convinced of the disparity between the native and European soldiers when it came to handling pressure on the battlefield. After the Maratha cavalry charge had scattered the King's 74th, he concluded that 'if the enemy had pushed the sepoys, they could never have stood what had overpowered the 74th'. G.W. Forrest (ed.), *Selections from the Minutes and other Official Writings of the Honourable Mountstuart Elphinstone*, London: Bentley, 1884, p. 12.

[42] OIOC Orme India III, p. 547.

the Second Mysore War the failure of an attack on Tricatapalli was explained as being due to the 'want of a few Europeans to serve as an example to the Black troops'[43] and Thomas Munro was quick to attribute the defeat of the Maratha regulars to the treachery of their European officers and the lack of 'the support and animating example of European regiments'.[44]

It would be correct then, to say that besides functioning as the main strength of the British forces in India, European troops were also expected to replicate the role of the European officer within the sepoy units. Just as the European officers provided leadership by being superior leaders, the European troops led the sepoys due to their being superior soldiers. In other words, the British saw the sepoy as dependent on Europeans—officers and soldiers—even for his limited effectiveness.

The fact that the sepoys did not show any marked deficiency in steadiness and resolve in combat did not undermine this attitude. The sepoys behaved creditably in all the actions described earlier—and in many others. For example, at the Battle of Sholinghur in September 1781, several battalions of Madras sepoys held their fire until Hyder's household cavalry, the flower of the Mysore Army, came within point-blank range before opening fire[45] and when Tipu's army made 'a most Furious and unprecedented attack' during British operations against Mysore on the west coast in November 1782, the 8th battalion of Bombay sepoys reserved their fire with great discipline until the Mysoreans came close.[46] Sometimes the sepoys even put the Europeans to shame with their resolve. For instance, during the British siege of Cuddalore in 1782, a battalion of Bengal sepoys stood up to a night

[43] OIOC Mss. Eur. F. 190, box 1.

[44] Munro to Colonel Read, 6 March 1804. Owen, *Wellesley Despatches*, pp. 791-2. It is interesting to note that similar sentiments existed in the French camp as well. This is quite evident from the plan for a proposed expedition to India drawn up sometime in 1798-9 by the former French Resident at the Maratha Court (1781-8), M. de Montigny. Speaking of the raising of a sepoy force, Montigny was of the opinion that 4 Europeans per company would be sufficient to lead the sepoys 'confidently into action'. He also added that animated 'by the presence of the French army, they could be trained to be excellent soldiers'. Hatalkar (ed.), *French Records*, 6, p. 490.

[45] OIOC Mss. Eur. F. 190, box 1.

[46] Colonel Macleod to Coote, 12 December 1782. *Correspondence During the Incapacitation*, p. 72.

attack by French troops when the European grenadiers who formed a picket broke and ran.[47]

Such gallantry earned high praise. I have already noted Eyre Coote's admiration for the sepoys at Porto Novo. Likewise, Wellesley was 'astonished' at the steadiness of the sepoys at Assaye.[48] But such behaviour was not sufficient to change deep-rooted perceptions. On the contrary, as with the command structure, failure of any sort tended to reinforce the existing doubts and help rationalize the *status quo*. Thus, when an ambush laid for Mysorian troops failed due to the hasty firing of a sepoy in 1767, Colonel Robert Kelly remarked contemptuously that it 'will serve as a caution, never to trust sepoys with loaded arms on any service'.[49] Likewise, when an attack made with sepoys on the Fort of Panjalamkurichchi in September 1799 failed, the Commanding Officer, Major Bannerman attributed the repulse to the absence of Europeans in the assault party. 'I have little doubt in my mind that the place could be carried as soon as the Europeans arrive without waiting for cannon to make a breach', he assured his superiors, concluding that the 'circumstance of one native officer being only wounded contrasted with four European officers killed and two wounded, will sufficiently mark the want of energy on the part of the natives'.[50]

But panic in battle is common to soldiers of all ages and can be the result of many factors like exposure to heavy fire, surprise or simple fatigue. The best soldiers in eighteenth century Europe sometime panicked for the most trivial reasons; at the Battle of Fontenoy in 1746 the French infantry broke and fled after facing one volley from the British while in 1758, during the Battle of Kay Prussian infantry refused

[47] According to Colonel Cathcart, one of the King's officers present, the sepoys who saved the European troops belonged to the 24th regiment of Bengal native infantry. Crisp, *British India Analysed*, vol. 3, pp. 799-803. It is probably the same incident that Meer Hussein Ali Khan Kirmani describes in his history of Tipu Sultan's reign, although he identifies the sepoys as a Carnatic regiment. Meer Hussein Ali Khan Kirmani, *The History of the Reign of Tipu Sultan Being a Continuation of the Neshani Hyduri*, trs. W. Miles, Delhi: Oriental Publishers, 1980; 1st pub. 1842, pp. 27-8.

[48] Wrote Wellesley: 'I assure that their [Maratha] fire was so heavy that I much doubted at one time whether I should be able to induce our troops to advance, and all agree that the battle was the fiercest that had ever been seen in India. Our troops behaved admirably. Our sepoys astonished me.' Quoted in Pythian Adams, *The Madras Regiment*, p. 140.

[49] Mss. Eur. D. 1146/6, p. 58.

[50] Quoted in Bishop R. Caldwell, *A History of Tinnevelly*, Delhi: Asian Educational Services, 1982, p. 183.

to advance against Russian field fortifications inspite of physical assaults from their officers.[51] As I have already shown, European troops in India also panicked. Sepoys were no exception. But the sepoys' panic had the potential to reinforce long-standing doubts about their reliability under fire while Europeans' faltering was often treated with disbelief. Take for instance the retreat of a European picket during the Mysorean siege of Mangalore in 1783. The Commander-in-Chief castigated the soldiers for being 'so shamefully backward and dastardly, as to be afraid to face the few of the cowardly enemy that came into the trenches; a situation where three Europeans were equal to all that could oppose them'.[52] Clearly, great deeds were expected from European troops.

Thus, despite all the confidence the English had in the leadership of European officers and the benefits of rigorous training, there existed a pervasive belief in the sepoys' limitations as soldiers. Generally, the sepoys were sound—but good behaviour could not wholly eliminate deep-rooted prejudice, lurking just below the surface and liable to be voiced at moments of crisis.

How can one explain these perceptions? Interestingly, in broad terms, they appear remarkably similar to the observations made by British officers in the following century when racist thinking about the sepoys' innate weakness was beginning to assert itself. As noted earlier, nineteenth century racist observations of the sepoys portrayed the native soldier as innately inferior to the European in both courage and leadership qualities which made British control over them a part of the natural order. But it was also pointed out that there was little scope for such sentiments in the eighteenth century. In that case, to what can one attribute such a preference for European officers and soldiers?

One obvious reason for denying sepoys higher military command has already been alluded to. This was the question of security. The British were certainly not prepared to allow the natives of a conquered land to control the instrument that preserved that conquest. It is true that the British did not think very highly of the Indian's patriotism but still, they were perceived as belonging to one culture. The growing awareness of the distinctiveness of the Indian culture and the seemingly obsessive attachment of Indians to their religion only strengthened

[51] Childs, *Armies*, p. 126.

[52] *An Account of the Gallant Defence of Mangalore in 1783*, London, 1786, p. 179.

the perception that Indians on the whole shared a common background and heritage. The knowledge that many sepoys also shared local and family ties due to the prevailing recruitment practices enhanced this feeling even further, making it easier for the British to perceive their sepoys as a distinct group.

In short, Indians had a lot more in common with each other than with the British, a situation that was not very favourable to building trust. To make matters worse, one of the things Indian soldiers were perceived to have in common with each other was mercenary ambition. Under these circumstances, bestowing higher command on sepoys who had local and family connections with the men they were to command and little attachment to the Company's interest other than the pay they received meant a serious security risk. The British only had to think of the careers of Yusuf Khan and Hyder Ali who had revolted against their employers. As noted earlier, it was the sepoy officers who were usually punished during mutinies. Such circumstances did not offer bright career prospects for sepoy officers. As Cornwallis explained in August 1787:

> I think it must be universally admitted that without a large and well-regulated body of Europeans, our hold of these valuable dominions must be very insecure. It cannot be expected that even the best of treatment would conciliate the willing obedience of so vast a body of people, differing from ourselves in almost every circumstance of laws, religion and customs; and oppressions of individuals, errors of government and several other unforeseen causes will no doubt arouse an inclination to revolt. On such occasions it would not be wise to place great dependence on their countrymen who compose the native regiments to secure their subjection.[53]

Therefore, it is not surprising if the Company felt more assured of the loyalty of their European officers because not only were they culturally alienated from the subcontinent; they also shared common cultural ties as Europeans. This is exactly why the Company had employed Topasses in the early period. Moreover, most Europeans serving in the Company's army were British nationals. The European units of the EIC had usually included the men from many different European countries but by the late eighteenth century, foreign recruitment had been gradually phased out because the Company believed that Englishmen were more trustworthy than other

[53] Quoted in Wickwire and Wickwire, *Cornwallis*, p. 108.

Europeans.[54] Naturally they were attached to the Company's interest due to their national consciousness. As Gerald Bryant explains, the Company's British officers saw themselves as the representatives of Britain and performed their services with a patriotic fervor.[55] The willingness of Jaswant Rao Holkar's British officers to face death rather than fight the Company is telling proof of this.

The perceptions of the incompetence of sepoy officers can also be interpreted as an off-shoot of this fundamental insecurity. Not only could officers with mercenary ambitions and close ties with their men pose a direct challenge to the Company's authority, they could also not be expected to have a strong commitment to providing effective leadership in combat. Likewise, sepoys who had no strong attachment to the Company beyond their pay could not expect to fight hard. Therefore, the admission of only Europeans to the upper echelons of command helped preserve the integrity of military command at the top while at the level of the rank and file, the European soldiery added

[54] In the words of George Macmunn, the European troops in the early British settlements were formed 'from detachments sent from England, from runaway sailors, men of disbanded Fench corps, from Swiss and Hanoverians from prisoners-of-war and any white nationals in search of a livelihood', George MacMunn, *The Armies of India*, London: Dam and Charles Black, 1911, pp. 4-5. Sometimes whole units of Foreign Europeans were also employed. For instance, several companies of Swiss soldiers fought for the EIC during the Carnatic War in 1751-2. OIOC O.V. 288, p. 213; McCormack, *One Million*, pp. 151-2. During the height of the Second Mysore War the Company also negotiated unsuccessfully with the Dutch East India Company to obtain 1,200 Dutch troops. Gleig, *The Life*, vol. 2, p. 356. However, British officers often expressed a desire for more English troops. For instance, in February, 1759 Colonel Francis Forde who was in the Deccan at the time, wrote to Bengal, pleading them to make certain that all European soldiers sent to him in future were Englishmen. Bengal Sec. Cons., 18 February 1759, OIOC P/A/2. See also for example Joseph Smith to Madras, 18 January 1760. Madras Mil. and Sec. Cons., 31 January 1760, OIOC P/D/43, pp. 123-4 and Richard Smith to Madras, 26 November 1760. Madras Mil. and Sec. Cons., 4 December 1760, OIOC P/D/43, p. 1051. By late 1770s the EIC was already reviewing its policy of recruiting foreign Europeans. As one officer put it, foreign mercenaries, 'destitute of all national feelings are ready to act for the best paymaster, an event which should be alarming to Englishmen, as proprietors of the Honourable Company'. Arthur N. Gilbert, 'Military Recruitment and Career Advancement in the Eighteenth Century: Two Case Studies', *Journal of the Society for Army Historical Research*, vol. 57, no. 229, 1979, p. 37.

[55] Bryant, 'Officers', p. 209. Apart from the lack of the 'animating example of European regiments' Thomas Munro also attributed the failure of the Maratha regulars to the 'want of a national spirit among its officers'. Munro to Colonel Read, 6 March 1804. Owen, *Wellesley Despatches*, pp. 791-2.

a stability which could not be expected from sepoys. As such, depending mainly on Europeans—particularly British nationals—for military command and hard fighting may be taken as a matter of measuring effectiveness in terms of commitment.

Thus, the recognition of a higher morale and commitment in the European troops may have been a contributory factor in determining their role in combat. But was that all? It must also be remembered that the perception of the Indian soldier as a mercenary, deeply attached to his religion also meant that his loyalty could be solicited by anyone, including the Company as long as his needs were catered to. This was exactly the rationale behind pandering to the sepoys' prejudice and providing him with regular pay. As already seen, 'when their prejudices were humoured' Rajputs were considered 'the bravest and most devoted soldiers'.[56] There were many British officers who were convinced of the sepoys' attachment to the Company's service, even under extremely difficult circumstances. It is interesting that Colonel John Caillaud, despite criticizing the mercenary character of Indian soldiers, also had high praise for the loyalty shown by the Company's sepoys:

> Though I have not allowed publick [*sic*] virtue to the Indians in general they are not destitute of some good qualities, amongst which we may give the first rank to their fidelity as they express it (and not improperly) fidelity to those whose salt they eat. This may be termed the Indian point of honour and is most prevalent in the lowest class. To support this opinion we have the experience of almost twenty years since the natives have been employed in our service and every year increasing in number and consequence. There is not in that space of time an instance of their betraying the trust reposed in them, and this not only in success, but when our affairs have been doubtful and critical, when the service has been dangerous and hard, their payments irregular and they in the neighbourhood of an enemy who did not want the means and spared no pains to debauch them. Of their fidelity therefore we have sufficient proofs, not only from our own experience but from the knowledge of many instances in the course of service against our enemies in which they have given examples of attachment and steadiness that would do honour to the bravest and best men. That they desert frequently is true but not more, nor in greater numbers than is frequently amongst the common soldiers in all armies.[57]

Caillaud was not making an idle point. Sepoys often showed a remarkable attachment to the Company's cause under very adverse conditions. The Second Mysore War provided many examples of such

[56] Welsh, *Military Reminiscences*, 1, p. 14.
[57] OIOC Orme India III, p. 3746.

loyalty. During that war, we hear of sepoys and their families dying 'by dozens on the highway'[58] and sepoys having to sell their children to sustain themselves due to want of provisions and arrears in pay,[59] yet remaining staunchly behind the Company. This devotion was not lost on many British officers who served with the sepoys at the time. One of them wrote: 'I have known the Indian army,' he wrote, 'under the fatigue of two unfortunate campaigns, unpaid for more than 15 months, almost without clothing, and with a very scanty allowance and food from the public store, adhere with invincible attachment to our declining fortunes and refuse the most tempting offers of the enemy to withdraw them from our standard.'[60] Such observations show that there was also a recognition in the British camp that the sepoy could display astonishing loyalty that went beyond mere pecuniary gain. Indeed, to some British observers, it was the European troops who needed to be closely watched; as the Rev. William Tennant, who was an army chaplain and knew the European soldiers well, warned, the Company had more to fear from 'the treachery of its European troops' than from 'the insubordination or revolt of its native armies'.[61]

Thus, it is questionable whether the British had such strong doubts about the commitment of the sepoys as to make these doubts the sole foundation of their approach to deploying troops in battle. But what other possible reasons could have existed for the preference for European troops in combat?

This brings me to the British perception of Indian military inferiority. As shown already, the European troops were heavily depended on in situations where aggressive behaviour was required and that it was this lack of aggression or resolution that marked the Indian soldier as 'timid' and made British soldiers speak of 'bravery uncommon to Blacks'. Is it possible that what is seen in the organization and deployment of the sepoy army is the persistence of that perception?

The answer is certainly in the affirmative. It is true that many in the British camp saw indiscipline as the main weakness in Indian armies but it is doubtful whether they necessarily believed that discipline alone

[58] Footnote to the General's Minute 22 October 1782. *Correspondence During the Icapacitation*, p. 8.

[59] Mss. Eur. D. 799. During the Second Maratha War, a large number of sepoys captured by Holkar endured shocking torture and mutilation without abandoning the Company's service. Thorn, *A Memoir*, p. 369.

[60] OIOC Home Misc. 510, pp. 9-11.

[61] Tennant, *Indian Recreations*, vol. 1, p. 393.

could make an Indian soldier as good as a European. This is because the British probably recognized that the Indian and European military cultures contrasted too sharply with each other to enable Indian soldiers to fully embrace the spirit of European-style fighting. In other words, Indian indiscipline was an expression of a complex military culture with its own system of values. As such, indiscipline could not be isolated from other factors which formed the Indian way of fighting. For example, take the case of the widespread belief among Europeans that Indian soldiers refused to charge home for the fear that they might lose their horses. Does this mean that these Europeans also believed that the concern for the safety of his mount was the only factor that made Indian soldiers behave irresolutely in battle? To put it another way, did the British believe that, given reassurance by his employer that his horse will be promptly replaced, an Indian soldier would immediately return to the charge, carrying all before him? The problem was more complex than that and the Europeans who had seen the clumsy Indian gun carriages trundling towards massive mud fortresses and marauding cavalry devastating the fertile countryside would have certainly recognized it as such, as a part of a much bigger problem, not wholly eliminated merely by providing Indian soldiers with European-style training and uniforms. The perception of Indian passivity encouraged by religion would have certainly strengthened this belief that Indian military attitudes were a part of a broader, complex system of thinking and acting which could not be easily changed, while the strong, sometimes aggressive, demonstrations of religious prejudice by sepoys would have provided a telling example of the folly of trying to change beliefs and customs ingrained over centuries for the sake of discipline.

All this did not mean that Indian soldiers could not be made effective European-style soldiers but rather, that they could not be made as 'perfect' as European troops. Such skepticism probably explains the attitudes of many British officers in the Bengal Army who routinely sent sepoys and even sepoy officers returning from furlough back to the parade ground to learn their drill from scratch, no difference being made 'between the new raised soldier and the veteran of five and twenty'. The rationale was that after an absence of about a month or so from the army, 'the sepoy forgets his exercises and becomes as awkward as a recruit'.[62] The Rev. William Tennant even went so far as

[62] *Observations and Remarks (1798)*, p. 24.

to reassure his readers that there was no real danger of sepoys deserting to a hostile Indian army with their discipline because 'after a few month's disuse, [the sepoy] becomes as completely ignorant of his duty as if he had never learnt it'.[63] It is significant that there were no such observations made about the European troops. The British probably believed that once he was in his 'native' environment the sepoy lost touch with his European drill. Even the wisdom of drilling Indian soldiers too much was questioned. As Captain Blakiston observed, 'the frequent drills and roll calls, though absolutely necessary to preserve the Europeans, whose habits were anything but temperate or quiescent, in any degree of order, were by no means so to the sober and domestic sepoy, who, fond of his ease, becomes discontented when harassed by unnecessary duty'.[64]

Thus, although an Indian soldier could be trained to fight in the European manner, it was also believed that he did not respond to discipline in the same as a European soldier. Under these circumstances personal courage alone mattered very little because what counted was its translation into collective courage. Not that personal courage was unimportant; but it was not everything. This explains why Indian troops from temperate zones were not treated as the equals of European soldiers on the battlefield despite a strong belief in their capacity for personal courage. It is doubtful whether the admirers of the sturdy and brave Rajput peasantry ever forgot that they were talking first and foremost, about Indians. In other words, a north Indian peasant may have been perceived as hardy northerners and brave, but were these qualities not subordinate to the influence of culture? After all, it was the northerners who were most particular about religion and caste. It seems that in the eyes of the British the bravery of the northerners only placed them a notch above other Indians from the south; as one observer explained, the 'innate courage and athletic form' of the Bengal sepoy made him superior to his counterpart in the Carnatic.[65] In short,

[63] Tennant, *Indian Recreations*, vol. 1, pp. 392-3.

[64] Blakiston, *Twelve Years*', vol. 1, p. 325. Major John Carnac also expressed similar sentiments when he spoke of pecuniary inducement being the only way the Company could hope to gain the loyalty of sepoys, because Indian troops usually preferred to serve Indian rulers with whom 'they have considerably less duty and are free from all restraints of discipline'. Carnac to Vansittrat, 2 February 1761, OIOC Mss. Eur. F. 128/4.

[65] Crisp, *British India Analysed*, vol. 3, p. 797.

whether he was a Telugu from the Carnatic or a Rajput from Bhojpur, a sepoy was first an Indian soldier, very different to Europeans in habits and beliefs and as a result, could not and did not respond to European style discipline like the Europeans. They could be certainly improved, but only within the limits set by their beliefs and customs.

I contend that the British never expected the sepoys to become as efficient as Europeans at any time during the formation and expansion of the sepoy army. All they expected from the sepoys was to function in support of the European troops during major campaigns and keep the countryside in tranquility. Drill, discipline and European-style organization had a dual purpose: to actually improve the performance of the sepoys and to enable the European officers to control the sepoys so that they could be deployed in support of the European troops.

Therefore, all that the British expected from the sepoy through drill, discipline and European leadership and support was to be a superior type of *Indian* soldier. This is exactly what Colonel Robert Kelly meant when he said that the British officers had found the medium 'which so well suits the genius of the sepoys; and has certainly made them the *best black troops in the world*'.[66] It is also what many British officers meant when they praised sepoys for their expertness at drill and manoeuvers; they were complementing them as Indian troops. It is also what Cornwallis meant when he boasted about a battalion of sepoys conquering India. They all carry one basic message: that the sepoys were good *Indian* troops. Needless to say, sepoy failures could only reinforce this view.

Thus, it is possible to see British perceptions of Indian military weakness playing a role as important as the perception of European cultural isolation in relegating the sepoys to a secondary role in combat. The sepoys, as Indians steeped in the subcontinental military culture, were not expected to enter into the spirit of the European military culture despite European-style training and discipline. But the important thing is that the British were quite content with this situation; the sepoy army was cheap, on the whole very loyal and did what was expected of them, that is to maintain order in the countryside and support European troops in major campaigns. The British couldn't possibly ask for more. The fact is they didn't.

[66] OIOC Mss. Eur. D. 1146/6, p. 80. My emphasis.

# Conclusion

THE SECOND HALF of the eighteenth century witnessed not only the expansion of British dominion over India but also the development of British perceptions about the subcontinent. Led by a desire to 'know' the land and the people they were conquering, the British embarked on a quest for knowledge about the subcontinent. The foregoing discussion has focussed on the military dimension of the construction of this knowledge as it was reflected in the English East India Company's sepoy army. Although the sepoy was armed, disciplined and clothed in the European manner, he was always treated as an Indian soldier, the product of social and cultural conditions peculiar to the subcontinent. He was preferably recruited from the dominant social groups and once recruited, was treated with sensitivity towards his religious and material needs. Sensitive matters like overseas travel was made voluntary while efforts were made to encourage loyal service through regular pay and rewards.

Such attitudes showed the appreciation of the peculiarities of the Indian culture in general and the Indian military culture in particular. The growing awareness of the role of the caste hierarchy in Indian society and the appreciation of the mercenary nature of military service in India were largely responsible for the British policy of recruitment and general management of the sepoy army. This appreciation was not simply the result of scholarly study; the sepoys themselves, through frequent mutinous behaviour impressed on the Company the need to be sensitive to their religious and material needs.

Appreciation of cultural difference also resulted in British prejudice towards their sepoys. This was evident in the command structure and the deployment of the sepoy army in the field. Although Indian troops were considered good enough to receive European training and discipline but not fit to hold higher military command. Even under European command and up-to-date training, the sepoy was not trusted with highly demanding combat duties, particularly leading assaults on fortified places.

These British prejudices were influenced by simple factors. The British were simply unwilling to trust a people who did not share their cultural or national background. In other words, they felt insecure allowing Indians whose habits and values contrasted so sharply with their own, to hold responsible positions within such an important institution like the army. Such people could not be expected to fight hard for the Company's cause simply because they did not have anything in common with the British. The growing awareness of the distinctiveness of the Indian culture made certain that this prejudice was well entrenched.

However, there was more to this prejudice than simple insecurity. The British also perceived Indian difference in the form of the genuine disparities that existed between contemporary European and India ways of fighting. British, and indeed European perception of Indian military difference had a long history. Since the seventeenth century, European visitors to the subcontinent had been comparing the Indian military system unfavourably with European warfare. This perception of Indian military inferiority received a further boost when the EIC began intense military operations on the subcontinent from the mid-eighteenth century. What had hitherto been mere observation now turned into first hand experience enabling the British to construct a more complete picture of Indian military backwardness. Indian armies were now perceived as inferior to their European counterparts where all the salient features of European warfare were concerned. Indian troops lacked discipline, their artillery was clumsy and the troops themselves simple mercenaries.

It would be surprising if such a total contrast did not influence British attitudes to the formation and employment of an army of Indian soldiers. This was particularly so when the most palpable aspect of Indian military inferiority was the reluctance of Indian armies to stand and fight. The result was that although the British provided their sepoys with European training and discipline, they did not expect Indians to be as competent as European officers in carrying out their duties. In other words, European drill and discipline were not deemed sufficient to wholly eliminate the negative impact of a military culture that was almost the antithesis of its European counterpart. The result was that although Indians were given a measure of responsibility as officers and soldiers, Europeans were relied on to provide military leadership and do the tough fighting. The failures of sepoys only reinforced this perception.

Thus, the British perception of Indian soldiers in the eighteenth century was influenced by on a number of factors ranging from the insecurities of the conquerors to genuine differences that existed between the Indian military culture and the European military system rather than by a desire to construct Indian inferiority according to an imperialist agenda. Knowledge about Indian difference and inferiority was gained through scholarly study and interaction with Indian soldiers. The ultimate outcome of these perceptions was the creation of an army that was never treated as the equal of the European branch of the Company's army, but it was the result of fear, ignorance and even weakness, rather than an imperialist self-perception.

However, the basic discrimination between Europeans and sepoys on the basis of perceived reliability creates a new dimension for the understanding of the development of the English East India Company's army in the eighteenth century, suggesting that the sepoy army of the eighteenth century was something more than an institution of tolerance and understanding. It suggests that it was also the seedbed of future contempt towards the sepoy. The essential ingredient for the development of racist perception about Indian soldiers in the following century—the perception of unreliability in a crisis without European officers and soldiers—was already well and truly alive in the eighteenth century, and that the sepoy army was founded partly on that perception. In other words, the racist ideology of the nineteenth century provided a new interpretation for an old perception, giving it a more sinister twist. In the heady atmosphere of empire and scientific progress the inferiority of the Indian soldier came to be treated as the product of an innate weakness and the Indian cultural environment itself came to be seen as the manifestation of that inner weakness, turning simple prejudice into downright contempt and men into specimens.

# Appendix

COMPOSITION OF STORMING PARTIES

| *Date* | *Place* | *Composition of the Storming Party (in the order of precedence in the attack)* |
|---|---|---|
| 1764 | Madura | European grenadiers.<br>Remainder of the Madras European battalion.<br>Sepoys. |
| 1771 | Sultanpore | A detachment of the Bombay European regiment.<br>Two companies sepoys grenadiers. |
| 1771 | Broach | A detachment of the Bombay European regiment headed by one of the grenadier companies.<br>A body of sepoys. |
| September 1773 | Tanjore | European grenadiers.<br>Pioneers (workmen with tools to clear the debris).<br>Sepoy grenadiers. |
| 1 January 1780 | Ahmedabad | A detachment of the Bombay European regiment with the grenadiers leading. |
| 11 June 1782 | Cuddalore | European grenadiers of 71st and 72nd King's regiments.<br>The remainder of the above regiments.<br>Sepoys. |
| February 1791 | Dharwar | A detachment of the 2nd Bombay regiment. |
| 17 October 1791 | Nandidurg | Flank companies of the 36th and 71st King's regiments.<br>102nd King's regiment. |
| 21 December 1791 | Savandurg | Flank companies of the 52nd and 76th King's regiments.<br>Remainder of the above regiments. |

(Contd.)

APPENDIX (Contd.)

| *Date* | *Place* | *Composition of the Storming Party (in the order of precedence in the attack)* |
|---|---|---|
| 1792 | Bangalore | Grenadier companies of the European regiments. |
| 1792 | Srirangapattanam | *Right Column:*<br>Six flank companies of the 71st, 74th and 52nd King's regiments.<br>Battalion companies of the 52nd regiment.<br>One battalion Bengal sepoys.<br>*Centre Column:*<br>King's 71st regiment.<br>Two sepoy battalions.<br>*Left Column:*<br>King's 72nd regiment<br>Four sepoy battalions. |
| 1799 | Srirangapattanam | *Left column:*<br>Six flank companies King's troops.<br>King's 12th and 33th regiments.<br>Flank companies of 10 Bengal battalions.<br>*Right column:*<br>Flank companies of the Scotch brigade.<br>Swiss regiment de Meuron.<br>King's 73rd and 74th regiments.<br>Eight flank companies Madras sepoys. |
| 1803 | Gawilgur | North Breach: Grenadier company and 2 battalion companies of the King's 94th regiment.<br>Flank companies of 3 sepoy battalions. |

# Glossary

| | |
|---|---|
| *amuldar* | officer in charge of a district. |
| *bargir* | literally, a burden carrier; in Indian armies a cavalry man equipped and mounted by the state. |
| *condottieri* | mercenary soldiers serving Italian states during the Renaissance. |
| *cummerbund* | sash. |
| *deshmukh* | local chief in western India. |
| *gardis* | European-style infantry serving the Marathas in late eighteenth century. |
| *jagir* | an assignment of land revenue, usually in return for military service. |
| Kshatriya | the warrior caste in the Indian caste hierarchy. |
| *mansabdar* | in the Mughal empire a noble with the obligation to contribute a specified number of horsemen to the Mughal army. |
| Nayar | a caste with a martial tradition in south-western India. |
| *palaikkar* | a petty chief or ruler in south India, called poligars by the British. |
| *rattan* | cane. |
| *sardar* | a military captain, a petty chief. |
| *sat* | the rank denoting a *mansabdars* position within the Mughal army. |
| *sawar* | in the Mughal army a rank denoting the number of cavalrymen maintained by a noble. |
| *silahdar* | literally, equipment holder; in Indian armies a cavalryman riding his own horse. |
| *tope* | grove of trees. |
| *zamindar* | landholder, petty chief. |

# Bibliography

## PRIMARY SOURCES

### MANUSCRIPT SOURCES: BRITISH LIBRARY: ORIENTAL AND INDIA OFFICE COLLECTIONS

*Collections*

Factory Records, Fort St. David.
Factory Records, Karwar.
Bengal Military Consultations.
Bengal Secret Consultations.
Bombay Public Consultations.
Home Miscellaneous Series.
Orme India.
Orme Various.
Madras Public Consultations.
Madras Military and Secret Consultations.
Madras Select Committee Consultations.
Madras Military and Political Consultations.
Military Records.
Miscellaneous Letters Received by London.

*European Manuscripts*

'An anonymous account of the battles of Delhi and Laswari', Mss. Eur. B. 401.
'An unpublished account of the Bombay Army by Edward Sambrooke John Anderson', 2 vols., Mss. Eur. C. 155.
'Bombay Army General Orders, 1788-9', Mss. Eur. E. 419.
'Brigade Orders for the 2nd Brigade Bengal Army', Futtypore, 1796, Mss. Eur. D. 459.
Carnac Papers, Eur. F. 128/4.
Clive Papers, Mss. Eur. G. 37, box 20.
Eyre Coote Papers, Mss. Eur. F. 190, vol. 1 and box 1.

'General orders of the army before Seringapattanam', 1 January–27 June 1799, Mss. Eur. E. 386.

'Journal of Captain George Kinlock on the expedition to Nepal begun on the 26th August 1767', Mss. Eur. F. 128/40.

'Journal of General Mathew's campaign against Mysore', 1782-3, Mss. Eur. C. 154, notebook no. 6.

'Letter from an officer serving with the army before Srirangapattanam', Mss. Eur. B. 276.

'Memoranda of Colonel Robert Kelly', Mss. Eur. D. 1146/6.

'Memoir of James Oliver', Mss. Eur. D. 799.

'Memoir of an expedition to the East Indies undertaken in the year 1754 with some Observations on the Climate, People, Customs and Manners', Mss. Eur. B. 215.

'Minutes of the House of Commons Committee on the EIC', Mss. Eur. D. 1018.

BRITISH MUSEUM EUROPEAN MANUSCRIPTS DEPARTMENT

Journal kept by Lieutenant Colonel Henry Cosby during the campaign in the Carnatic including the expedition against Tanjore, Bombay and Pondicherry', Add. 29898.

Miscellaneous letters relating to the Second Maratha War, Add. 13857.

Orderly book of a detachment of the Madras Army Commanded by Colonel Sir Henry Cosby in 1785-6. Pasley Papers, Add. 29900.

NATIONAL ARMY MUSEUM, CHELSEA, LONDON

Mss. nos. 6309-619 and 8207-64.

## PUBLISHED SOURCES

*Collections of Official Documents, Despatches, etc.*

*Correspondence During the Incapacitation of the Commander-in-Chief in September 1782, With General Orders From the Above Date to April 1783, Collected by Major-General James Stuart,* 1785.

*Country Correspondence, Fort St. George, Military Department, 1749,* Madras: Government Printers, 1910.

*Diary and Consultation Book, Fort St. George, Military Department, 1753, 1754, 1755 and 1756,* Madras: Government Printers, 1910-13.

Dodwell, Henry H. (ed.), *A Calendar of Madras Despatches 1740-44,* Madras: Government Printers, 1920.

Forrest, G.W. (ed.), *Selections from the Letters, Despatches and other State Papers*

*Preserved in the Foreign Department of the Government of India 1772-1785*, 3 vols., Calcutta: Superintendent of Govt. Printing, 1890, vol. 1.

———, *Selections from the Minutes and other Official Writings of the Honourable Mountstuart Elphinstone*, London: Bentley, 1884.

*Fort St. George General Orders July 12, 1796*, Madras, 1796.

Gurwood, Lt.-Col. William (ed.), *Despatches of the Field Marshal the Duke of Wellington During his Various Campaigns in India, Denmark, Portugal, Spain and the Low Countries and France From 1799 to 1818*, 8 vols., London: John Murray, 1834, vol. 1.

Hatalkar, V.G. (ed and trs.), *French Records Relating to the History of the Marathas*, 9 vols., Bombay: Maharashtra State Board for Literature and Culture, 1980-5, vols. 6 and 8.

Hill, S.C. (ed.), *Bengal in 1756-57: a Selection of Public and Private Papers Dealing with the Affairs of the British in Bengal During the Reign of Siraj-ud-Daulah*, 3 vols., New York: AMS Press, 1968; 1st pub. 1905.

Long, J., *Unpublished Letters of Government for the Years 1748 to 1768 Inclusive Relating Mainly to the Social Condition of Bengal with a Map of Calcutta*, Calcutta: Firma K.L. Mukhopadhyay, 1973; 1st pub. 1869.

Martin, Robert Montgomery (ed.), *The Despatches, Minutes and Correspondence of the Marquess Wellesley During his Administration in India*, 5 vols., New Delhi: Inter India Publishers, 1984; 1st pub. 1836, vol. 3.

Moor, Edward (ed.), *A Compilation of all the Government, General, Brigade and Garrison Orders of the Bombay Army 1750-1800*, Bombay, 1801.

Owen, Sydney J. (ed.), *A Selection From the Indian Despatches, Memoranda & ca of the Duke of Wellington*, Oxford: Clarendon, 1880.

———, *A Selection From the Despatches, Treaties and Other Papers of the Marquess Wellesley, K.G. During his Government of India*, Oxford: Clarendon, 1877.

Prasad, B. (ed.), *Fort William India House Correspondence and Other Papers Relating Thereto*, 21 vols., Delhi: National Archives, 1975, vol. 19.

*Public Consultations, Fort St. George, 1741*, Madras: Government Printers, 1910.

*Records of the Government of Bengal: Letter and Copy Book of the Resident at Durbar at Murshidabad 1769-70*, Calcutta: Bengal Secretariat Press, 1919.

Singh, Raghubir (ed.), *Poona Residency Correspondence, volume 10: the Treaty of Bassein and the Anglo-Maratha War in the Deccan in 1803-04*, Bombay: Sri Gauranga Press, 1951.

Sinha, N.K. (ed.), *Fort William India House Correspondence and Other Contemporary Papers Relating Thereto*, Public Series, 21 vols., New Delhi: National Archives, 1949, vol. 5.

Wilson, C.R. (ed.), *Old Fort William in Bengal: a Selection of Official Documents dealing with its History*, 2 vols., London: John Murray, 1906.

*Other Published Works*

*A Memoir of a War in India from 1780 to 1784 Including a Narrative of the Imprisonment and Suffering of our Officers and Soldiers by an Officer of Colonel Baillie's Detachment*, London, 1789.

*An Account of the Gallant Defence of Mangalore in 1783*, London, 1786.

Alexander, Alexander, *The Life of Alexander Alexander Written by Himself*, 2 vols., London, 1830, vol. 1.

Beatson, Alexander, *A View of the Origin and Conduct of the War with Tippoo Sultan Comprising a Narrative of the Operations of the Army Under the Command of Lieutenant-General George Harris and of the Siege of Seringapattam*, London, 1800.

Bernier, Francois, *Travels in the Mughal Empire, A.D. 1656-1658*, trs. Archibald Constable, New Delhi: S. Chand, 1968; rpt. of 1891 edn.

Blakiston, Captain John, *Twelve Years' Military Adventures in Three Quarters of the Globe: or, Memoirs of an Officer Who Served in the Armies of His Majesty and of the East India Company, Between the Years 1802 and 1814, in Which are Contained the Campaigns of the Duke of Wellington in India, and his Last in Spain and the South of France*, 2 vols., London, Henry Colburn, 1829, vol. 1.

Bland, Major-General Humphrey, *A Treatise of Military Discipline in which is Laid Down and Explained the Duty of the Officers and Soldiers thro' the Several Branches of the Service*, London, 1753.

Caraccioli, Charles, *The Life of Robert Lord Clive, Baron of Plassey*, 3 vols., London, 1775, vol. 1.

Cambridge, Richard Owen, *An Account of the War in India Between the English and the French on the Coast of Coromandel from the Year 1750 to the Year 1761*, London: printed for T. Jeffreys, 1762.

Crisp, Burrish (trs.), *British India Analysed: the Provincial and Revenue Establishments of Tippoo Sultaun and of Mahomedan and British Conquerors in Hindustan, Stated and Considered in Three Parts*, 3 vols., Delhi: Crown Publications, 1988; 1st pub. 1793, vol. 3.

Dirom, Major Alexander, *A Narrative of the Campaign in India Which Terminated in the War With Tippoo Sultan in 1792*, Delhi: Asian Educational Publications Services, 1985; 1st pub. 1793.

Downing, Clement, *A History of the Indian Wars*, with an introduction and notes by William Foster, London: OUP, 1924; 1st pub. 1737.

Dubois, Abbe J.A., *Hindu Manners, Customs and Ceremonies*, trs. Henry K. Beauchamp, London: OUP, 1959; 1st pub. 1906.

Dundas, Colonel David, *Principles of Military Movements, Chiefly Applied to the Infantry*, London: T. Cadell, 1788.

Fullerton, William, *A View of the English Interests in India and an Account of the Military Operations in the Southern Part of the Peninsula During the Campaigns of 1782, 1783 and 1784. In Two Letters Addressed to the Right*

*Honourable the Earl of... and to Lord Macartney and the Select Committee.* At Fort St. George, London, 1787.

Grose, John Henry, *A Voyage to the East Indies with Observations on Various Parts there*, London: S. Hooper and A. Morely, 1757.

Hastings, Warren, *A Narrative of the Insurrection in the Zameendary of Benaris in 1781 and the Transactions of the Governor-General in the District*, Calcutta, 1782.

Khan, Seid Gholam Hussain, *The Seir Mutaqherin or Review of Modern Times Being a History of India as Far Down as the Year 1783*, 4 vols., Lahore: Sheikh Mubarak Ali, 1975; rpt. of 1905 edn., 1st pub. 1789, vol. 2.

Kindersley, Mrs, *Letters from the Island of Teneriffe, Brazil, the Cape of Good Hope and the East Indies*, London, 1777.

Kirmani, Meer Hussein Ali Khan, *The History of the Reign of Tipu Sultan Being a Cotinuation of the Neshani Hyduri*, trs. W. Miles, Delhi: Oriental Publisher, 1980; 1st pub. 1842.

M.M.D.L.T., *Hyder Ali and the Revolution in India (the History of Hyder Shah Alias Hyder Ali Khan Bahadur*, Delhi: Daya Publishing House, 1988; 1st pub. 1848.

McPherson, W.C. (ed.), *Soldiering in India 1764-1787: Extracts from Journals and Letters Left by Colonel Allan Mcpherson and Lieutenant John Mcpherson of the East India Company's Service*, London: William Blackwood & Sons, 1928.

Manucci, Niccolo, *Storia do Mogor or Moghul India 1653-1708*, trs. William Irvine, 4 vols., Delhi: Editions Indian, 1965, vols. 1 and 2.

Martin, Francois, *India in the Seventeenth Century (Social, Economic and Political): Memoirs of Francois Martin, 1670-1694*, trs. Lotika Varadarajan, 2 parts, Delhi: Manohar, 1983, part 2.

Michaud, Joseph, *History of Mysore under Hyder Ali and Tippoo Sultan*, trs. V.K. Raman Menon, Delhi: Asian Educational Services, 1985; 1st French edn., 1801-6; 1st English edn. 1926.

Moor, Edward, *A Narrative of the Operations of Captain Little's Detachment and of the Maratha Army Commanded by Purseram Bhow; During the Late Confederacy in India Against the Nawab Tippoo Sultan Bahadur*, London, 1794.

Munro, Innes, *A Narrative of the Military Operations on the Coromandel Coast Against the Combined Forces of the French, Dutch and Hyder Ali Cawn, From the Year 1780 to the Peace in 1784*, London, 1789.

*Observations and Remarks on the Dress, Discipline & ca of the Military by a Bengal Officer*, Calcutta, 1798 and 1809.

Orme, Robert, *Historical Fragments of the Mogul Empire, of the Morattoes, and of the English Concerns in Indostan from the Year MDCLIX*, edited with an introduction by J.P. Guha, New Delhi: Associated Publishing House, 1974; 1st pub. 1782.

———, *History of the Military Transactions of the British Nation in Indostan, from the Year MDCCXLV to Which is Prefixed a Dissertation on the Establishments Made by Mahomedan Conquerors in Indostan*, 2 vols., vol. 2 in 2 parts, New Delhi: Today and Tomorrow's Publishers, 1975; 1st pub. 1778.

Pandey, Sita Ram, *From Sepoy to Subedar, Being the Life and Adventures of Subedar Sita Ram, a Native Officer of the Bengal Army, Written by Himself*, ed. James Lunt, London: Routledge and Kegan Paul, 1973.

Pester, John, *War and Sport in India: an Offier's Diary*, London: Heath, Cranton and Ousley Ltd., 1914.

Pillai, Ananda Ranga, *The Private Diary of Ananda Ranga Pillai, Dubash to Joseph Francois Dupleix, Governor of Pondicherry*, ed. H. Dodwell, 13 vols., Delhi: Asian Educational Services, 1985; 1st pub. 1922, vol. 8.

Rennel, Major James, *The Marches of the British Armies in the Peninsula of India during the Campaign of 1790 and 1791*, London, 1792.

Shipp, John, *Memoirs of the Extraordinary Military Career of John Shipp, late a Lieutenant in His Majesty's 87th Regiment*, Chichester, London: T.F. Unwin, 1890; 1st pub. 1829.

Smith, Lewis Ferdinand, *A Sketch of the Rise, Progress and Termination of the Regular Corps Formed and Commanded by Europeans in the Service of the Native Princes of India with Details of the Principal Events and Actions of the Late Maratha War*, Calcutta, 1805.

Tavernier, Jean-Baptiste, *Travels in India, Six Voyages de Jean-Baptiste Tavernier 1605 -1609*, trs. V. Ball and William Crooke, 2 vols., Delhi: Oriental Books Reprint Corporation, 1977; rpt. of 1889 edn., vol. 1.

Tennant, Rev. William, *Indian Recreations, Consisting Chiefly of Strictures on the Domestic and Rural Economy of the Mahomedans and Hindoos*, 2 vols., London, 1804, vol. 1.

Thorn, William, *Memoir of the War in India Conducted by General Lord Lake, Commander-in-Chief and Major-General Sir Arthur Wellesley, Duke of Wellington; From its Commencement in 1803 to its Termination in 1806, on the Banks of the Hyphasis*, London: Military Library, 1818.

## SECONDARY SOURCES

### BOOKS

Alavi, Seema, *The Sepoys and the Company: Tradition and Transition in Northern Indian Military Culture 1770-1830*, Delhi: OUP, 1995.

Ali, M. Athar, *The Mughal Nobility under Aurangzeb*, Bombay: Asia Publishing House, 1996.

Anderson, B., *Imagined Communities: Reflections on the Origin and Spread of Nationalism*, London: Verso, 1991.

Anderson, M.S., *War and Society in Europe of the Old Regime 1618-1789*, London: Fontana, 1988.

Ascoli, David, *A Companion to the British Army 1660-1983*, London: Harrap, 1983.

Avineri, Shlomo, *Karl Marx on Colonialism and Modernization: his Despatches and other Writing on China, India, Mexico, the Middle East and North Africa*, New York: Doubleday, 1968.

Aziz, Abdul, *The Mansabdari System and the Mughal Army*, Delhi: Idarah-i-Abiyat-i-Delhi, 1972.

Banton, Michael, *The Idea of Race*, London: Tavistock Publications, 1977.

Barnes, Major R. Money, *Military Uniforms of Britain and the Empire: 1742 to the Present Time*, London: Seeley Service and Co. Ltd., 1960.

Barres, Jean-Baptiste, *Memoirs of a Napoleonic Officer*, trs. Bernard Miall, New York: The Diall Press, 1925.

Bayly, C.A., *Empire and Information: Intelligence Gathering and Social Communication in India 1780-1880*, Cambridge: CUP, 1996.

Barat, Amiya, *The Bengal Native Infantry: its Organisation and Discipline*, Calcutta: Firma K.L. Mukhopadhyay, 1962.

Best, Geoffrey, *War and Society in Revolutionary Europe 1770-1870*, Leicester: Leicester University Press, 1982.

Beloff, Max, *The Age of Absolutism*, London: Hutchinson University Library, 1967.

Bennet, G. (ed.), *The Concept of Empire: Burke to Attlee 1774-1947*, London: Black, 1962.

Bidwell, Shelford, *Swords for Hire: European Mercenaries in Eighteenth Century India*, London: John Murray, 1978.

Black, Jeremy, *European Warfare 1660-1815*, London: UCL Press, 1994.

Bolt, Christine, *Victorian Attitudes to Race*, London: Routledge and Kegan Paul, 1971.

Boxer, C.R., *The Dutch Seabone Empire*, London: Hutchinson, 1965.

Brittlebank, Kate, *Tipu Sultan's Search for Legitimacy: Islam and Kingship in a Hindu Domain*, Delhi: OUP, 1997.

Broome, Captain Arthur, *History of the Rise and Progress of the Bengal Army*, Calcutta: 1850.

Buchanan, Francis, *An Account of the Districts of Bihar and Patna in 1811-1812*, New Delhi: Usha Publications, 1986, 1st edn. 1934.

Cadell, Patrick, *History of the Bombay Army*, London: Longmans Green, 1938.

Caldwell, Bishop R., *A History of Tinnevelly*, Delhi: Asian Educational Services, 1982.

Callahan, Raymond, *The East India Company and Army Reform*, Cambridge, Massachussetts: Harvard University Press, 1972.

Caplan, Lionel, *Warrior Gentlemen: 'Gurkhas' in the Western Imagination*, Providence: Berghahn Books, 1995.

Chandler, David, *The Art of War in the Age of Marlborough*, London: B.T. Batsford Ltd., 1976.

Chandra, Satish, *Parties and Politics at the Mughal Court*, Delhi: People's Publishing House, 1972.

Childs, John, *Armies and Warfare in Europe*, Manchester: Manchester University Press, 1982.

———, *The Army, James II and the Glorious Revolution*, Manchester: Manchester University Press, 1980.

Cohn, Bernard, *Colonialism and its Forms of Knowledge: the British in India*, Princeton, New Jersey: Princeton University Press, 1996.

———, *An Anthropologist Among the Historians and Other Essays*, Delhi: OUP, 1987.

Cohen, Stephen P., *The Indian Army: its Contribution to the Development of a Nation*, Berkeley: University of California Press, 1971.

Colebrooke, T.E., *The Life of the Honourable Mountstuart Elphinstone*, 2 vols., London: John Murray, 1884, vol. 1.

Compton, Herbert, *A Particular Account of the European Military Adventurers in Hindustan*, London: OUP, 1976; 1st pub. 1895.

Contamine, Philippe, *War in the Middle Ages*, trs. Michael Jones, Oxford: Basil Blackwell, 1984.

Corvisier, Andre, *Armies and Societies in Europe 1494-1789*, Bloomington: Indiana University Press, 1979.

Cowie, Leonard W., *Hanoverian England 1714-1837*, London: Bell, 1967.

Dasgupta, Atis K., *The Fakir and Sanyasi Uprisings*, Calcutta: K.P. Bagchi, 1992.

Delbruck, Hans, *History of the Art of War Within the Framework of Political History*, trs. Walter J. Renfroe, Jr., 4 vols., Westport, Connecticut: Greenwood, 1975-85, trs. of 3rd German edn. 1920, vol. 4.

Desai, W.S., *Bombay and the Marathas up to 1744*, Delhi: Munshiram Manoharlal, 1970.

Dirks, Nicholas B., *The Hollow Crown: Ethnohistory of an Indian Kingdom*, Ann Arbor: University of Michigan Press, 1993.

Dodwell, H.H., *Sepoy Recruitment in the Old Madras Army*, Calcutta: Superintendent, Govt. Printing, 1922.

Duffy, Christopher, *The Military Experience in the Age of Reason*, London: Routledge and Kegan Paul, 1987.

———, *The Army of Frederick the Great*, Melbourne: Wren, 1974.

Egerton of Tatton, Lord, *A Description of Indian and Oriental Armour*, London: Arms and Armour Press, 1968, 1st pub. 1896.

Embree, Ainslie T., *Imagining India: Essays on Indian History*, Delhi; OUP, 1989.

Fawcett, Sir Charles, *The English Factories in India*, n.s., vols. 1, 3 and 4, Oxford: Clarendon, 1936, vol. 1.

Feiling, Keith, *Warren Hastings*, London: Macmillan, 1954.

Fisher, Michael H., *The Travels of Dean Mahomet: an Eighteenth Century Journey Through India,* Berkeley: University of California Press, 1997.

Fortescue, John, *History of the British Army*, 13 vols., London: Macmillan, 1902-30, vol. 3.

Foster, Sir William, *English Factories in India,* 13 vols., Oxford: Clarendon, 1906-27, vol. 13.

Fox, Richard, G., *Kin, Clan, Raja and Rule: State Hinterland Relations in Pre-industrial India,* Berkeley: University of California Press, 1971.

Gleig, G.R., *The Life of Sir Thomas Munro*, 2 vols., London: Murray, 1849, vol. 2.

Gommans, Jos, *The Rise of the Indo-Afghan Empire c. 1710-1780*, Leiden: E.J. Brill, 1995.

Gordon, Stewart, *The Marathas 1600-1818,* The New Cambridge History of India II. 4, New York: CUP, 1993.

———, *Marathas, Marauders and State Formation in Eighteenth Century India,* Delhi: OUP, 1994.

Guha, Nikhilesh, *Pre-British State System in India: Mysore 1761-1799,* Calcutta: Ratna Prakashan, 1985.

Gupta, Maya, *Lord William Bentinck in Madras and the Vellore Mutiny 1803-07,* Delhi: Capital Publishers, 1986.

Habib, Irfan, *The Agrarian System of Mughal India,* New York: Asia Publishing House, 1963.

Hall, Bert S., *Weapons and Warfare in Renaissance Europe: Gunpowder, Technology and Tactics,* Baltimore, Maryland: John Hopkins University Press, 1997.

Heesterman, J.C., *The Inner Conflict of Tradition: Essays in Indian Ritual, Kingship and Society,* Chicago: University of Chicago Press, 1985.

Hill, S.C., *Yusuf Khan, the Rebel Commandant,* London: Longman Green, 1914.

Horn, Paul, *Das Heer und Kriegswesens der Grossmughals,* Leiden, 1894.

Houlding, J.A., *Fit for Service: the Training of the British Army, 1715-1795,* Oxford: Clarendon, 1981.

Holman, Dennis, *Sikander Sahib: the Life of Colonel Thomas Skinner 1778-1841,* London: William Heinemann Ltd., 1961.

Howard, Michael, *War in European History*, London: OUP, 1970.

Hughes, B.P., *Open Fire: Artillery Tactics from Marlborough to Wellington,* Chichester, Sussex: A. Bird Publications, 1983.

Hutchins, F.G., *The Illusion of Permanence: British Imperialism an India,* Princeton, New Jersey: Princeton University Press, 1967.

Inden, Ronald, *Imagining India,* Oxford: Basil Blackwell, 1990.

Irschick, Eugene F., *Dialogue and History: Constructing South India 1795-1895,* Berkeley: University of California Press, 1994.

Irvine, William, *The Army of the Indian Moghuls: its Organisation and Administration,* New Delhi: Eurasian Publishing House, 1962.

Irvine, William and Sir Jadunath Sarkar, *Later Mughals,* Calcutta: Sarkar, 1922.

Jamulluddin, Syed, *The State under Timur: a Study in Empire Building,* Delhi: Har-Anand Publications, 1995.

Kaye, John William, *Life and Correspondence of Charles, Lord Metcalfe,* 2 vols., London: Bentley, 1854, vol. 1.

Keegan, John, *The Face of Battle,* London: Jonathan Cape, 1976.

Kennet, Lee, *The French Armies in the Seven Years' War: a Study of Military Organisation and Administration,* Durham: Duke University Press, 1967.

Knox, Robert, *Races of Men: a Fragment,* London: Renshaw, 1850.

Kolff, Dirk A., *Naukar, Rajput and Sepoy: Ethnohistory of the Military Labour Market in Hindustan 1450-1850,* Cambridge: CUP, 1990.

Kopf, David, *British Orientalism and the Bengal Renaissance: the Dynamics of Indian Modernization 1773-1835,* Berkeley: University of California Press, 1969.

Kucklick, Henrika, *The Savage Within: The Social History of British Anthropology 1885-1945,* Cambridge, New York: CUP, 1991.

Kuper, Adam, *The Invention of Primitive Society: the Transformation of an Illusion,* London: Routledge and Kegan Paul, 1988.

Lauren, Paul Gordon, *Power and Prejudice: the Politics and Diplomacy of Racial Discrimination,* Boulder, Col.: Westview Press, 1996.

Larus, Joel, *Culture and Political-Military Behaviour: the Hindus in Pre-modern India,* Calcutta: South Asia Books, 1979.

Lawford, James P., *Britain's Army in India,* London: Allen and Unwin, 1976.

Love, H.D., *Vestiges of Old Madras,* 3 vols., London: John Murray, 1913, vols. 1 and 3.

Lynn, John A., *The Bayonets of the Republic: Motivation and Tactics in the Army of Revolutionary France 1791-94,* Chicago: University of Illinois Press, 1984.

McCormack, John, *One Million Mercenaries: Swiss Soldiers in the Armies of the World,* London: Leo Cooper, 1993.

MacMunn, Sir George, *The Martial Races of India,* London: Sampson Low, Marston & Co., 1933.

———, *The Armies of India,* London: Dam and Charles Black, 1911.

Mcneill, William H., *Keeping Together in Time: Dance and Drill in Human History,* Cambridge, Massachusetts: Harvard University Press, 1995.

———, *The Pursuit of Power: Technology, Armed Forces and Society Since A.D. 1000,* Chicago: University of Chicago Press, 1982.

Mainwaring, Arthur Edward, *Crown and Company: the Historical Records of the 2nd Battalion Royal Dublin Fusiliers, Formerly the 1st Bombay European Regiment,* 2 vols., London: Arthur and Humphreys, 1911-23, vol. 1.

Mallet, Michael, *Mercenaries and their Masters: Warfare in Renaissance Italy,* London: Bodley Head, 1974.

Marshall, P.J., *Bengal, the British Bridgehead: Eastern India 1748- 1828*, The New Cambridge History of India II. 2, Cambridge: CUP, 1988.

———, *The Great Map of Mankind: British Perceptions of the World in the Age of Enlightenment*, London: Dent, 1982.

———, *The British Discovery of Hinduism in the Eighteenth Century*, Cambridge: CUP, 1970.

Marshall, Dorothy, *Eighteenth Century England*, London: Longman, 1965.

Mason, Phillip, *A Matter of Honour: the Story of the Indian Army, its Officers and Men*, Hammondsworth: Penguin, 1976.

Metcalfe, Thomas R., *Ideologies of the Raj*, The New Cambridge History of India III.4, Cambridge: CUP, 1984.

Mill, James, *History of British India*, with notes and continuation by H.H. Wilson, 9 vols., London: James Madden, 1840, vols. 1 and 2.

Millar, Gilbert John, *Tudor Mercenaries and Auxiliaries 1485-1547*, Charlottesville: University Press of Virginia, 1980.

Moreland, W.B., *India at the Death of Akbar*, Delhi: Atma Ram and Sons, 1962.

Mukherjee, S.N., *Sir William Jones: a Study in Eighteenth Century British Attitudes to India*, London: Sangam, 1987.

Oman, Charles, *The History of the Art of War in the Middle Ages*, 2 vols., New York: Burt Franklin, 1924, vol. 1.

Omissi, David, *The Sepoy and the Raj: the Indian Army 1860-1940*, Bassingstoke: Macmillan in association with King's College, 1994.

*Oxford English Dictionary*, Oxford: Clarendon, 1989, vol. 2.

Panikkar, K.M., *A History of Kerala 1498-1801*, Annamalainagar: Annamalai University Press, 1960.

Parker, Geoffrey, *The Military Revolution: Military Innovation and the Rise of the West 1500-1800*, Cambridge, New York: CUP, 1988.

———, *The Thirty Years' War*, London: Routledge and Kegan Paul, 1984.

Pearse, Hugh, *Memoir of the Life and Military Services of Viscount Lake*, London: Robert Blackwood, 1908.

Peers, Douglas, *Between Mars and Mammon: Colonial Armies and the Garrison State in India 1819-1835*, London and New York: Tauris Academic Studies, 1995.

Pythian-Adams, Lieutenant-Colonel E.G., *The Madras Regiment 1758-1958*, Wellington: Defence Services Staff College Press, 1958.

Richards, John F., *The Mughal Empire*, The New Campbridge History of India I. 5, Cambridge: CUP, 1993.

Richardson, Major-General F.M., *Fighting Spirit: a Study of Psychological Factors in War*, London: Leo Cooper, 1978.

Rao, Velcheru Narayana, David Schulman and Sanjay Subramaniyam, *Symbols of Substance: Court and State in Nayaka Period Tamilnadu*, Delhi: OUP, 1992.

Ratnawat, Shyam Singh, *Rajput Nobility: With Special Reference to the*

*Kachchawaha Nobility of Jaipur During 1700-1858,* Jaipur: Panchsheel Prakashan, 1989.

Raye, N.N., *The Annals of the Early English Settlements in Bihar,* Calcutta: Kamal Book Depot, 1927.

Redlich, Fritz, *The Greman Military Enterpriser and his Workforce: a European Economic and Social History,* 2 vols., Wiesbaden: Steiner, 1964.

Riencourt, Amoury de, *The Soul of India,* London: Honeyglen, 1986.

Roberts, Michael, *Essays in Swedish History,* London: Weidenfield and Nicholson, 1968.

Ross, Steven T., *From Flintlock to Rifle: Infantry Tactics, 1740-1866,* London: Frank Cass, 1996.

Said, Edward, *Culture and Imperialism,* London: Chatto and Windus, 1993.

———, *Orientalism: Western Conception of the Orient,* New York: Pantheon Books, 1978.

Sarkar, Sir Jadunath, *A Military History of India,* Bombay: Orient Longman, 1970.

———, *The Fall of the Mughal Empire,* 4 vols., New York: AMS Press, 1949-50, vol. 1.

Saxena, K.M., *The Military System of India 1850-1900,* Delhi: Sterling, 1974.

Seeley, J.R., *The Expansion of England,* Chicago: University of Chicago Press, 1971.

Sen, Surendranath, *The Military System of the Marathas,* Calcutta: K.P. Bagchi, 1979; 1st pub. 1959.

Sen, S.P., *The French in India 1763-1816,* Calcutta: Firma K.L. Mukhopadhyay, 1958.

Sheppard, E.W., *Coote Bahadur: a Life of Lieutenant-General Sir Eyre Coote, K.B,* London: Werner Laurie, 1956.

Simpson, Peter, *The Independent Highland Companies 1603-1760,* Edinburgh: J. Donald, 1996.

Singh, Saint Nihal, *India's Fighters: Their Mettle, History and Services to Britain,* London: Sampson, Law, Marston and Co., 1914.

Singh, Madan Paul, *Indian Army Under the East India Company,* New Delhi: Sterling, 1976.

Spear, Percival, *The Nabobs: a Study of the Social Life of the English in the Eighteenth Century India,* London: OUP, 1963.

Snyder, Louis L., *The Idea of Racialism: its Meaning and History,* New York: Van Nostrand, 1962.

Stein, Burton, *Peasant State and Society in Medieval South India,* Delhi: OUP, 1980.

Stepan, Nancy, *The Idea of Race in Science: Great Britain: 1800-1960,* Hamden, Connecticut: Archon Books, 1982.

Stokes, Eric, *English Utilitarians in India,* Delhi: OUP, 1982; 1st pub. 1959.

———, *The Peasant and the Raj: Studies in Agrarian Society and Peasant Rebellions in Colonial India,* Cambridge: CUP, 1978.

Streusand, Douglas E., *The Formation of the Mughal Empire*, Delhi: OUP, 1989.

Swift, Eric, *The Brave and the Prejudiced*, Chelmsford, Essex: Sprinfield, 1982.

Thompson, I.A.A., *War and Government in Habsburg Spain 1560-1620*, London: Athlone Press, 1976.

Treasure, Geoffrey, *The Making of Modern Europe 1648-1789*, New York: Methuen, 1985.

Van Creveld, Martin, *Supplying War: Logistics From Wallenstein to Patton*, Cambridge: CUP, 1977.

Van de Berghe, L., *Race and Racism: a Comparative Perspective*, London: Wiley, 1967.

Ward, William, *A View of the History, Literature and Religion of the Hindus*, 4 vols., London, 1817-20, vol. 1.

Welsh, James, *Military Reminiscences Extracted from a Journal of Nearly Forty Years' Active Service in the East Indies*, 2 vols., London: Smith, Elder & Co., 1830, vol. 1.

Wickwire, Francklin and Mary Wickwire, *Cornwallis: the Imperial Years*, Chapel Hill: University of North Carolina Press, 1980.

Wilks, Mark and Murray Hammick, *Historical Sketches of the South of India*, 3 vols., London, 1818, vols. 2 and 3.

Williams, Captain John, *An Historical Account of the Rise and Progress of the Bengal Infantry from its Formation in 1757 to 1796*, London, 1810.

Wilson, W.J., *History of the Madras Army*, 5 vols., Madras: Government Press, 1882-8, vols. 1, 2, 3.

Wink, Andre, *Land and Sovereignty in India: Agrarian Society and Politics Under the Eighteenth Century Maratha Swarajya*, Cambridge: CUP, 1986.

Wurgaft, Lewis D., *The Imperial Imagination: Magic and Myth in Kipling's India*, Middletown, Connecticut: Wesleyan University Press, 1983.

Wylly, H.C., *Life of Lieutenant-General Sir Eyre Coote, K.B.*, Oxford: Clarendon, 1922.

Yule, Henry and A.C. Burnell, *Hobson-Jobson: a Glossary of Colloquial Anglo-Indian Words and Phrases and of Kindred Terms, Etymological, Historical, Geographical and Discursive*, London: John Murray, 1903.

Zaman, M.K., *Mughal Artillery*, Delhi: Idarah-i-Abiyat-i-Delhi, 1983.

ARTICLES

Alavi, Seema, 'The Company Army and Rural Society: the Invalid Thana 1780-1830', *Modern Asian Studies*, vol. 27, no. 1, 1993, pp. 147-78.

Barua, Pradeep, 'Military Developments in India 1750-1850', *Journal of Military History*, vol. 58, no. 4, 1994, pp. 599-616.

Bayly, Susan, '"Caste" and "Race" in the Colonial Ethnography of India', in Peter Robb (ed.), *The Concept of Race in South Asia*, Delhi: OUP, 1995, pp. 165-218.

Belich, James, 'The Victorian Interpretation of Racial Conflict and the New Zealand Wars: an Approach to the Problem of one-sided Evidence', *The Journal of Imperial and Commonwealth History*, vol. 15, no. 2, 1987, pp. 123-47.

Boxer, C.R., 'Asian Potentates and European Artillery in the 16th-17th Centuries: a Footnote to Gibson-Hill', *Journal of the Malayan Branch of the Royal Asiatic Society*, vol. 38, 1996, pp. 156-72.

Bowen, H.V., 'The East India Company and Military Recruitment in Britain, 1763-1771', *Bulletin of the Institute of Historical Research*, vol. 59, no. 139, 1986, pp. 78-90.

Bryant, Gerald James, 'Pacification in the Early British Raj 1755-85', *Journal of Imperial and Commonwealth History*, vol. 14, no. 1, 1985, pp. 3-19.

———, 'East India Company and the Crisis in Madras 1783', *Journal of the Society for Army Historical Research*, vol. 62, no. 249, 1984, pp. 13-27.

———, 'Officers of the East India Company's Army in the Days of Clive and Hastings', *Journal of Imperial and Commonwealth History*, vol. 6, no. 2, 1978, pp. 203-27.

Caplan, Lionel, 'The Bravset of the Brave: Representations of the Gurkha in Modern British Military Writings', *Modern Asian Studies*, vol. 25, no. 3, 1991, pp. 571-97.

Chattopadhyay, B.D., 'The Emergence of the Rajputs as Historical Process in Early Medieval Rajasthan', in Karine Schomer (ed.), *The Idea of Rajasthan: Explorations in Regional Identity*, 2 vols., Delhi: Manohar, 1994, vol. 2, pp. 161-91.

Chauduri, K.N., 'From Barbarian and the Civilised to the Dialectic of Colour: an Archaeology of Self-Identities', in Peter Robb (ed.), *Society and Ideology: Essays in South Asian History,* Delhi: OUP, 1993, pp. 22-48.

Cooper, R.G.S., 'Wellington and the Marathas 1803-04', *International History Review*, vol. 11, no. 1, 1989, pp. 31-8.

Dewey, Clive, 'Images of the Village Community: a Study in Anglo-Indian Ideology', *Modern Asian Studies*, vol. 6, no. 3, 1972, pp. 291-328.

Duffy, Michael, 'Military Revolution and the State 1500-1800', in Michael Duffy (ed.), *The Military Revolution and the State 1500-1800*, Exeter: University of Exeter, 1980, pp. 1-9.

Gilbert, Arthur N., 'Military Recruitment and Career Advancement in the Eighteenth Century: Two Case Studies', *Journal of the Society for Army Historical Research*, vol. 57, no. 229, 1979.

Greenhunt, Jeffrey, 'Sahib and Sepoy: an Inquiry into the Relationship Between the British Officers and Native Soldiers of the British Indian Army', *Military Affairs*, vol. 48, no. 1, 1984, pp. 15-18.

Gommans, Jos, 'Warhorse and Gunpowder in India c. 1000 - 1850', in Jeremy Black (ed.), *War in the Early Modern World*, London: UCL Press, 1999, pp. 105-28.

———, 'Indian Warfare and Afghan Innovation During the Eighteenth Century', *Studies in History*, n.s., vol. 11, no. 2, 1995, pp. 261-80.

Hill, S.C., 'The Old Sepoy Officer', *English Historical Review*, vol. 28, no. 110, 1913, pp. 260-91 and no. 111, 1913, pp. 496-514.

Howard, Michael, 'Empire Race and War in pre-1914 Britain', in Hugh Lloyd Jones, Valerie Pearl and Blair Worden (eds.), *History and Imagination: Essays in Honour of H.R. Trevor-Roper*, London: Duckworth, 1981, pp. 340-55.

Inden, Ronald, 'Orientalist Construction of India', *Modern Asian Studies*, vol. 20, no. 3 1986, pp. 401-46.

Inikori, J.E., 'The Import of Firearms into West Africa 1750-1807: a Quantitative Analysis', *Journal of African History*, vol. 18, no. 3, 1977, pp. 339-68.

Jones, Colin, 'The Military Revolution and the Professionalisation of the French Army in the Ancien Regime', in Michael Duffy (ed.), *The Military Revolution and the State 1500-1800* , Exeter: University of Exeter, 1980, pp. 29-48.

Kanta, Ragat, 'Race, Religion and Realm: the Political Theory of "The Reigning Raj Indian Crusade of 1857"', in Mushirul Hasan and Naryani Gupta (eds.), *India's Colonial Encounter: Essays in Memory of Eric Stokes*, Delhi: Manohar, 1993, pp. 132-82.

Kiernan, V.G., 'Foreign Mercenaries and Absolute Monarchy' in Trevor Aston (ed.), *The Crisis in Europe 1560-1660*, London: Routeledge, 1965, pp. 117-40.

Khan, Rafi Ahmad, 'New Light on Mughal Cavalry' in Irfan Habib (ed.), *Medieval India: a Miscellany*, Bombay: Asia Publishing House, 1972, pp. 70-98.

Kolff, Dirk H., 'The End of an Ancien Regime: Colonial War in India 1798-1818', in J.A. Moor and H. Wesseling (eds.), *Imperialism and War: Essays in Colonial War in Africa and Asia*, Leiden: Universitaire Press, 1989, pp. 22-50.

Knaap, G. 'Europeans, Mestizos and Slaves: the Population of Colombo at the End of the Seventeenth Century', *Itinerario*, vol. 5, no. 2, 1981, pp. 84-101.

Lenman, Bruce, 'The Transition to European Military Ascendancy in India 1600-1800', in John Lynn (ed.), *Tools of War: Instruments, Ideas and Institutions of Warfare, 1445-1871*, Chicago: University of Illinois Press, 1990, pp. 100-30.

Leonard, Karen, 'The Hyderabad Political System and its Participants', *Journal of Asian Studies*, vol. 30, no. 3, 1974, pp. 569-82.

Leopold, Joan, 'British Application of the Aryan Theory of Race to India, 1850-1870', *English Historical Review*, vol. 89, no. 352, 1974, pp. 578-603.

Lynn, John A., 'The Evolution of Army Style in the Modern West 800-2000', *International History Review*, vol. 18, no. 3, 1996, pp. 505-45.

Macaulay, J.A., 'The Dublin Fusiliers', *Irish Sword*, vol. 6, no. 25, 1964, pp. 257-70.

Marshall, P.J., 'Lord Macartney, India and China: the Two Faces of the Enlightenment', *South Asia*, vol. 19 (special issue), 1996, pp. 121-32.

———, 'Western Arms in Maritime Asia in the Early Phase of Expansion', *Modern Asian Studies*, vol. 14, no. 1, 1980, pp. 13-29.

Miller, James, 'The Diary of James Miller', *Journal of the Society for Army Historical Research*, vol. 3, no. 14, 1924, pp. 208-26.

Nissan, Elizabeth and R.L. Stirrat, 'The Generation of Communal Identities', in Jonathan Spencer (ed.), *Sri Lanka: History and the Roots of Conflict*, London: Routledge, 1990, pp. 19-44.

Peeler, Sue Pyatt., 'Land Forces of the East India Company in the Seventeenth Century', *Journal of Indian History Golden Jubilee Volume*, 1973, pp. 550-64.

Peers, Douglas, 'The Habitual Nobility of Being: British Officers and the Social Construction of the Bengal Army in the Early Nineteenth Century', *Modern Asian Studies*, vol. 25, no. 3, 1991, pp. 545-69.

———, 'Sepoys, Soldiers and the Lash: Race, Caste and Army Discipline in India 1820-1850', in *Journal of Imperial and Commonwealth History*, vol. 23, no. 3, 1995, pp. 211-47.

Pemble, John, 'Techniques and Resources in the Second Maratha War', *Historical Journal*, vol. 19, no. 2, 1976, pp. 375-404.

Poliakov, Leon, 'Racism from the Enlightenment to the Age of Imperialism', in Robert Ross (ed.), *Racism and Colonialism: Essays in Ideology and Colonial Structure*, The Hague: M. Nijhoff Publishers for Leiden University Press, 1982. pp. 54-65.

Richards, John F. and Velcheru Narayan Rao, 'Banditry in Mughal India', *Indian Economic and Social History Review*, vol. 17, no. 1, 1980, pp. 95-120.

Richards, John F., 'Norms and Comportment among Imperial Mughal Officers', in Barbara Metcalfe (ed.), *Moral Conduct and Authority*, Berkeley: University of California Press, 1984, pp. 255-89.

Richards, W.A., 'The Import of Firearms into West Africa in the Eighteenth Century', *Journal of African History*, vol. 21, no. 1, 1980, pp. 43-59.

Ritchie, C., 'A Sepoy Muster Book of 1768', *Journal of the Society for Army Historical Research*, vol. 32, 1954, pp. 18-23.

Rickword, G.O., 'Note on an Announcement in Ipswich Journal 15/11/1766', *Journal of the Society for Army Historical Research*, vol. 32, no. 83, 1954, p. 149.

Robb, Peter, 'South Asia and the Concept of Race', in Peter Robb (ed.), *The Concept of Race in South Asia*, Delhi: OUP, 1995, pp. 1-76.

Showalter, Dennis E., 'Caste, Skill and Training: the Evolution of Cohesion in

European Armies from the Middle Ages to the Sixteenth Century', *Journal of Military History*, vol. 57, no. 3, 1993, pp. 407-30.

Sinha, Mrinalini, 'Gender and Imperialism: Colonialist Policy and the Ideology of Moral Imperialism', in Michael S. Kimmel (ed.), *Changing Men: New Directions in Research on Men and Masculinity*, Newbury Park, Calif: Sage Publications, 1987.

White, Gavin, 'Firearms in Africa: an Introduction', *Journal of African History*, vol. 12, no. 2, 1971, pp. 173-84.

Ziegler, Norman, 'Some Aspects of Rajput Loyalty During the Mughal Period', in John F. Richards (ed.), *Kingship and Authority in South Asia*, Wisconsin: University of Wisconsin, 1972, pp. 215-25.

———, 'Evolution of the Rathor State of Marvar: Horses, Structural Change and Warfare', in Karine Schomer (ed.), *The Idea of Rajasthan: Explorations in Regional Identity*, 2 vols., Delhi: Manohar, 1994, vol. 2, pp. 192-217.

UNPUBLISHED THESIS

Bryant, Gerald James, 'The English East India Company and its Army 1600-1778', unpublished Ph.D. thesis, University of London, King's College, 1975.

# Index


Abbe' Dubois 76, 84
Abu'l Fazl 39
Adams 81
Adolphus, Gustavus 54
Afghans 38-9, 67
Agra, battle of 170
Alavi, Seema 27-8, 126, 128
Ali, Hyder 68-9, 135, 139 141, 143-4, 171, 174
Ali, Mohamed 18, 66, 88, 93, 106, 117
Amol, Hadjee 96
'amoral' society 23
amuldars 133
Anderson, Benedict 37
Anglo-French War 88, 121
Anglo-Maratha War II (1803-5) 74
Anglo-Mysore War III (1790-2) 77-8
Arcot, siege of 81
aristocratic-military nexus 63
*Army of the Indian Mughals* 30
Arni, battle of (1751) 120
Articles of War 125
Aryan race 19-20
'ashrafi' gentry 159
Asiatic Society of Bengal 13
Assaye, battle of (1803) 46, 71, 135, 147-51, 156-7

Baillie, William 69
Bannerman 172
Barat, Amiya 99
Barbosa, Duarte 49
Bayly, Christophar 23
Bell 91
Bengal Army 27, 99-101, 109, 112, 114, 125-6, 159, 161, 164-5, 178
Bernier, Francis 76, 79, 81
Bhao, Purseram 77
Bharat, Amiya 109
Bhonsle 151
Black, Jeremy 30
black commandant 111-12, 115
Blakiston, John 71, 83-4, 179
Bombay Army 26, 98-9, 104, 128-9, 165, 168
Bombay sepoy 93
Boscawen 93
Bourquin, Louis 72, 74, 151
Boxer, C.R. 19
British attitude towards Gujars 25; Gurkhas 25-6; Indian civilization and culture 13-16, 19-24, 27; Indian soldiers 24-9; Jats 25; Sikhs 25; source of study 29-31; Tamils 25
British perception and sepoys, command and deployent 166-80; management and control 158-66, 183
Broome, A. 109-10, 118
Bryant, Gerald 26, 175
Bulkley, Phillip 93, 106
Buxer, battle of 135-9

Cadell, Patrick 26
Cader, Abdul 125

Caillaud, John 40, 79, 81, 176
Cambridge, Richard 82-3, 118
Campbell, Charles 133
Caplan, Lionel 24
Carnac, John 161
Carnatic Nawab army 77
Carnatic War (1740 & 1750) 66-7, 88, 130
Carnatic War II (1757-61) 131
Cassim, Mir 68
Cawder, Abdul 105-6
Champion 138
Chanda Saheb 81, 118
Charles VII of France 58
Chengama, battle of (1767) 115
Childs, John 30
Clive, Robert 18, 93-4, 100, 102, 106, 109-10, 112, 118, 120-1, 124, 131, 166
Coffrees (African slaves) 91
conquest meaning in eighteenth century 36
Cooke 139, 141
Coote, Eyre 123, 131, 133, 141, 143-4, 170, 172
Cornwallis 20, 95, 99-100, 174, 180
Craddock 164
Crecy, battle of (1346) 53
Cuddalore, British siege of 171
Cullier, Pierre, *see* Perron, Cullier
*Culture and Imperialism* 22

Dalton, John 77
Darwin, Charles 18
De Boigne, Benoit 70, 72-3
De Gobineau, Arthur 17
De Guibert, Comte 65
De Lauristen, Jean Law 76
De Meuron 146
decadent society 23
Delhi, battle of (1803) 70
*deshmukh* 35
Dirom, Alexander 46
Dow, Alexander 14
Drudgeon 74
Duffy, Christopher 30
Dumas 117
Dundas, David 123, 148
Dupleix, Francois 117

8th battalion of Bombay sepoy 171
English East India Company (EIC) sepoy army, division of labour in wars 154-7; during 1746-1805 92-5; emergence of 76, 85, 92-5; expansions of natives in 94; garrison in India during 1600-1746 85-8; native recruitment 87-8; organization of 29; perception on formation of 30; replacement of peons by sepoy in 93, 96; *see also* sepoy, sepoy army
European army, discipline in 64-6; Indian military and 66-75; mercenary armies 57-9, 62; officers and men 62-6; organization of 56-62; permanent armies 58-9; polygot nature of 56; professionalism in 62; recruiting system 57; superiority over Indian military 66-75; supply system 59-60; tactics in battlefield 51-5
European state and military organization 56-62
European warfare, revolution in tactics of 51-5
evolution theory 17

firearms, innovations in 51-4
Fitzclarence 47
Fitzgerald 115
Flanders 79
Fontenoy, battle of 63, 172
Forbes, James 84, 159
Ford, Francis 94, 110, 124, 132

Fort St. David Council 91, 93, 101, 117-18
Fort St. George Council 93, 102, 120, 133, 166
Fort William Council 88
Fraser, William 110
French East India Company 33, 66

Glorious Revolution 60
Godwin 132
Golconda army 81
Golden Past for south India 23
Golden Rock 131
Gommans, Jos 67
Gordon, Robert 168
Gordon, Stewart 30
Grant 126

Habib, Irfan 35
Hasting, Warren 13, 100-1, 161
*havildars* 96-8, 106, 111, 114, 128-9
Heesterman, J.C. 37
Heron, Alexander 108
Hindu warriors, European perception about 83-4
Hinduism 15
*History of the Military Transactions of the British Nations in Indostan* 29
Holkar, Jaswant Rao 74, 175
Holland 99

Inden, Ronald 22-3
Indian army, command and control of 34, 38, 42-3, 158-66
Indian battle-tactics 46
Indian inferiority, scientific evidence of 20-1
Indian military organization 79
Indian military system, inferiority of 28
Indian soldier, British perception of 84, 158-83; European perception 76-85; recruitment of 85-8, 96-105
individual skill and courage, ethos in war in India 47-50
Inglia, Ambaji 147, 151
Irvine, William 30

Jaocb, John 24
Jacobite rebellion 60
Jalleel, Abdul 66-7
*jamadar* 39, 96-9, 105-6, 111, 114-15, 128
*jamadari* system of recruitment 40, 42, 79
*jamadari* units 56
James II 60
Jemal Sahib 107, 112, 133-4
Jones, William 13-14, 19

Karwar, Raja of 87
Kay Prussian, battle of 172
Keegan, John 63, 66
Kelly, Robert 128, 167, 172, 180
Khan, Ibrahim 129
Khan, Sher 33
Khan, Yusuf 107-9, 125, 129, 134, 174
Kilpatrick 120, 124
King's 12th regiment 146
King's 39th regiment 89
King's 73rd regiment 146
King's 74th regiment 146, 150
King's 76th regiment 153, 156
King's 78th regiment 83, 148, 150, 156
Kinlock, George 115
Kolff, Dirk 30, 36, 39, 101
Kshatriya 48

Lake 74, 147, 151, 153, 156, 170
Lally 110
Laswari battle of 135, 151-4, 156-7
Lawrence, Henry 21
Lawrence John 21
Lawrence, Stringer 89, 93, 120-1, 133-4
linear formation at battlefield 54

Louis XI 58
Lucan 74
Lynn, John A. 61

Macartney 19
Maclean, Lauchlin 106
Madras Army 26, 99, 102-5, 112, 116; caste composition in 102-5
Madras Military Regulation of 1766 102
Madras Regulation of 1759 122
*mansabdari* system 38-9
*mansabdars* 39
*mansabs* 39
Manucci, Niccolo 76-7
Maratha army 42, 70-5, 77-8, 161, 164, 167; change to European style 70-5
Maratha-Mughal battles 44-6
Maratha War II (1803) 74, 135, 147-54
Marathas 33-8, 42, 44-6, 69-70, 83, 88-9
martial classes 48
martial races, theory of 25-6
Martin, Francois 33-4, 42
Maurice 52
Medoc 138
Meer Sahib 144
mercenary armies 57-9, 62
Michand, Joseph 83
military castes of south eastern coastal region of Kerala 49-50
military organization, in pre-modern Europe 61, 64
*Military System of the Marathas* 30
Mill, James 78
*mofussil* 99
Moor, Edward 29, 78, 83, 168
Moorish language 116
Mughal army 38, 42, 76
Mughal artillery 67
Mughal battles 43-6
Mughal cavalry 38
Mughal empire 37-9
Muhammad, Nasir 33
Munro, Hector 125, 135-6, 138, 143
Munro, Innes, 29, 98, 115, 167
Munro, Thomas 171
Muslims, European perception of 83
Mysore Army 77, 143-4, 171
Mysore battles 139-57
Mysore War I, 97, 139
Mysore War II (1780-4) 68, 82, 97, 144, 167-8, 171, 176
Mysore War III (1790-2) 69, 144
Mysoreans 69, 139, 141, 171-3
Mysorian cavalry 81-2

*naiks* 96-7, 106, 111, 114
*Narrative of the Military Operations on the Coromandal Coast* 29
*Narrative of the Operations of Captain Little's Detachment* 29
Nasir Jang 118
Nayak, Kolaique Achamail 33-4, 42
Nellore Subedar 108-9, 134
Nizam's army 46
Noles, W.A. 106

Omissi, David 24
ordonnance companies 58
orientalism, concept of 24
*Orientalism* 22
*Origin of Species* 18
Orme, Robert 29, 77-8, 84, 118, 121, 134, 159

*palaikkars* 35
Pandey, Sita Ram 99
Panjab Style government 21
Parker, Geoffrey 30
Peers, Douglas 24
Perron, Cullier 70, 72-3, 147
Phalked campaign of Marathas 44
Plassey, battle of 79, 89, 110, 130
Pohlman 74
Pondicherry 68

Popham 115
Porto Novo, battle of 135, 141-4, 157, 172
Portuguese 86-7
pyramidally segmented type of state 35-6

racism, European attitude towards 17-18, 20-1
Rajputs 48-9, 84, 100-2, 160
Raza, Muhammad 33-4, 42
Reinhardt, Walter 68
Renne, James 164
Richards, John 39
rulers and soldiers in War in India 33-43

Said, Edward 22-3
Samugarh 76, 77
*sardars* 35
*Saturday Review* 18
Scindia, Mahadji 70, 72-3, 75, 147, 150-1
segmented armies 38
segmented states 38
Sen, Surendranath 30
sepoy, British perception and 158-80, 183; command and deployment 166-80; cultural distinctiveness 161; management and control 158-66; religious sensitivities 161-4; *see also* sepoy army
sepoy army, active military campaigns 134-5; battalion formation 109-12; big battles 135-57; Assaye 147-51; Buxar (1764) 135-9; division of labour in 154-7; Laswari 151-4; Maratha War II 147; Mysore 139-57; Porto Novo (1781) 141-4; Srirangapattanam 144-7; Tiruvannamalai (1767) 139-41; EIC approach to control 124-9; European control over 112-17; European-style organization of 111; rate of pay 128; *see also* English East India Company (EIC) sepoy army recruitment of 96-105; tactical organization of 105-9; training of 117-23; war during (1746-1805) 130-57; years of apprenticeship 1746 to 1760 130-5
Seven Years' War in Europe 89
Shivaji 37, 42
Sholinghur, battle of 171
Shuja 136
Sidis, campaign against 167
Singh, Cheyt 27
Singh, Kesar 107, 112
Siraj-ud-Daulah 40, 89, 94, 130
Smith, Joseph 108
Smith, Lewis Ferdinand 73
soldiers, individualistic approach to training for wars 46-7; and rulers in war in India 33-43; welfare 60
Spanish Succession War (1702-13) 61
Sparkes 115
square formation at battlefield 54
Srirangapattanam, battle of 135, 144-7, 169
Stein, Burton 35
Stevenson 147-8
Stuart 143
*subedars* 96, 99, 106-7, 111, 114-15, 125-6, 128, 134
Sugar Loaf Rock, battle of 121
Sumroo 136, 138; *see also* Reinhardt, Walter

Tavernier, Jean-Baptiste 79
Tellicherry sepoy 93
Tennant, William 177-8
Thirty Years' War (1618-48) 57, 62
35th battalion of Madras native infantry mutiny in Colombo 116, 126, 163
33rd royal regiment 146
Tiger of Mysore 147

Timur, Amir 43
Timur's army 43
Tipu Sultan 68-9, 135, 144, 146
Tiruvannamalai, battle of 123, 135, 139-41, 157
Tone, William 78-9
Topasses 86-8, 91-2, 139, 174

Usanbech, Mohamed 96

Vansittrat, Henry 161
Vellore mutiny 163-4
Vijayaraghava 49-50

Wallenstein, Count Albrecht von 56
War, in Europe, European superiority and Indian Military Revolution 66-75; military organization and 56-62; officers and men 62-6; revolution in tactics 51-5; in India, demand for troops and 88-92; individual skills and courage ethos 47-50; rulers and soldiers 33-43; tactics, weapons and training 43-7
Wardlow, W. Ralph 106
Wellesley, Arthur 147-8, 151, 156, 168-70, 172
Welsh, James 102-3, 156, 160
Westphalia treaty 58
White, Henry 103, 161
Wilkins, Charles 13
Wilks, Mark 82-3
William of Orange 60
Williams 109-10
Wilson, W.J. 26, 109
Wood 97, 139, 141

Yonge, Robert 20

*zamindari* infantry 39
*zamindari* war bands 40, 42
*zamindars* 35
Ziegler, Norman 30, 48